The ABCs of Structured Discovery Cane Travel for Children

Have cane, will travel

A Volume in:
Critical Concerns in Blindness

Series Editor:
Edward Bell

Critical Concerns in Blindness

Edward C. Bell
Series Editor

Books in This Series

Encyclopedia of Sports & Recreation for People with Visual Impairments (2012)
Andrew Leibs

Getting Ready for College Begins in Third Grade:
Working Toward an Independent Future for Your Blind/Visually Impaired Child (2010)
Carol Castellano

The Blind Need Not Apply:
A History of Overcoming Prejudice in the Orientation and Mobility Profession (2007)
Ronald J. Ferguson

Accessible Education for Blind Learners: Kindergarten through Post-Secondary (2007)
Shelley Kinash & Ania Paszuk

Independent Movement and Travel in Blind Children: A Promotion Model (2007)
Joseph Cutter

Making It Work: Educating the Blind/Visually Impaired
Student in the Regular School (2006)
Carol Castellano

Seeing Beyond Blindness (2006)
Shelley Kinash & Ronald J. Ferguson

The Blindness Revolution: Jernigan in His Own Words (2006)
James H. Omvig

Education and Rehabilitation for Empowerment (2005)
Ed Vaughan & James H. Omvig

The ABCs of Structured Discovery Cane Travel for Children

Have cane, will travel

Merry-Noel Chamberlain

INFORMATION AGE PUBLISHING, INC.
Charlotte, NC • www.infoagepub.com

Library of Congress Cataloging-in-Publication Data

The CIP data for this book can be found on the Library of Congress website (loc.gov).

Paperback: 978-1-64802-555-6
Hardcover: 978-1-64802-556-3
E-Book: 978-1-64802-557-0

Printed in the United States of America

CONTENTS

PART III

PART IV

PREFIX

The field of Orientation and Mobility (O&M) for the blind did not give serious consideration to providing training to children until the 1980s. This changing philosophy coincided with the creation of canes suitable for children by the National Federation of the Blind and the formation of the National Organization of Parents of Blind Children. Parents began to advocate for O&M training for their school aged children because previously canes were not given to young people until they were about 16 years old. Children were taught according to a model that had been used with returning blinded veterans from World War II. In the 1960s in Iowa and the1970s in Nebraska, rehabilitation programs for adult blind began employing blind people as O&M instructors. In addition, they were using a curriculum based upon what was described by Dr. Alan Dodds as structured discovery. In the 1990s this philosophy was used as the basis for a program to train mobility instructors at Louisiana Tech University in Ruston, Louisiana. This program was inclusive of all applicants, blind or sighted. Other university programs training students to become mobility instructors had a history of discrimination, excluding blind and low vision people on the basis of their visual impairment.

In the 2000s mobility instructors schooled in Structured Discovery Cane Travel began to work with children and adults alike. As with adults, children were expected to be independent and competent users of the long white cane as well as critical thinkers. These skills were transformational and allowed the students to adapt to different environments.

In *The ABCs of Structured Discovery Cane Travel for Children*, Dr. Merry-Noel Chamberlain shows with evidence based best practices that blind children learn independent travel successfully by using a Structured Discovery Cane Travel curriculum. She presents an overview of the theoretical basis for the existence of the practice of Structured Discovery Cane Travel. Also, she draws comparisons with Sequential Learning and Structured Discovery learning revealing that Sequential Learning is less conducive to independent travel. Dr. Chamberlain then relates these concepts to the use of Structured Discovery Cane

Travel as a basis for a curriculum for children, from infant to high school. She provides descriptions of the tools and techniques to promote an independent paradigm for working with children in the home, the school and in the community environment. Furthermore, Dr. Chamberlain presents a system where parents are an essential element in promoting their child's daily use of the long white cane.

Dr. Chamberlain culminates her book by presenting a large number of activities and games which promote positive cane techniques and transformational learning. She recommends the use of games and activities to develop cognitive skills which promotes the basic concepts of critical thinking. In addition, she gives resources for IEP goals and assessment tools. Her examples help the reader of this book to have abundant resources which promote the use of the skills of Structured Discovery Cane Travel.

The ABCs of Structured Discovery Cane Travel for Children is a tremendous resource for professionals and parents alike. As both an educator and a parent of a blind child, Dr. Chamberlain shows a keen insight into the needs of children with visual impairments to become confident and independent cane travelers. This is a must read for individuals who have an interest in fostering the independence and success of blind children.

—Denise Mackenstadt, NOMC
Mackenstadt Rehabilitation Services

PART I

CHAPTER 1

INTRODUCTION

Dear Reader,

The ABCs of Structured Discovery Cane Travel for Children explains the basics of Structured Discovery Cane Travel regarding the use of the long white cane; the purpose of the cane; and why it is important for individuals who are blind, legally blind or partially sighted to use the cane for independent travel. Although some of this text is technical, my desire is for you to find it informative. My goal is for children to obtain the essential skills necessary to travel independently, safely, confidently, efficiently, and gracefully, in order to successfully step forward in life.

Sincerely,
Merry-Noel

The *Orientation and Mobility (O&M) curriculum* focuses on the foundational skills necessary to develop future independence and sovereignty for individuals who are blind or visually impaired. The instructors of O&M teach concept development, techniques and skills to students so they may efficiently, gracefully and safely travel independently in a myriad of locations (Jacobson, 1993; Pogrund & Griffin-Shirley, 2018). *The ABCs of Structured Discovery Cane Travel* concentrates on the education of children, though the principals may be applied to adults as well. *Structured Discovery Cane Travel (SDCT)* is an O&M curriculum that utilizes transformational knowledge, hands-on experiences, problem-solving opportunities within natural environments, and personal reflection through teachable moments to develop physical and mental mapping skills which can be utilized post instruction. In addition, SDCT has been proven to yield higher self-confidence levels in consumers than those who received mobility instruction by way of a Sequential Learning O&M curriculum (Chamberlain, 2019).

For individuals, who will be referred to as *students* throughout this text, the proficiency of O&M skills is necessary for them to live an active and self-sufficient life (Geruschat, & De L'Aune, 1989). Having the necessary O&M skills to maneuver within one's home and community is considered one of the most critical aspects of human abilities as demonstrated by proficient cane travelers, referred to here as *consumers*. According to Long (1990), limitations of independent mobility severely negatively impacts vocational and social opportunities. People (blind or sighted) venture further from their native soil now than in earlier centuries due to the industrial revolution (Koestler, 1976) which opened doors for opportunities of economic betterment. This created a growth in social mobility and for consumers to be productive members of our society, they need to have superior O&M skills whereby they are able to locate and enter familiar and unfamiliar environments "safely, efficiently, gracefully, and independently" (Hill & Ponder, 1976, p. 1).

DISTANCE VISION CATEGORIES OF VISUAL IMPAIRMENTS

Before moving forward, let's have a clear understanding of *vision*, rather… the lack of *sight*. The Center for Disease Control and Prevention (CDC) (2017) estimates 27 million American citizens will be visually impaired by 2030. Keep in mind that *vision* is a directional foreground modality (Kratz et al., 1987) and visual impairments are identified in categories based on visual acuities. It is estimated that about 90% of individuals with visual impairments have various degrees of vision loss with unique functional limitations, which leaves about 10% as totally blind (American Optometric Association, 2018; Blasch et al., 1997; Koestler, 2004; Orr & Rogers, 2001; Stein et al., 2000). The majority of individuals with visual impairments fall into the *Legal Blindness* Category. Legal blindness includes those who have a visual acuity of 20/200 or worse in their better eye, with correction, or those who have a combined (meaning both eyes) visual field of 20 degrees or less (CDC, 2017; Social Security Administration, 2018) and this includes individuals whose visual acuity may be 20/20 within that limited field of view.

Understanding visual acuities can be confusing. Basically, *normal vision* is considered to be 20/20. This means people who have 20/20 visual acuity can all see the same thing when standing 20 feet away from that visual target. *Mild visual impairment* is a visual acuity between 20/30 and 20/60. These individuals need to be a little closer to the visual target in order to see the same objects that a person with 20/20 is able to see as far as 60 feet away. Individuals are considered to have a *moderate visual impairment* if their visual acuity is between 20/70 and 20/180. A person who falls into this category must be as close as 20 feet from the visual target while those with 20/20 visual acuity can be as far away as 70 to 180 feet to see that same target. As previously stated, legal blindness is when a person's visual acuity is worse than 20/200 and this category has two subcategories: *severe* and *profound*. Those who are severe have a visual acuity between 20/200 and 20/480 while those who are profound have an acuity worse than 20/500. That is, individuals with profound vision loss may only be able to count fingers held very close to their eye(s)

TABLE 1.1. Visual Categories Based on Distance Visual Acuities

20/20 or better	20/30 to 20/60	20/70 to 20/180	20/200 to 20/480	20/500 or worse	No Vision
Normal	Mild or Near Normal	Moderate, Low Vision, or Partially Sighted	Legally Blind		Blind
			Severe	Profound	

Source: American Optometric Association, 2018; Blasch et al., 1997; Chamberlain, 2019, p. 3; Koestler, 2004; Stein et al., 2000.

and/or may have limited light perception. Provided in Table 1.1 is a breakdown of the various categories of visual impairments based on distance visual acuities (Chamberlain, 2019, p. 3).

Visual acuities may fluxuate throughout the day depending on physical strain, lighting and perhaps weather patterns (Gould & Sullivan, 1999). For some visual impairments such as Stargargts or Macular Degeneration, individuals may turn their head to use their peripheral vision or their *sweet spot* to see targeted items. In addition, some individuals may move targeted visual items closer to or farther from their eyes while others may physically move their bodies closer to or farther away in order to focus to the best of their abilities.

SERVICES

Services for the blind or visually impaired within the school system for children (birth—age 21) or Vocational Rehabilitation (for over age 14) require documentation indicating the individual has a visual impairment which is detrimental to their educational performance or livelihood. The level of services provided differs between the educational and the rehabilitation systems. In the rehabilitation system, a person who is not yet legally blind *may* qualify by having a visual condition known to get worse. If an individual qualifies for services in either the education or the rehabilitation system, then that person will most likely automatically meet the requirements for O&M, as well.

In the educational system, some states have two categories, Legally Blind or Blind, while other states may include an additional Partially Sighted category (See *Nebraska Verification Guide for Blind, Legally Blind and Partially Sighted*, Appendix). Visual acuities and/or cause of vision loss is used to determine services such as large print, Braille, and/or O&M. Keep in mind that in the educational system, accommodations may only be recommended for the current visual acuity of the student without regard for future possible visual decline. Also, Gould and Sullivan (1999) state 60% of visually impaired children have additional disabilities such as cerebral palsy, mental disabilities and hearing impairments.

HISTORY OF THE
VISUAL MINORITY

The visual minority, known throughout this book as *consumers* is a diverse group of individuals who may consider themselves as many society members considers them: dependent on others, helpless, hopeless, inferior, and objects of pity, without the right or the ability to obtain employment, according to Baldwin (2016), Blasch, et al. (1997), and Omvig (2002). Dweck (2008) states when negative stereotypes are evoked, students and consumers often conform to those stereotypes without self-awareness. Sadly, parents and educators sometimes fall into the trap whereby, according to Salisbury (2018), consumers who exhibit similar characteristics of any minority group automatically receive membership status, implications, and treatments. This philosophy supports Dodds (1988) who states some believe the goal of mobility training is to make consumers travel as indistinguishable as possible. Hence, there has been a history of utilizing techniques to hide blindness by (1) using folding or telescoping canes (which can be stowed away), (2) using a human guide rather than a long white cane (so as not to bring attention to the mobility tool), or (3) simply attempting to maneuver about using a monocular or unreliable vision. When the latter method is utilized, the opposite effect often occurs whereby these individuals attract attention through their bumping into objects, tripping over objects, or standing within people's comfort zone, etc., which supports the stereotypical image of blindness as stated above.

However, when individuals have positive mindsets, their performance will not be disrupted by stereotypes, says Dweck (2008). Therefore, it is important to instill positive mindsets regarding blindness and the long white cane within ourselves and others. The direction of our young adults begins at home, then continues at school and beyond where they may be employed, well-educated, live independently, and participate within society. This young visual minority group, when given the proper techniques of blindness, including O&M training, can and will compete equally with their sighted peers to become adult taxpayers rather than barely surviving on Social Security Disability Insurance checks, states Omvig (2002).

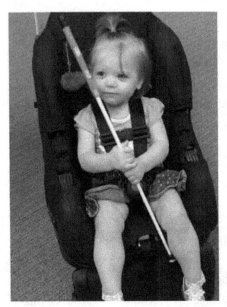  

CHAPTER 2

WHAT IS ORIENTATION AND MOBILITY?

Orientation and Mobility (O&M), also known as *Cane Travel* or simply *Mobility* is the skill and ability to maneuver from one location to another. For consumers, the tool used for mobility is the long white cane with a metal tip which, when used properly, offers a safe and efficient method of (1) terrain interpretation; (2) location of obstacles; (3) a means to negotiate around obstacles; and (4) a tool used to perform elevation changes (Sauerburger & Bourquin, 2010). The *long white cane* is the main tool used by consumers to gain surface information from the environment and to identify the user as being visually impaired or blind (Pogrund & Griffin-Shirley, 2018). Simply put, consumers use the cane "to maintain contact with the horizontal surface, while avoiding contact with the vertical ones" (Dodds, 1993, p. 50).

Since it has been verified through "anecdotal evidence reported by low-vision rehabilitation workers and visually impaired adults" that O&M training supports independent travel skills (Soong et al., 2001), let's take a closer investigation of the definitions of *Orientation* and *Mobility*. According to Sarid (2012), there are two interrelated metaphorical senses for *orientation* which include: (1) positioning and awareness (i.e., where one is in location relative to the world) and (2) knowledge awareness which dictates direction leading to desired targets or destinations. *Mobility* is simply the ability to facilitate movements (Jacobson, 1993) whereby movement may occur by crawling, scooting, or perhaps using a wheelchair or crutches. Pogrund and Griffin-Shirley (2018) state orientation is the self-knowledge of where one is located within a particular space while mobility is the ability to efficiently and safely maneuver from one location to another. The *profession of O&M* is teaching the above concepts, techniques and skills to individuals so they are able to *independently* travel safely in a myriad of locations, efficiently and gracefully (Aditya, 2004; Cutter, 2007; Jacobson, 1993) by way of using a long white cane with a metal tip as the mobility tool.

HISTORY OF ORIENTATION & MOBILITY

The use of a cane is not a new concept or technique used by visually impaired mankind. Research has revealed that blind people have used a stick (i.e., a makeshift cane, of sorts) since the beginning of human history (Bryant, 2009; First Steps, n.d.; Foundation Fighting Blindness, n.d.; Kim & Wall Emerson, 2012; Roberts, 2009; Sauerburger & Bourquin, 2010; Williams, 1967). For example, a British gentleman named Lieutenant James Holman (1786–1857), used a walking stick with a metal tip, according to Roberts (2009). He adds Holman was a *self-taught navigator* who placed metal on the end of his wooden stick to prevent it from splitting and considered this tool as "standard strolling equipment for gentlemen of the day" (pp. 75–76). Lieutenant Holman used the metallic sound of the stick as it hit various surfaces for detection of nearby objects such as walls and described this sound as a *quick burst of noise* (Roberts, 2009). Today, consumers use the metal tip for "echo-ranging cues and force-impact information" about the terrain (Pogrund & Griffin-Shirley, 2018, p. 178) as well as a method to obtain auditory information regarding the surrounding environment. Thus, "tap, tap, tap, [is] the sound of independence" (Winter, 2015) when a cane with a metal tip is used. Subsequent to Holman was Mr. W. Hanks Levy, who in the 1870s expressed theories for cane use and design in England which are similar to those used today (First Steps, n.d.) by consumers in the United States. Levy stated in 1872 that the importance of walking independently could scarcely be exaggerated (First Steps, n.d.; Koestler, 1976, p. 302) which implies walking without the assistance of another (that is, a human guide) is extremely important.

In the early 1900s little research was conducted regarding independent mobility (O'Donnell, 1988) and the development of a curriculum to instruct independent travel to newly blinded consumers. According to Williams (1967), formal O&M instruction is unknown prior to the 1960s while First Steps (n.d.) adds that consumers simply designed methods that met their needs. However, it wasn't until World War II when America began to utilize the cane as a formal tool in mobility for wounded veterans (Williams, 1967). Thus, the profession of O&M in the United States is moderately short which, according to Baldwin (2016), officially began with the rehabilitation of veterans who became blind due to WWII. However, at that time, "no thought or consideration had been given to the development or the needs of young blind children" (Pogrund & Rosen, 1989, p. 431).

THE MOBILITY PROFESSION

As a profession, there is a dreadful shortage of O&M instructors throughout the United States (Chamberlain, 2019; Pogrund & Griffin-Shirley; 2018, Wells, 2008) and this deficiency is even more pronounced within school districts. Instructors of O&M serve a diverse population from infants to the elderly, who have single to multiple disabilities (Wells, 2008). Therefore, there are two types of O&M instructors—those who work with adults in a rehabilitation facility and those who work with children birth to age 21 in the educational system. Since its inception, the traditional O&M training for children, although somewhat down-sized, has been similar to the adult rehabilitation that was established during WWII (Wells, 2008). *The Structured Discovery Cane Travel curriculum does not follow this traditional approach.*

In many cases in the educational system, one instructor is required to serve several students who are spread out among numerous districts, towns or counties. Thus, time with students can be limited and/or scarce. In some academic areas consistent and frequent instruction is vitally important for on-going progress towards success. However, by having a mobility instructor who uses the SDCT curriculum, students benefit from perfecting problem-solving techniques which offers transformational knowledge whereby they learn and master mobility skills which can be transferred outside of instruction time and utilized within their natural environment.

Orientation and Mobility instructors ensure their students are provided a myriad of opportunities to achieve maximum independence, often through self-dependent mobility, also known as *independent cane travel* (Ballemans et al., 2011; Leonard, 1968; Malik et al., 2018; Williams, 1967). Students gain mobility skills with the use of the long white cane whereby the cane is (1) a symbol of independence (Heinen, 2014; Omvig, 2005); (2) a cherished and positive tool for autonomy (Vaughan, 1993); (3) a probe to navigate and identify the environment (Foundation Fighting Blindness, n.d.); and (4) an identifier that the user's vision is impaired (Ballemans et al., 2011; Kaiser et al., 2018).

O&M GOALS

As with any educational program, O&M instructors establish goals for their students in conjunction with the desires and concerns of the students' parents and educational team which are documented on the child's *Individual Education Plan (IEP)*. Although instructors assist students in gaining the necessary skills to travel independently from one location to another, they also prepare students to maneuver safely to desired locations (Aditya, 2004) both on and off school campuses. The Museum of the American Printing House for the Blind (n.d.), states mobility is considered the core skill necessary for daily living, while Castellano (2005) adds that movement is necessary to stimulate curiosity and socialization skills. When students perfect the skills of O&M, they gain the utmost human ability, which is the capability to travel independently when and how they decide (Long, 1990; Maurer et al., 2007).

Basically, O&M instructors provide specialized training to students on how to safely and efficiently travel independently using a long white cane to and within a myriad of desired locations (Aditya, 2004; Crudden, 2015). While the cane is considered the primary tool used for mobility, it is up to the curriculum to offer the richest knowledge incorporating O&M techniques. This specialized curriculum must include problem-solving and practical approaches which have been developed through the collective travel experiences of former students (i.e., consumers), in addition to the experiences of their O&M instructors (Long & Giudice, 2010; Long, 1990) who may be blind or visually impaired themselves.

Beyond the basic skills of using the long white cane, O&M students work on becoming competent, independent, and safe travelers by developing transformational mobility skills. While venturing to students' Points-of-Interest (POIs), "a progression of environments, from simple to complex is typically used when teaching the long cane or introducing road crossing concepts and skills" (Deverell, 2011, p. 68). In addition, students work on mobility skills in areas which are most familiar (i.e., near) to areas which are further away such as from their classroom to hallways, to cafeteria to playgrounds or from residential to businesses (Hudson, 1997). While doing so, students work on transformational skills. Some of those skills are listed below, although they are not necessarily acquired in this order:

- Cane basics, mechanics, and etiquette.
- Skills in gathering and interpreting environmental information through echolocation and cardinal directions.
- Obstacle detection and problem-solving skills.
- Self-monitoring and self-expectations skills that emerge while building self-confidence and enhancing independent mobility.
- Understanding, creating, and enhancing mental mapping skills.

INDEPENDENT TRAVELERS

The instruction of orientation, along with training in mobility must be combined in order to build the self-confidence to ensure that successful and independent travel may occur. Pogrund and Griffin-Shirley (2018) state consumers who can do one but not the other cannot be independent travelers. See Table 2.1.

TABLE 2.1.   Possibility of Independent Travel for Consumers

Orientation		+	Mobility		=		Possibility
Students who are able to orient themselves to their surroundings…	✓	and	have the skills to maneuver about efficiently and safely…	✓	=	✓	*Can* become Independent Travelers.
Students who are able to orient themselves to their surroundings…	✓	but	do not have the skills to maneuver about efficiently and safely…	✗	=	✗	Cannot be Independent Travelers.
Students who become easily disoriented…	✗	despite	having the skills to maneuver about efficiently and safely…	✓	=	✗	Cannot be Independent Travelers.

CHAPTER 3

NATIONAL ORIENTATION AND MOBILITY CERTIFICATION (NOMC)

Using the cognitive learning theory, the educational psychology department at Louisiana Tech collaborated with the Louisiana Center for the Blind to develop a new Orientation and Mobility Master's level program in 1997 (Bell & Mino, 2011; Schroeder, 1997). This was made possible through a Federal Experimental and Innovative grant from the Rehabilitation Services Administration, U.S. Department of Education (Aditya, 2004). Prospective college students learned the SDCT curriculum used by instructors who hold *National Orientation and Mobility Certification (NOMC)* obtained through the *National Blindness Professional Certification Board (NBPCB)* which includes: 1) Cane Basics and Cane Techniques; and 2) problem-solving opportunities.

Rather than following a *Sequential Learning* (SL) curriculum model limited to addressing only an aggregate list of learning objectives (i.e., skills and knowledge) used to guide instruction (Education Reform, 2015), the SDCT curriculum addresses *all* aspects of a student's life through a holistic curriculum (Vaughan & Omvig, 2005) through its occluded requirement during mobility lessons. Keep in mind that *curriculums* are built around objectives which "always reflect the values of those who created it" (Wiles, 2009, p. 14) which is evident within the SDCT curriculum that was implemented by and for consumers due to their concerns with the development of the VA training program for wounded soldiers in the 1940s (Baldwin, 2016; Ferguson, 2007).

Historically individuals with visual impairments were excluded from obtaining certification in mobility instruction. However, all prospective future O&M instructors (sighted, visually impaired, or blind) may attain NOMC certification even though, according to Bell and Mino (2011), it was originally designed for blind or visually impaired individuals to obtain credentials in order to enter O&M employment opportunities. Prospective O&M instructors must be occluded during mobility training, if they have any usable vision. That is, sighted prospective O&M instructors spend 500–650 hours of *immersion* training while legally blind prospective O&M instructors spend up to 2000 hours (approximately one year) depending on their mobility skills upon entry (Aditya, 2004). The VA prospective O&M instructors in the 1940s also exercised this occluded immersion training prior to employment (Miyagawa, 1999).

The National Orientation and Mobility Certification is the only O&M certification confirming that the holder has fully met the rigorous standards required in the SDCT curriculum and principles without a visual monitoring requirement (NOMC, 2017; Vaughan & Omvig, 2005). Unique to O&M is that NOMC is performance-based, which means that NOMC instructors are required to demonstrate their ability to perform the necessary Orientation and Mobility techniques for both outdoor and indoor activities while occluded, that is, if the candidate has any vision (Aditya, 2004).

Two men were the first to graduate the innovated O&M program and the following year three men and two women graduated. Of those seven individuals, one was sighted and at the time of this writing, 30% of the nation's NOMCs are sighted (Bell, 2018). Currently, if a person is interested in becoming an NOMC instructor using the SDCT curriculum, there are two avenues from which to select: (1) graduate from a NBPCB approved university program; or (2) successfully complete an approved NBPCB supervised agency apprenticeship (Kaiser et al., 2018; NOMC, 2017).

IN THE BEGINNING

In 1997, Louisiana Tech University and Louisiana Center for the Blind, both in Ruston, Louisiana, collaborated to design an Educational Psychology Master's level program that utilized Discovery Learning which mirrored principles from a *Cognitive Learning Theory* (Bell & Mino, 2011; Schroeder, 1997). Cognitive learning instructional design employs an environment whereby students acquire knowledge and improve comprehension to build and expand upon (Tennyson & Rasch, 1988) which is key in Discovery Learning, now known as Structured Discovery Cane Travel (SDCT). Instructors using the SDCT curriculum begin with direct instruction to master simple Cane Basics, then quickly focus on hands-on problem-solving opportunities (Mino, 2011) because improved cognition happens through the practice and development of independent reasoning without constraints to meet certain criteria. Structured Discovery Cane Travel instructors comprehend that students of all ages are capable of learning for themselves (Koestler, 2004).

Before the term Structured Discovery Cane Travel was adopted, *Discovery Learning* was used. Dr. Kenneth Jernigan, Director of Iowa Department for the Blind (1958–1978), infused into its training curriculum the discovery learning philosophy (Bell & Mino, 2011), that "a teaching strategy in which the material to be learned is uncovered by the learner in the course of solving a problem or completing a task" (Fazzi & Barlow, 2017, p. 254). Therefore, *Discovery Learning* is a curriculum in which participants use action-based activities in mobility to unlock the doors of transformational knowledge (Mezirow, 1991). Structured Discovery Cane Travel was adopted for and by blind people (Baldwin, 2016; Ferguson, 2007) and uses a curriculum which emphasizes *Teachable Moments* and hands-on experiences. These teachable moments include real-life educational opportunities during novel and unexpected encounters which ensures strong personal impacts through which students develop long-lasting concepts or memories of the learning experience (Hansen, 1998).

Under the direction of Dr. Jernigan, the Iowa Department for the Blind became an experimental rehabilitation site in 1958 to embrace the discovery approach (Omvig, 2002). Within ten short years, Dr. Jernigan received the Presidential Citation for his pioneering work in Vocational Rehabilitation (VR) (Omvig, 2002). "Our approach is fundamentally based upon the belief that techniques used by sighted teachers," states Dr. Jernigan, a successful blind cane traveler, "and the alternative techniques which we use are equally effective and that ours are in no way inferior" (Morais et al., 1997, p. 2). Students use cognitive abilities to build and develop self-confidence through action-based, hands-on experience of independent travel to locations which are meaningful for that student (Tigges, 2004). In addition, when given the freedom to explore, students utilize their senses to make discoveries whereby they build strong mental connections (Dodge, & Heroman, 1999).

The discovery learning philosophy significantly and positively impacted vocational rehabilitation throughout the country. It spread from Iowa to Nebraska, Colorado, Louisiana, and Minnesota (Aditya, 2004; Bell & Mino, 2011). In 1984, Alan Dodds, a British O&M instructor, devised the term *Structured Discovery* while at the Nebraska Commission for the Blind when he described his mobility experience of cognitive problem-solving under the direction of an agency-trained blind O&M instructor (Dodds, 1984). Dodds (1984) states that he did not receive sighted information second hand; rather he was permitted to experiment through making mistakes and actively exploring his environment to determine possible solutions without external assistance while occluded.

REHABILITATION TRAINING FOR THE BLIND

Although, the SDCT philosophy was implemented by and for individuals who were blind or visually impaired due to their concerns with the development of the VA O&M training program in the 1940s (Baldwin, 2016; Ferguson, 2007), the NOMC has only been around since 1999. Therefore, Certified Orientation and Mobility Specialists (COMS) has monopolized rehabilitation since its inception in 1962, which historically excluded blind or visually impaired perspective instructors until 1997 (Bell & Mino, 2011; Baldwin, 2016; Vaughan & Omvig, 2005) even though "mobility involves a great deal of mental processing that may not always be measured through direct observation" by their instructor (Geruschat & Turano, 2002, p. 80). One major reason for COMS notoriety is that only one university in the United States offers NOMC certification (ACVREP, 2018; Aditya, 2004; Chamberlain, 2019) to serve the approximate 1.9% of the American population who have visual disabilities (Annual Disability Statistics Compendium, 2017).

Of the over 250 Vocational Rehabilitation (VR) training centers across the United States where O&M is taught to adults (VisionAware, 2018), a high majority of them only have instructors with COMS certification while a very few offers both COMS and NOMC instructors. As an essential component of VR services, consumer choice emerged in the 1900s (Kosciulek, 2004). Yet, due to perceptions and instructional bias of O&M stakeholders (Vaughan, 1993; Wall Emerson & Corn, 2006) and availability of both O&M options, newly blinded consumers are not offered a choice as to which mobility curriculum they receive.

Structured Discovery Cane Travel curriculum is taught in National Blindness Professional Certification Board (NBPCB) approved training centers whereby they are consumer-focused (i.e., collaboration with blind consumer organizations) and meet the NBPCB standards (i.e., concentration on maintaining SDCT methods with an empowering philosophy regarding training) (NBPCB, 2018). The NBPCB approved agencies include the following private centers: (1) Blindness: Learning In New Dimensions, Incorporated (BLIND, Inc) in Minnesota; (2) Colorado Center for the Blind (CCB); and (3) Louisiana Center for the Blind (LCB); and at the following state-operated centers: (1) Ho`opono Services for the Blind Orientation Center in Hawaii; (2) Nebraska Commission for the Blind and Visually Impaired, Orientation Center; and (3) New Mexico Commission for the Blind, Orientation Center (NBPCB, 2018).

O&M INSTRUCTION IN THE EDUCATIONAL SETTING

The National Orientation and Mobility Certification is the only O&M certification confirming that the holder has fully met the rigorous standards required in the SDCT curriculum and principles without a visual monitoring requirement (NOMC, 2017; Vaughan & Omvig, 2005).

The U.S. educational system utilizes O&M certified individuals to provide services for their students. Depending on the size of the district, they either hire their own O&M instructors, contract with an Educational Service Unit or Area Education Agency, or independently contract directly with the O&M professional. Because of COMS longevity, and the unawareness of the NOMC, educational organizations maintain their status quo. However, although the Sequential Learning (SL) curriculum may work well in academics, it has been proven to lower self-confidence in O&M by 32% (Chamberlain, 2019). The COMS curriculum begins with human guide techniques while the NOMC curriculum begins with instruction of the long white cane (Aditya, 2004; Chamberlain, 2019; COMS Handbook, 2018).

CHAPTER 4

FUNDAMENTALS OF SDCT

The fundamentals of the Structured Discovery Cane Travel (SDCT) curriculum are action-based, hands-on activities conducted in real-world settings. That is, students obtain knowledge by way of independent movement through space which requires multi-tasking, a method which has been proven to be more beneficial than if students were to remain static (Deverell, 2011). Through physical actions, students gain spatial orientation that, according to Kaiser et al. (2018) and Payne (2002), is necessary for the brain to register positioning of where the body is and that can be conducted through touch. Many consumers use the long white cane as a mobility tool (Tuttle, 1984) because it provides tactile information about the terrain as one of its many functions. Cutter (2007) adds the long white cane offers near space knowledge through touch while the metal tip provides distance sense awareness through echolocation (i.e., reflected sound) for efficient exploration (i.e., movement) in the world.

The fundamentals of SDCT are based on perceptions, other than the initial instruction of the long white cane. Students work one-on-one with their O&M instructors for individualized training beginning with *Cane Basics* as this is the primary tool consumers use for life. Cane Basics is the only Sequential Learning (SL) component of the SDCT curriculum in the sense that it is introduced prior to *Cane Mechanics*. However, students need not "master" Cane Basics before venturing toward Cane Mechanics in the SDCT curriculum. (Chapter 6 delves further into Cane Basics and Cane Mechanics). Rather, mastering occurs henceforth, that is, directly after the cane techniques are introduced, or as Blaha (1967) states, instruction progresses to more advanced travels. While students are occluded, the SDCT curriculum proceeds with developing Problem-Solving Skills, Echolocation (via the metal tip), Intrinsic Feedback/Motivation, Transformational Knowledge, and Mental Mapping skills.

GLASSER'S CHOICE THEORY

When students are actively involved in the decision-making process, such as the SDCT curriculum which is hands-on, an increase in training effectiveness is probable (Coulter et al., 1999; Glasser, 1998). Glasser's *choice theory* is an internal control psychology in which the direction of people's lives are determined by how and why choices are made (Glasser, 1998). In other words, when students are given options, they have the freedom of choice which, according to Glasser (1998), is necessary for growth. Cutter (2007) states when students are not given the personal freedom of choice during training, they tend to make risky decisions regarding independent movements post-training.

LOCUS OF CONTROL

In all levels of the educational system from preschool to graduate school, it is clearly understood that teachers hold *Locus of Control*. The same is true for O&M instructors during cane travel lessons involving young children within the school setting. "Locus of control is a psychological concept that refers to how strongly people believe they have control over the situations and experiences that affect their lives" (Glossary of Education Reform, 2013, par. 1). For older students, mainly those outside of the school setting, Mettler (1995) states the unambiguous training goal in SDCT is for students to accept and maintain locus of control. Transition of locus of control from instructor to student occurs as students work through problem-solving opportunities (i.e., obstacles) while traveling to *their* desired locations. Young children within the school setting also have some level of locus of control as they progress in their O&M skills. Yet, the locus of control transition from teacher to student cannot occur if students are not given travel opportunities to face obstacles to independently develop problem-solving skills.

> The unambiguous training goal in SDCT is for students to accept and maintain locus of control (Mettler, 1995)

Older students maintain locus of control directly after receiving Cane Basics, states Mettler (1995). Henceforth, as students complete each travel experience, the satisfaction remains with the student through their own successes. Students of all ages who have self-confidence in their travel abilities understand and believe that they are in control of their actions directing their whereabouts. That is, students maintain locus of control and believe they determine what happens (Dodds, 1988). When lessons are completed, *it is the student who gains personal satisfaction* and this feeling of success transfers to their next lesson. Of course, their mobility instructor may also find satisfaction when the students are successful.

INTRINSIC FEEDBACK/MOTIVATION

During each lesson, the instructor remains silent in order for students to focus on obtaining information through internal processing or senses known as *Intrinsic Feedback* such as: 1) any auditory sounds available either through the metal cane tip or elsewhere; 2) any olfactory information available; 3) any terrain information provided by tactile feedback through the cane; 4) internal perception (kinesthetic cues); and 5) prior knowledge, experience, and/or memory of spatial information (Long & Giudice, 2010). Perception or focusing strategies need to be conducted within the mobility lesson, states Baldwin (2016). He adds that since the environment is ever changing, students need to pay attention to their intake of raw perceptual data; this information is gathered internally and organized into their cognitive mental map for later retrieval (Baldwin, 2016).

Depending on the student's needs, external verbal information regarding the environment (i.e., the number of doorways, hallways, etc.) is not provided to the student before and/or during the lesson. Some extrinsic information, even if well intended, delivers useless facts which may simply cause the student to become overwhelmed attempting to organize and memorize that information. Keep in mind that this extrinsic data is from the providers' point-of-view and what that person considers pertinent. Students need to discover and determine for themselves if the environmental encounter is worthy of retention.

Verbal external information restricts students from the opportunity to develop intrinsic feedback and the creation of mental mapping skills. In addition, some students can become dependent on information provided externally (i.e., cue dependency) and this can lower self-confidence and hinder internal problem solving. Often cue dependent students will halt their mobility and wait for external information, or the *ok* to travel forward, before proceeding.

However, at times during mobility, students may encounter obstacles which, after some contemplation, they think are unsolvable. When that happens, instructors assist students to work through the problems by asking trigger questions to help them expose previous knowledge and/or experiences to hypothesize or arrive at possible solutions. Such probing, open-ending questions help students to tap into their transformational knowledge, and according to Mettler (1995), this helps students develop their intrinsic skills while being actively engaged in their mobility development.

Intrinsic Motivation is another fundamental of the SDCT curriculum because it establishes goals which are meaningful or significant only to that student (Sarid, 2012). According to Sullo (2007) "internal control psychology is based upon the belief that people are internally, not externally, motivated" (p. 7). Thus, when students have a choice regarding the locations they visit, they enter Choice Theory, which Sullo (2007) states satisfies one's basic internal psychological needs of: (1) belonging or connecting; (2) power; (3) freedom; and (4) fun (p. 8). Sullo (2007) adds, as students develop self-confidence, they gain power through proficiency, competence and achievements. Therefore, the mobility instructor has the responsibility to encourage and facilitate learning opportunities for their students in a variety of natural environments so they can explore and build new concepts which support the internal psychological needs. While students develop intrinsic motivation, their mobility instructor continuously monitors their travel skills and abilities to ensure that there are no gaps of prerequisite skills, knowledge, or concepts during skill-building opportunities.

> **When students comprehend that their movement (via travel) represents personal choices, they discover freedom to make effective and responsible decisions. (Sullo, 2007)**

Maurer et al. (2007) states that SDCT instructors assist students toward enabling and building the discovery of environmental concepts through sound profiles. This method is intentionally designed to guide students to use and develop intrinsic feedback and/or transformational knowledge which helps construct independent travel skills through extensive practice and training (Maurer et al., 2007). According to Sullo (2007), when students are internally motivated, they are active learners who are "not controlled by outside events or stimuli" (p. 14). Instead they are able to cultivate essential perceptual-cognitive skills to use in similar experiences outside of class (Mettler, 1995). When students comprehend that their movement (via travel) represents personal choices, they discover freedom to make effective and responsible decisions (Sullo, 2007).

OCCLUDED TRAINING

Many legally blind students receiving mobility instruction are unaware that their remaining vision is unreliable. Regardless, they often consider their unreliable vision as true and dependable. However, this may place the student in dangerous situations. *Occluded training* provides students the abilities and skills they can depend on, regardless of how much vision they have now or how little vision they may have in the future. Therefore, the SDCT curriculum requires students to be occluded (i.e., wear sleep-shades, blindfolds, bandanas) during O&M instruction. Occluding, according to Kappan (1994), Pogrund and Griffin-Shirley (2018), is used to block or restrict visual input and build self-confidence while perfecting nonvisual skills.

Keep in mind that being occluded during mobility is not intended to be what Herbert (2000) states is a powerful experience to enhance disability awareness and/or to promote positive attitudes towards individuals with disabilities. Rather, spending extensive hours in total immersion helps students gain self-confidence while focusing on the development of non-visual mobility techniques. When students learn O&M while wearing sleep-shades, regardless of how much vision is lost over time, the skills they obtained in mobility training are maintained.

> When skills are mastered without vision, regardless of lighting conditions or level of decreased vision over time, students are still able to perform the task.

In some cases, students may need additional time to adjust to wearing the sleep-shades. When this happens, mobility instructors may need to begin lessons in areas that are extra familiar to the student. Time may be needed for them to gather enough courage to leave their comfort zone and, more importantly, to trust the information their long white cane offers. If the student is still struggling with the adjustment to wearing sleep-shades, a hearing test may be necessary. Due to extremely rare extenuating circumstances, occlusion training during O&M lessons may be impossible for some students.

According to Maurer et al. (2007) and Mino (2011), one of the most critical mental processes necessary in mobility is having self-confidence in the *nonvisual* techniques of problem-solving. The SDCT curriculum focuses on these mobility skills as students use the long white cane while occluded, which significantly reduces the overall time spent in training. When skills are mastered without vision, regardless of lighting conditions or level of decreased vision over time, students are still able to perform the task. In contrast, if skills are mastered with minimal available vision, that skill may not be usable in poor lighting conditions or additional training will be necessary if or when sight decreases. Therefore, SDCT students who have any remaining vision benefit from occlusion training because sleep-shades allocate attention toward learning as well as…

1. Removes the need for additional training in various lighting conditions and/or as vision decreases, reducing the time students spend in training.
2. Blocks unreliable, distracting vision which may subconsciously affect the students' ability to build nonvisual knowledge and skills necessary for travel (Maurer et al., 2007).
3. Reduces visual fatigue which happens when attempts are made to utilize old skills while simultaneously trying to develop and perfect new ones (Maurer et al., 2007).
4. Improves performance levels by removing the dependency on lighting conditions.

According to Kappan (1994), minimal occluded disability awareness training possibly creates false impressions of the true capabilities of consumers. Thus, prospective mobility instructors learning the SDCT curriculum spend extensive hours occluded (i.e., 500–650 hours for sighted instructors; 500–2000 hours for legally blind) (Aditya, 2004) which models the Veteran's O&M training program in the 1940s (Miyagawa, 1999). Instructors who undergo extensive occluded mobility training can actively, without hesitation, demonstrate nonvisual mobility tasks. Thus, through the actions of the instructor demonstrating self-confidence and ability, students may internally believe in the mobility skills they are striving to obtain. Therefore, National Orientation and Mobility Certified instructors are able to demonstrate that they have acquired the skills that they are requesting from their students, just as algebra teachers are able to demonstrate the necessary steps to complete complex mathematical formulas.

Through the SDCT curriculum, instructors help students build constructive (problem-solving) travel strategies while they are occluded. These strategies can be transferred from the lesson setting to other locations post-instruction whereby students are able to solve a myriad of travel obstacles or challenges. When students have confidence in their travel abilities without using their limited or remaining vision, they are more likely to be self-motivated during off-training hours when they are able to use the vision they may still have. This was evident with blinded soldiers who, on weekends, traveled independently to local establishments when off duty (Miyagawa, 1999). When people learn to pay attention to their surroundings, rather than be told about their surroundings, they learn to tune into their other senses, states Gravel (2006), a consumer who wrote this observation to his former SDCT instructor:

> Instructors who undergo extensive occluded mobility training can actively, without hesitation, demonstrate nonvisual mobility tasks.

I'm unafraid to venture out on my own now, even when traveling in a new city. You gave me the understanding and courage to simply "get the job done," no matter the supposed obstacles. You taught me—undeniably—that I can be dropped off anywhere, not even knowing exactly where, and still find the location where I need to go (pp. 23–25).

MENTAL MAPPING

To create a diagram of the environment within the mind is considered *Mental Mapping Skills* (Chamberlain, 2005) and this essential ability depends on the development of nonvisual senses, according to Guerreiro et al. (2017). When given the freedom to explore, students utilize their senses to make discoveries whereby they build strong mental connections and spatial relationships within their environment (Dodge, & Heroman, 1999; Hudson, 1997). These skills help students understand their surroundings, relating a comprehensive representation of future travel opportunities (Guerreiro et al., 2017). Long and Giudice (2010) state that mental mapping involves a higher cognitive spatial ability than memorization of sequential actions or *landmarks*. Landmarks are Points of Interest (POI) which are stationary, meaning they may be used as reference points that are unlikely to be moved such as water fountains, support columns, texture change on the floor (carpet to tile) (Chamberlain, 2017). Through spatial orientation by way of physical actions within the environment, students utilize intrinsic feedback in the creation of mental mapping skills whereby, during mobility, they discover and determine for themselves what is worthy of retention. Furthermore, ongoing mental spatial updates are necessary for knowledge awareness while traveling (Hudson, 1997). In addition, Kaiser et al. (2018) and Payne (2002) state the ability of touch is necessary for the brain to register body positioning and develop spatial orientation. Touching the environment occurs through the mobility tool (i.e., the long white cane), states Tuttle (1984), which provides tactile information about the terrain. Mental mapping is paramount through the use of the cane because, as Cutter (2007) states, the cane with a metal tip offers near space information through touch as well as distance information through echolocation sense awareness (i.e., reflected sound) and this occurs effectively via movement. Through active involvement and self-responsibility, students learn by multi-tasking while performing movement (i.e., walking) which develops spatial orientation simply by their use of the cane within the environment (Deverell, 2011; Kaiser et al., 2018; Payne, 2002).

> When given the freedom to explore, students utilize their senses to make discoveries whereby they build strong mental connections (Dodge, & Heroman, 1999)

Active physical interactions are paramount in the SDCT curriculum whereby students engage in environmental characteristics using residual senses. Tuttle & Tuttle (1996) state this hands-on sense (touch) utilizes a physical interaction of exploration and perhaps curiosity as a conceptual whole. This physical interaction, according to DuFour et al. (2006), effectively "develops a deeper and more profound knowledge and greater commitment than learning by reading, listening, planning, or thinking" (p. 4). Mental mapping, through movement, may actually replace vision in regards to environmental clarification (Barraga & Erin, 1992). Furthermore, this transformational skill is fundamental for successful mobility post-training.

TWO TYPES OF MEMORY

Memory, as part of the cognitive process, is often relied upon during rehabilitation (Iskow, 2010) and that includes mobility training. Educators use two types of memory systems embedded within curriculums: 1) *Locale* (long-term) with an unlimited capacity and 2) *Taxon* (short-term) with a capacity of approximately five tasks (Payne, 2002). Sequential Learning (SL) is a curriculum that follows the Taxon memory system which needs continuous rehearsals and extrinsic motivation to reach perfection (Payne, 2002). For example, students often use Taxon memory for mathematics and spelling tests whereby they develop new skills while simultaneously attempting to improve retention, which challenges retention capacity and adds stress (Dodds, 1988). O'Donnell (1988) states the memorization of routes decreases mobility performance because of the negative correlation between short-term (Taxon) memory and stress.

Dodds (1988) states Taxon memory challenges retention capacity before and during mobility lessons and Payne (2002) adds when travel lessons are arranged (i.e., fixed), isolated knowledge chunks are created which are insignificant in nature. In addition, continuous rehearsals are required along with extrinsic motivation for successful completion. As stated above, when students discover and determine for themselves the importance of environmental encounters, mental mapping skills develop. Therefore, it is no surprise that participants of a study conducted by Guerreiro et al. (2017) struggled with the retention of precise sequential information that was provided to them prior to the physical action requirement because this data was insignificant in nature. Guerreiro et al.'s (2017) study agrees with Payne (2002) which proved short-term memory hinders transformational knowledge and generates problem-solving roadblocks through lack of flexibility toward detours, shortcuts or even curious exploration.

Locale Memory system is used in the SDCT curriculum in which students are internally motivated by curiosity and intrinsic expectations which leads to successful achievement. According to Payne (2002), Locale memory systems are interconnected as they create personal and meaningful mental mapping skills. Since travel opportunities "will never be accomplished or experienced in exactly the same way" (Deverell, 2011, p. 67) it is vital that students develop problem-solving skills to handle travel woes that may create anxiety. Alan Beggs (1992) states, aside from self-confidence, the difference between poor travelers and accomplished travelers is their capabilities to handle anxiety and their recall proficiencies.

Through purposeful movements to desired destinations, students actively build attention, intention, perception, consciousness, and memory (i.e., Locale/long-term memory with an unlimited capacity) (Baldwin, 2016). Blasch et al. (1997), states consumers travel best while utilizing their senses to (1) gather information about the environment; (2) develop cognitive abilities of reasoning and memory; (3) interpret the sensory information; and (4) develop spatial orientation. Guerreiro et al. (2017) adds consumers also use landmarks known as Points of Interest (POI) to help with navigation. When students are given opportunities to develop sensory and motor skills, they are able to utilize their transformational knowledge to retrieve the skills from their long-term memory which requires less mental effort than memorizing all aspects of the travel route (Soong et al., 2001).

PROBLEM-SOLVING SKILLS

Having the ability to problem solve is related to being capable independent travelers (Alan Beggs, 1992).

After the introduction of Cane Basics, activities quickly focus on Cane Mechanics through discovery learning, which is the foundation of Structured Discovery Cane Travel. In order for optimal performance, Fay and Funk (1995) state students need to be cognitively aware. This is where the shift from instructor to student takes place regarding who maintains locus of control. This transition is brought about through intrinsic feedback where students utilize plenty of time to contemplate options and consider and weigh alternatives during their mobility lessons to become active problem-solvers. Alan Beggs (1992) determined through a study that having the ability to problem solve is related to being a capable independent traveler.

Opportunities to problem solve occur during teachable moments when a travel woe is discovered in the SDCT curriculum. In other words, lessons are *discovered* by the students through opportunities to problem-solve (Blasch et al., 1997) and these occasions help develop transformational knowledge for future retrieval. These are real-life new and/or unexpected environmental encounters that engage and stimulate long-lasting concepts and/or memory of specific learning experiences (Hansen, 1998). The amount of time used to contemplate and resolve the travel woe increases the probability that students will be successful in solving problems (Fay & Funk, 1995).

Through the SDCT hands-on curriculum, which encourages active physical interactions, students are able to learn environmental characteristics via their residual senses, states Tuttle & Tuttle (1996). They add, these senses include touch, physical interaction by way of utilization of exploration, and possibly curiosity as a conceptual whole. This effective, hands-on experience "develops a deeper and more profound knowledge and greater commitment than learning by reading, listening, planning, or thinking" (DuFour et al., 2006, p. 4). Actually, according to Barraga and Erin (1992), movement may replace vision in environmental clarification. (Chapter 5 will further explain Problem Solving Techniques in SDCT.)

TRANSFORMATIONAL KNOWLEDGE

Transformational Knowledge is the ability to learn and master techniques within a plethora of settings during training through hands-on experiences and then transfer those skills post-training to other settings. This technique is paramount in the SDCT curriculum which enables the development of higher self-confidence. Directly after students are introduced to the basics of how to use the cane, they begin to develop transformational knowledge through independent environmental exploration along with some generalized instruction focused on problem-solving, states Tigges (2004), former Director of the Orientation Center at the Iowa Department for the Blind. She adds, this phase includes information gathering and internal processing development when students encounter opportunities to problem-solve because they are encouraged to use their own resourcefulness instead of depending on external guidance and/or reassurances from a mobility instructor. The Orientation Center has used Discovery Learning since its inception to support long-term and retainable knowledge that increases students' self-confidence and ensures better developed independent travel skills (Tigges, 2004) which has proven to be successful in Chamberlain's (2019) study. Since it is impossible to look into students' minds to gain insight as to the cognitive process as they are undergoing while comprehending travel woes, instructors assess students' actions or self-reports to evaluate independent travel and transformational knowledge. Thus, their behavior represents cognitive problem-solving capabilities.

SELF-CONFIDENCE

The ability to utilize transformational knowledge builds self-confidence. Keep in mind that consumers' sense of adequacy, value, competence, worth and satisfaction are considered forms of self-confidence, self-esteem, and self-determination (Tuttle & Tuttle, 1996). As with transformational knowledge, self-confidence cannot be observed visually; rather the measurement is through consumers' action. For example, novice drivers demonstrate lack of confidence through their actions by way of driving slower with spasmodic movements while expert drivers operate their vehicles smoothly and methodically. The same is true through observation of beginners and expert cane travelers, in that beginners tend to walk slowly with a gait that is not smooth or methodical. Spatial intelligence (i.e., Mental Mapping) is necessary for movement to take place. Lazear (1999) state proficient cane travelers often have greater self-confidence and accuracy in their mobility skill than sighted people wearing sleep-shades. Overall, **self-confidence** is how much a person feels certain or capable of their decisions, actions, and/or behaviors (Bearden et al., 2001).

The independent travel habits of students may correspond to the students' self-perceptions of their O&M abilities and skills states Bénabou and Tirole (2002), who indicate when students have higher self-confidence, they have enhanced motivation and decreased or extinguished self-handicapping habits. It is fair to say that in mobility, actions represent self-confidence levels in O&M (Chamberlain, 2019). In fact, according to Schreiber and Moss (2002), students' actions represent their personal beliefs, self-confidence, and their perceived ability. Some researchers have used walking speed and gait to evaluate self-confidence (Geruschat & Turano, 2002), yet that method of study was proved to be inadequate through Chamberlain's (2019) study where frequency and distances independently traveled, post-instruction were measured.

According to Dodds (1988) and Tigges (2004), students acquire essential mental processing skills, and this cognitive development is how they gain self-confidence in their independent mobility in ways that are meaningful to them. Building self-confidence and self-efficacy is a critical component in O&M because, according to Aditya (2004), individuals with high levels of self-confidence in their travel skills are less likely to be involved in accidents compared to those with low self-confidence. Mobility instructors using the SDCT curriculum consider their students' self-confidence when addressing their psychological aspects of independent and safe travel through purposeful movements.

EVIDENCE SUPPORTING SDCT

The measurement of rehabilitation goals and equivalent outcomes which were evaluated to prevent the wasting of governmental resources (Vaughan, 1993) supported the fundamentals of SDCT. This evaluation was conducted through a survey in 1991 which measured the activities of consumers post training of

TABLE 4.1. Activity After Training: 1991 Post-Training (Vaughan, 1993)

| Category | Sequential Learning (SL) | | Structured Discovery Cane Travel (SDCT) |
	Minnesota State Services for the Blind	Duluth Lighthouse for the Blind	Blind: Learning in New Directions (Blind, Inc.)
Total participants	57	50	52
Gained Employment	5 (9%)	6 (12%)	14 (27%)
Went to College	14 (25%)	11 (22%)	38 (73%)
Did Nothing Post-Training	38 (67%)	33 (66%)	Zero

three rehabilitation training centers in Minnesota: Minnesota State Services for the Blind (MSSB), Duluth Lighthouse for the Blind (DLB), and Blind: Learning In New Dimensions (BLIND, Inc.) (Table 4.1).

Of the three rehabilitation agencies, BLIND, Inc. was the only agency that used a discovery-learning (i.e., SDCT) method of instruction whereby post-training 100% of their consumers were either gainfully employed or enrolled in higher education (Vaughan, 1993). This survey revealed only 34% of the MSSB and 34% of DLB consumers followed the same aspirations. Therefore, this demonstrated that the discovery-learning approach results in greater self-confidence; leading to higher employment and independent living outcomes post instruction (Vaughan, 1993).

Another example supporting SDCT with transformational knowledge was revealed through a comparison study conducted by Chamberlain (2019) which measured self-confidence levels of consumers post O&M instruction. Keep in mind that self-confidence and self-determination are forms of competence in meeting life's demands (Tuttle & Tuttle, 1996) and how much a person feels assured and capable can be represented by their self-confidence levels (Bearden et al., 2001). In particular, Chamberlain's (2019) study was conducted to evaluate the relationship of two curriculums: (1) when students were first introduced to a guide compared to (2) those who were first introduced to the long white cane.

Chamberlain's (2019) study evaluated 40 consumers' O&M travel habits post-training to predict self-confidence levels by comparing their travel habits post-training. Half of the students received human guide instruction as their first lesson while the other half received instruction with the long white cane. These participants were spread throughout the United States whereby a single region or O&M instructor were not singled out. The states included:

- Arkansas
- California
- Colorado
- Florida
- Georgia
- Hawaii
- Idaho
- Indiana
- Louisiana
- Mississippi
- Missouri
- Montana
- Nebraska
- Nevada
- New Jersey
- New York
- Plus, three unknowns

TABLE 4.2. Self-Confidence Level Calculations

		SL	SDCT
Travel Outside City Limits (TOCL):	Never	15%	0
	Sometimes	55%	25%
	*Always	30%	75%
Travel independently to visit friends/relatives		50%	95%
Frequency Score		75%	90%
No need for future O&M training		50%	70%
Average score (* = score used for TOCL)		51%	83%
Difference			+32%

Chamberlain, 2019, p. 137

Since self-confidence and belief directs behavior (Glasser, 1998), the same must hold true for consumers' travel habits post-training through measuring their transformational efficiency. Chamberlain's (2019) study revealed consumers who received the SDCT O&M curriculum yielded higher self-confidence levels than those who received mobility instruction by way of a SL O&M curriculum by 32%. (See Table 4.2)

As stated in Chapter Three, prospective NOMC O&M instructors spend 500–2000 hours of *immersion* training (Aditya, 2004). This training has a strong impact on future independent travel because they are able to perform the tasks they are instructing their students to perform. This letter was written to her former NOMC O&M instructor, who she referred to has her *blind role model*. Allison (2013) states:

You were my O&M instructor when I was in the LCB STEP program at 16. I admit I couldn't have been much fun to work with at that time. I didn't hate my cane or sleep-shades or anything like that; I knew I had signed up for that when I chose to go to LCB instead of my lame local training center. But, even so, I was alternatingly scared and sarcastic and generally an annoying teenager. Anyway, I remember that first I didn't really buy what you said about being able to safely travel as a totally blind person. I really wanted to believe it, but I didn't. Partly because I knew you traveled as someone who seemed to have more sight than I did. So, I half listened to what you said and continued to lack confidence. Until one day you actually put on sleep-shades before we crossed a street together. I have no idea why, I think it was part of your O&M program internship? Anyway, that really impacted me. I doubt I mentioned it to you at the time, but I was impressed. I realized that you were so confident in your ability to travel as a totally blind person that you actually made yourself blinder to travel with me. And that was something I had never seen before. And over time it helped me to believe that the amount of sight I did or didn't have wasn't directly proportional to how much success I could have in life. I knew you believed that blind people could travel because you yourself traveled as a blind person. How in the world could I think that I couldn't do it when you were doing it right in front of me? And whether I ever told you about it or not, I've used my cane every single day since that summer. I was only a sporadic cane user before that.

Today I have a job and live on my own…I've lost a ton more sight and am completely night blind. But I still cross streets at night safely and don't worry about it because I have the skills and confidence to do it. And you were part of how I learned that so I wanted to say thank you…I know from personal experience how seldom we get to hear that the work we do ever helps anyone… I wanted you to know that one small thing you did 15-ish years ago made a big difference to one person. So, thanks again.

Best,
Allison

The SDCT curriculum is student focused whereby their mobility training is designed around their destination desires.

Left: Oliver was interested in the Military tanks for his mobility lesson.

Right: Noah wanted to go to the laundromat for one of his mobility lessons.

NOTES

_____

_____

_____

_____

_____

_____

_____

_____

_____

_____

_____

_____

_____

_____

_____

_____

CHAPTER 5

PROBLEM-SOLVING SKILLS IN O&M

Basically, *Structured Discovery*, Discovery Learning, and Problem-Solving are intertwined whereby students discover the necessary techniques or skills to be learned or completed to perform a task. *Structured Discovery* is the experience of cognitive problem-solving under the direction of an educator (Dodds, 1984) while *Discovery Learning* is "a teaching strategy in which the material to be learned is uncovered by the learner in the course of solving a problem or completing a task" (Fazzi & Barlow, 2017, p. 254). *Problem-solving* in O&M is the process of utilizing techniques to alleviate travel woes. It is a "metaphor for most higher-order thinking tasks and for most assessment tasks that tap higher-order thinking" (Brookhart, 2014, p. 12). This philosophy led to *Structured Discovery Cane Travel (SDCT)* which combines Structured Discovery and Discovery Learning and Problem-Solving Skills. SDCT is an O&M curriculum which utilizes transformational knowledge, hands-on experiences, problem-solving opportunities within natural environments, and personal reflection through teachable moments to develop physical and mental mapping skills which can be utilized post instruction, outside the O&M lesson. Specifically, SDCT involves the experience of cognitive problem-solving under the direction of a mobility instructor who has National Orientation and Mobility Certification. In mobility training, this discovery learning closely resembles the Veterans Administration O&M program (Sauerburger, 2007) whereby instructors do not create an artificial environment for students to discover. Rather, these are actual encounters that the student may and are most likely to face post mobility instruction.

> SDCT is an O&M curriculum which utilizes transformational knowledge, hands-on experiences, problem-solving opportunities within natural environments, and personal reflection through teachable moments to develop physical and mental mapping skills which can be utilized post instruction, outside the O&M lesson.

Structured Discovery Cane Travel instructors assist students to develop problem-solving techniques through exploration and/or discovery of transformational knowledge whereby they are able to utilize those intrinsic techniques post instruction. Unlike the general public, these instructors do not avoid potential

The ABCs of Structured Discovery Cane Travel for Children, pages 27–34.

minor, non-harmful obstacles within the student's path. Rather, they permit students to independently discover and explore the obstacles to determine possible solutions to alleviate the travel woe in order to continue toward desired destinations. Problems in cane travel are simply unexpected occurrences which may include and are surely not limited to the following examples:

- Any unforeseen obstacles within the travel path (i.e., mop bucket in the hallway, trashcans on the sidewalk, closed doors, chairs or any items presenting inaccessible pathways, etc.).
- Accidental veering or undetected curves.
- Unexpected or undetected changes in the terrain such as curb cuts, texture changes (i.e., carpet to hardwood to tile, etc.).
- Unexpected sensation of ascending or descending (i.e., ramps or slopes).
- Disorientation within the environment.
- Unexplained changes in the environment obtained through other senses (i.e., olfactory, auditory, temperature changes or wind gusts on the skin).

Encountering a problem is an unexpected occurrence which may sometimes evoke fear in students; however, the avoidance of travel woes prevents them the opportunity to problem-solve. This avoidance can hinder students from generating alternative travel routes as well as create fears of traveling independently. Thus, SDCT instructors welcome opportunities for students to develop problem-solving techniques in real-life situations. According to Mino (2011), these opportunities are "ill-structured because, by definition, they emerge from a real-world environment that is in constant and unpredictable change." When students master problem-solving skills, they are able to utilize those techniques outside of O&M class as proven by Chamberlain's (2019) study.

Students of all ages need opportunities to explore their environment so they can develop mental mapping skills. As they explore, students determined expectations as to what lies ahead. Then, they are able to comprehend that a problem exists when the environment or perceptions do not match their expectations based on experiences or knowledge prior to encountering the incident (Long & Giudice, 2010). Preferably, the problems students encounter during their mobility lessons are not solved by instructors, but rather the students engage in the problem solving to resolve their incorrect assumptions (Blasch et al., 1997). Long and Giudice (2010) state that the components of these hypothesis-testing, problem-solving opportunities include the following steps: (1) acknowledge that a problem exists; (2) identify workable solutions or strategies to proceed; (3) select a self-concluded option; (4) implement selected alternatives; and (5) evaluate the selected strategy. In addition, the capability to successfully problem-solve is severely influenced by external & internal factors which includes: students' conceptual knowledge; their ability to manage stress; their mobility skill and experiential levels; and the present environment (Perla & O'Donnell, 2004, 47). See Table 5.1.

In the SDCT curriculum, students learn independent travel by actually performing mobility functions independently, with the guidance of their mobility instructor, if needed. However, the level of guidance can be minimal to extreme—depending on the students' individual needs. For example, let's say a student has a desire to go to the lunchroom but believes this is only possible with the assistance of a guide. The lesson may begin with the student leaving the current location and walking toward the lunchroom. The path to the lunchroom is not verbally provided to the student in advance. Instead, the student leads the way, taking the direction he assumes is the path to the lunchroom. When the student faces an obstacle in the path, makes an incorrect move or misses an important turn, the student begins the problem-solving component of the lesson. By doing this independently, the student will be able to access transformational knowledge and build skills which can be utilized when the instructor is not present and/or in other settings.

TABLE 5.1.   Components of Successful Problem-Solving

STEPS	INFLUENCES Internal & External
1. Acknowledge problem exists	1. Conceptual knowledge
2. Identify workable solution/strategy	2. Ability to manage stress
3. Select self-concluded solution/strategy	3. Mobility skill and experiential levels
4. Implement selected solution/strategy	4. The present environment
5. Evaluate selected solution/strategy	
(Long & Giudice, 2010)	(Perla & O'Donnell, 2004)

However, if students begin to demonstrate frustration, then the mobility instructor may provide Socratic type of open-ended and/or probing questions to help them overcome their frustration through acknowledging the obstacle exists and recalling possible solutions. Through such questions, students often discover that solutions are found from within or from their previous experiences. With this method, they develop skills which can be transferred to other travel situations post- instruction. In the beginning of the training process, SDCT can be time consuming but as students' experience increases, so do their travel speed and confidence, thereby reducing instruction time.

Understandably, in the school system, instructional time may be limited. With that in mind, students in the above example can still be successful even if they do not entirely reach their desired location. The instructor may suggest walking *toward* rather than *to* the targeted goal. Then, the next time, the students' goal will be able to walk closer to that location. Problems that occur within the path are addressed as they are presented. This means, if a student needs to ascend stairs along the route and had never worked on stairs before, then the lesson of ascending stairs would be addressed <u>when</u> it was presented.

Problem-solving opportunities are simply teachable moments during a mobility lesson which provide discovery learning for the students. Teachable moments, or problem-solving opportunities, arise because they are ill-structured and these opportunities present themselves within an ever-changing, unpredictable environment during real-world activities (Mino, 2011). Keep in mind that "the environment encountered in O&M is itself a living thing, a dynamic interplay between physical, social, and sensory elements" (Deverell, 2011, p. 64). These educational encounters enhance on-the-spot learning with deeper meanings. In addition, teachable moments encourage critical reflection and skill building with self-assessment (Hansen, 1998). This enhanced mental processing is essential for students to engage in when traveling in familiar and unfamiliar environments (Mino, 2011). Since the process of problem-solving in mobility is cognitive and self-directed (Mettler, 1995; Wehmeyer, 2004), it "involves a great deal of mental processing that may not always be measured through direct observation" by their instructor (Geruschat & Turano, 2002, p. 80). Therefore, students need to gain skill in navigating practical environments as they are presented (e.g., poor sidewalk conditions, less than perfect weather conditions, and lack of assistance from the general public) in order to be exposed to a plethora of problem-solving opportunities (Mino, 2011; Perla & O'Donnell, 2004). Thus, students will gain the self-confidence to address environmental barriers, as well as be knowledgeable of alternative techniques of navigating in various environments (Kaiser et al., 2018) which they may utilize outside of class.

Novice and proficient cane travelers may make mobility *mistakes*, such as venturing off the desired travel route from time-to-time. These mistakes are *natural* opportunities to learn, known as teachable moments. For students these problem-solving encounters may be solved independently or with instructor guidance, if needed. Keep in mind that successful independent problem-solving cannot occur if students are overprotected, that is, not given opportunities to commit mistakes (Perla & O'Donnell, 2004) or are overwhelmed with verbal reports of approaching cautions or obstacles (i.e., stairs, doorways, wet floor signs or parked cars) when traveling (Mettler, 1995). When students are not permitted to make mistakes, they lose the opportunity to recognize that problems exist (Perla & O'Donnell, 2004), and this recognition is the first component of problem-solving opportunity, state Long and Giudice (2010). They add that students need to realize for themselves that a problem may exist if the environment in which they are traveling is different from their previous expectations or encounters. If students become dependent on someone to inform them of possible problems, they will (1) not pay attention to their environment during mobility; (2) not be able to recognize problems for themselves; and (3) decrease independent travel, whereby they become embedded within the Custodial Paradigm.

Many opportunities to encounter challenges are given to students throughout their lessons in the SDCT curriculum (Aditya, 2004). Students learn to use intrinsic feedback and hypothesis-testing to overcome challenges and, if needed, their instructor may offer probing, open-ending questions (Mettler, 1995). These types of questions help students conclude possible solutions to overcome obstacles are located within. Actually, helping students by posing challenging questions is a component of the *synthesis* category of Bloom's Taxonomy and provides students the necessary time to problem-solve, learn new skills, or internalize values or behavior (Fay & Funk, 1995). Mobility involves mental processing whereby students "need time to mull over ideas, contemplate, and weigh the alternatives before" making conclusions (Fay & Funk, 1995, p. 181; Geruschat & Turano, 2002).

Since experience leads to change (Baldwin, 2016), the SDCT O&M curriculum offers students opportunities in an abundance of environments such as "subways to nature trails, Capitol Hill to the mountains of Arkansas, and Mardi Gras to New Jersey" (Bell, 2015). These opportunities help students encounter both positive and negative mobility adventures rather than focusing only on positive outcomes. When O&M lessons focus entirely on positive outcomes, students may learn to avoid problems developing fears of the unknown and even fears of failure, which may result in low self-confidence and decreased independent travel (Perla & O'Donnell, 2004).

In the SDCT curriculum, students are encouraged to focus on skill development rather than memorization of landmarks and directions from one point to another. Cognitive environmental awareness and mental mapping skill development can hinder independent travel when there is an over emphasis on memorization, especially when encountering unexpected obstacles or incorrect turns (Perla & O'Donnell, 2004). The same is true of the need to memorize the number of steps from one location to another, for this technique is unreliable since individuals are unable to maintain the same gait between opportunities. Furthermore, if the number of steps is provided externally, this number may not coincide with the actual steps used by the student.

Some consider the lack of lesson time as a potential obstacle to problem-solving (Perla & O'Donnell, 2004); however, the SDCT curriculum provides ample time for students to be successful because *every problem-solving encounter is a learning opportunity*. Curriculums that use sequential methods limit instructors to the allotted time to complete the targeted lesson at hand. According to Payne (2002), adequate time is necessary for students to comprehend important aspects of the lesson (i.e., problem-solving) in order to determine and retain essential experiences which may be utilized in future settings. Since problem-solving encounters are learning opportunities, each lesson is considered successful.

The SDCT curriculum is individualized in that instructors closely monitor students' mobility progress and concept development to avoid *splinter skills* from occurring. Splinter skills, also known as *gaps of knowledge*, happen when students comprehend only fragments of a skill (Fazzi & Petersmeyer, 2001; Perla & O'Donnell, 2004). It is critical for instructors of young children and students with additional special needs to work closely with the school team and focus on deficient areas based on the students' Individual Educational Plan (IEP). These students may need extended opportunities to develop environmental concepts, such as curbs, and/or to practice basic prerequisite skills, such as how to identify or step up/down a curb. This additional learning occurs in conjunction with the skills and concepts being addressed in each mobility lesson. As students maneuver to targeted locations, splinter skills can be avoided through direct and meaningful experience. The SDCT curriculum avoids fixed routes which, according to Payne (2002), foster isolated knowledge chunks that are insignificant in nature and hinder flexibility of shortcuts, detours and/or curious exploration. **Fixed routes** are routes that have a relationship from one landmark to another regardless of the students' perspective (Long & Giudice, 2010). Rather, the SDCT lessons focuses on walking to locations which are meaningful to the student and provide flexibility for teachable moments, structured discovery, and problem-solving opportunities.

SOCRATIC METHOD

When students find themselves at a travel woe or mental roadblock, sometimes they become frustrated or confused. Mobility instructors will use this opportunity as a teachable moment rather than coming to their rescue, for if the latter happens, the student will not learn how to resolve the encounter independently, thereby losing potential growth in transformational knowledge. Rather, mobility instructors will utilize a modified form of the *Socratic Method* via probing, open-ending questions to assist students to determine their own possible solutions. "The principle underlying the Socratic method is that students learn through the use of critical thinking, reasoning, and logic" (Fabio, 2019, par. 3). This method need not be used as a *rapid* question session because students need time to ponder and problem-solve (Fay & Funk, 1995, p. 181; Geruschat & Turano, 2002). Thus, the Socratic questions are open-ended and probing in nature so students can conduct intrinsic thinking and focus on the task at hand (Fabio, 2019). Keep in mind that this curriculum technique is established at the very beginning of the SDCT training. So, when students encounter the travel woe during independent mobility, they are able to problem-solve, through transformational knowledge, possible questions asked by their mobility instructor during training to resolve their current predicament.

HANDS-ON EXPERIENCE

Orientation and Mobility is performance based and not something that can be learned by listening to a lecture, watching an educational film, or watching a YouTube video because it involves intrinsic feedback and hands-on experience. "Experiential learning remains the most powerful method of acquiring and retaining new skills and knowledge-no matter the age of the learner" states Golon (2017, p. 2). The SDCT curriculum follows a **kinesthetic** philosophy whereby students learn best through hands-on activities involving movement which improves focus by utilizing all senses (Golon, 2017). Kinesthetic experience includes a multi-sensory learning environment whereby internal learning occurs through active engagement (Macmillan, 2018) and problem-solving possibilities to enhance the development of transformational learning. This involves "movement, testing, trial and error and a non-traditional learning environment to retain information and excel" (Macmillan, 2018). Thus, students are active participants through excursions as while perfecting cane techniques and developing mental mapping skills. The SDCT curriculum utilizes fieldtrips to enhance hands-on experiences (Chamberlain, 2019):

- Banks
- Barbecues
- Beach
- Bowling
- Camping
- Carnivals
- Consumer state and national conventions
- Department & small-town stores
- Fair
- Fishing
- Grocery stores
- Hiking
- Museums
- Nature centers
- Parks
- Restaurants
- Shopping
- Sporting events
- State Capitol
- State Fair
- Various community outings
- YMCA
- Zoo

AUTOMATICITY AND PROBLEM-SOLVING

"The more complex the process an individual is involved in, the more parts of that process need to be at the level of automaticity" (Payne, 2002, p. 60). When students are able to interweave the process and the content of cane mechanics without thinking about the continuous operation, they are able to develop intrinsic automaticity (Leonard, 1968; Payne, 2002). This means students are "able to notice unexpected obstacles and steps even when distracted and knowing how to negotiate obstacles and steps safely" (Sauerburger & Bourquin, 2010, p. 203). Such automaticity occurs during on-going hands-on practice of problem-solving tasks while focusing on the process of perception, recall, recognition, and memory (Mezirow, 1991). Intrinsic automaticity develops without thinking when the continuous operation of incorporating a task into the physical body schema is performed (Leonard, 1968; Payne, 2002). Mezirow (1991) adds that automaticity occurs while focusing on problem-solving and involves the process of recall, perception, recognition, and memory.

> When students do not consistently use the cane, the lack of opportunities to develop automaticity results in lower self-confidence and unsafe skills (Dodds, 1988).

When students do not consistently use the cane, the lack of opportunities to develop automaticity results in lower self-confidence and unsafe skills (Dodds, 1988). Thus, the SDCT curriculum provides ample opportunities to perfect problem-solving abilities which increase time to develop automaticity. This process leads students on the path toward becoming highly skilled travelers. Maurer (2011) states skilled travelers demonstrate the following characteristics: (1) automaticity of routine travel skills; (2) awareness of auditory information, (3) understanding and accepting that travel mistakes will occur; and (4) the ability to correct and recover from travel errors.

ORIENTATION AND MOBILITY: STEPS TO PROBLEM SOLVING

Independent problem-solving during O&M training builds skills which activates transformational knowledge to be used beyond mobility instruction. However, often times, when students are faced with an obstacle, they immediately jump to the conclusion that they are *lost*. Generally, students know their whereabouts (i.e., in the building, park, zoo, or store), they simply may not know where they are *within* that setting. Therefore, *disoriented* is a better word to represent their state of confusion for *lost* and *disoriented* are semantically related in confused topic. In O&M being *lost* is not knowing the way to a given location or whereabouts while being *disoriented* is loss of directional sense. Thus, *disoriented* is used in place of *lost* when off-course (Lost and Disorientated, 2016).

That being said, when students become disoriented they need to utilize problem-solving techniques to regain orientation. *The Orientation and Mobility Steps to Problem-Solving* offers a step-by-step guide to help mobility students regain orientation. These steps include: (1) Acknowledging there is a problem; (2) Identifying & selecting a possible solution (i.e., continue walking, stop to check cardinal directions, re-trace steps, or seek other options); (3) Evaluating the solution; and (4) Determining the next option based on the evaluation. If the problem is resolved, then the student may continue toward the destination. However, if the problem is not resolved, then the student needs to select a different solution.

Although chapters and chapter could be written about problem solving techniques during O&M, the best way to understand non-visual problem solving is through action. An option to problem-solve first-hand through literature is available in Part II (*O&M Encounters: Going to Mickey's House*). Readers are in charge of their own destiny through a fictional adventure where they will encounter obstacles, make decisions toward possible solutions and evaluate those choices. The Orientation and Mobility Steps to Problem-Solving may be used as a reference, if needed.

Left: Reuben, a preschooler, successfully demonstrates his ability to shoreline the cafeteria wall.

Right: Noah, a middle school student, props his cane under his arm when saying the pledge in the mornings.

Bottom: This teachable moment was captured when Oliver, a middle school student, discovered pine cones during a mobility adventure. He demonstrates his "invented" technique to maintain contact with his cane while he investigates and searches for pine cones. Also, Oliver demonstrates his value of the cane as a mobility tool by keeping it close.

ORIENTATION AND MOBILITY STEPS TO PROBLEM-SOLVING

NOTE: *Disoriented* is not the same as *lost*. Travelers know their general whereabouts (i.e., in the building, park, zoo, or store). They simply may not know where they are *within* that setting.

Steps to problem-solving	1) 💡	2) Select a possible solution (and their symbols)	3) Evaluate solution and reselect	4) Options based on evaluation
1) Acknowledge there is a problem 2) Identify & select a possible solution 3) Evaluate solution 4) Options based on evaluation - If problem is resolved – continue to destination - If problem is not resolved – select another solution	ACKNOWLEDGE THERE IS A PROBLEM	**Continue to Destination**	a) Discovered problem was a minor distraction	Problem resolved – continue to destination
			b) Determined problem 💡 still exists	Select one: STOP ↩ 🤔
		STOP	a) Check 🧭 cardinal directions	Problem is resolved – continue to destination
			b) Use senses for cues (i.e., listen, feel sun & wind) c) Investigate/ explore nearby	If problem is not resolved STOP First, repeat: Second, select one: ↩ 🤔
		Retrace Steps ↩	a) Regained orientation	Continue to destination
			b) If problem 💡 still exists, First: ↩	Second, if problem not resolved, select one STOP 🤔
		Seek Other Options 🤔	a) Double check directions via Braille/written notes or phone	Continue to destination
			b) * Verify current location	
			c) Call destination for clarification of directions	
			d) Follow a trusted guide (i.e., school staff, police officer, store employee, friend) only until oriented	
			e) Call a cab, family member or friend for assistance or a ride, but **NEVER accept a ride from a stranger!**	

find joy in the journey

Dr. Merry-Noel Chamberlain, NOMC, TVI

* It is not safe to reveal the targeted destination to strangers. Rather, find a business and ask an employee, "What street is this?" or "Is this (name) Street?" to help regain orientation.

CHAPTER 6

THE CANE, THE TOOL

The mechanics of using the long white cane in a myriad of locations is the foundation in the SDCT curriculum. According to Baldwin (2016), when veterans returned blinded in WWII, the basic assumptions was that "blind people were fully capable of independent movement—all they needed was some training and a few basic tools . . . the long cane that probes space as the blind person moves about" (p. 42). This assumption results in the cane becoming "the focal point for the creation of an entire profession" (Baldwin, 2016, p. 42).

In SDCT, students learn O&M with long canes that closely resembles the example of 1st Chief Williams (Miyagawa, 1999) which are from toes to nose or somewhere between the individuals' chin and the nose (Aditya, 2004). Dodds (1984) states the longer cane is "infinitely more comfortable" because it is "held about two inches in front of the stomach, with the elbow bent" (p. 7). According to Rodgers and Wall Emerson (2005), surface information is alerted sooner for those who use longer canes than shorter canes because they contact the surface sooner. Thus, this advance warning provides students more reaction time to interact or avoid unexpected objects such as stairs, curbs, or other unforeseen drop-offs.

The cylinder-shaped handle offered in the SDCT curriculum utilizes two grips: (1) open-palm (Aditya, 2004) and (2) pencil grip for mobility. Keep in mind that the open-palm technique is not suited for canes with a golf-handle (Aditya, 2004). Furthermore, cylinder cane handles are smaller in diameter which makes them child-friendly, especially for little toddler-size hands.

INTRODUCTION OF THE LONG WHITE CANE

The first mobility lesson is critical for students because it establishes the framework which sets the direction of future independent travel. Students of all ages directly enter the Independence Paradigm in the SDCT curriculum, where they are exposed to problem-solving activities, development of transformational

The ABCs of Structured Discovery Cane Travel for Children, pages 35–49.

knowledge and mental mapping skills while using the long white cane. *Cane Basics*, that is introduction to the long white cane, is the first lesson in the SDCT curriculum because the cane is the tool consumers use for life. The "shift from extrinsic to intrinsic feedback begins" and skills are progressively refined (Mettler, 1995, pp. 15–16) in *Cane Mechanics* through problem-solving activities to master self-initiated correction procedures and internal error-detection mechanisms. Instructors assist students through adaptation to master "the physical mechanics of cane travel to the cognitive skills which undergird it" (Mettler, 1995, p. 15). Then, it is through transformational knowledge that students apply their previous experiences to independent travel post-training which quickly leads to success. As Welsh (2005) states, it is very important that students quickly experience success.

CANE TECHNIQUE

Before independent mobility occurs, students must first learn *Cane Basics*. Aside from *Cane Etiquette* (i.e., where to store the cane when not in use), students learn the physical components of holding the cane as well as the mechanics of using it. During this instructional stage, mobility instructors maintain locus of control to ensure students grasp the techniques correctly. Hence the reason this is the only Sequential Learning component of the SDCT curriculum.

Cane Basics include two *hand grips*: (1) *Pencil Grip* (helps to prevent the cane from going under obstacles such as tables and chairs); and (2) *Open Palm Grip* (helps to prevent the cane from thrusting into the user's abdomen when the cane encounters objects). Following the hand grips, students learn Cane Mechanics which includes: (1) *Extended Technique* (helps to travel quickly and confidently in open spaces); (2) *Cane Arc* (moving the cane tip to the right and left of the body, as wide as the user's shoulders, to ensure the area is clear of obstacles as well as wide enough for the body to proceed); (3) *Walk-in-Step* (provides *continuous* information that the area which is about to be traveled is clear of objects); (4) *Two-Point Touch* (creates auditory, and possible tactile, feedback in various locations); (5) *Touch & Slide* (provides tactile information regarding the terrain and locates peripheral landmarks that are best found using tactile methods); (6) *Constant Contact* (also helps to locate small, hard to detect, landmarks that are best found using tactile, and sometimes auditory methods); and (7) *Shore-lining* (helps when searching for tactile landmarks or items).

ECHOLOCATION SKILLS

The metal tip used in the SDCT curriculum is paramount in *echolocation* (i.e., reflective sound) because it offers *active* and *consistent* sounds for the user which produces specific signals that reflect off objects. In fact, individuals who are blind or visually impaired have used metal tips on the bottom of canes since the 1800s which offers detection of environmental features such as walls, streets, nearby houses, mailboxes, parked automobiles, open and closed-in spaces, etc. (Chamberlain, 2013; Roberts, 2009). Mobility instructors lay the foundation of self-confidence by encouraging students to focus on their auditory skills whereby they begin to identify various sounds offered by the metal cane tip when tapped against a plethora of available environmental objects, such as a wall, trash cans or doors (Chamberlain, 2013). Maurer (2011) emphasizes that when auditory information is mastered, travel is unlimited. Although some O&M professionals underestimate the ability to retrieve sensory information (Vaughan, 1993), consumers are environmentally illiterate if they are unable to master echolocation skills (Baldwin, 2016).

> Consumers are environmentally illiterate if they are unable to master echolocation skills (Baldwin, 2016).

CANE LENGTH

Cane length is normally based on what is appropriate for the student. According to Kaiser et al. (2018), O&M instructors account "for factors such as height, gait, walking speed, proprioceptive and tactile sensitivity, travel environments and personal preferences" (Kaiser et al., 2018, p. 11). However, when the focus is on young children, the above aspects may not be applicable especially if the child has not had experience with cane or not had the opportunity to developed proper mobility skills. Generally, the cane length in SDCT is determined by the height of the user. When standing upright, the cane needs to reach a height between the user's nose and mouth. For babies, the smallest cane is recommended, which is 25 inches. Once the child begins to maneuver about, proper measurements may be obtained.

Longer canes allow increased reaction time for the user. For example, an automobile driver would want at least four seconds rather than two seconds of reaction time before applying the brakes in order to avoid colliding with a suddenly stopped vehicle. Longer canes offer users more time to react when drop-offs, such as the edge of the sidewalk or stairs, are encountered. The longer cane also permits the user to travel with better posture and to travel faster which, in turn, builds self-confidence. For fast walkers, an even longer cane may be necessary.

When a cane is too short, the user may walk hunched over and take shorter steps which can create low self-confidence. In the United States, Lieutenant Richard Hoover was a primary leader in using the cane as the adjustment tool used for mobility based on his prior experience working at the Maryland School for the Blind as a teacher and physical training coach (Koestler, 2004). It was through Lieutenant Hoover's guidance that the cane was introduced to soldiers with its length reaching to the individual's sternum (Aditya, 2004; Koestler, 2004). Although the cane's function is to check an area for obstacles prior to actually encountering the object, Dodds (1988) noted that a cane at the sternum height requires the arm to be in an unnatural and unreasonable position. He adds this position causes the arm to tire quickly and to relax to the side, whereas Bryant (2009) states that when canes are shorter than the chest-bone, individuals must walk bent over with the arm extended (to increase the preview area). Therefore, the shorter cane technique causes the arm to quickly become uncomfortable which eventually leads to cane misuse post training (Dodds, 1984).

FREE CANE

At the time of this printing, individuals who are blind or visually impaired may obtain a free cane by going to: https://www.nfb.org/programs-services/free-white-cane-program. Before ordering a cane, be sure to read *The Cane Length* above to ensure the correct length is ordered. (See Appendix)

TRAVEL

Being able to travel beyond one's home environment has been proven to predict the likelihood of full-time employment (Cmar, 2015), whereas when mobility is only conducted on school grounds, problem-solving opportunities in novice or more complex environments are limited. When students only travel within their comfort zone, that is, within the home or school campus, they develop a perceived normality, just as older individuals do within their community (Ball & Nicolle, 2015). Thus, when venturing outside of the comfort zone (i.e., home environment), fear may arise. However, O&M training off campus and/or outside the comfort zone helps to overcome this fear.

FINAL DROP-ROUTES

Finally, rehabilitation agencies use *drop-routes* as a method to enhance self-confidence and problem-solving mobility skills. Drop-routes are also used to increase mobility competency and to evaluate skills as students' final instructional training exam in mobility training. The Veterans in the 1940s also participated in this mobility problem-solving curriculum when they were given the objective to independently figure things out (Welsh, 2005). As with the Veterans, the SDCT drop-routes consists of the following: (1) Creating confusion for the student such as taking the student on a meaningless automobile ride with numerous twists and turns so they are unable to use mental mapping to determine their whereabouts; (2) Dropping the student off at an unknown location where they are given the objective to (a) use mobility training abilities to return to home-base or (b) given a predetermined location to which they need to walk (Walsh, 2005b). For older students in the school system, the same lesson is practiced except the confusion is conducted through a confusing human guide experience.

STRUCTURED DISCOVERY CANE TRAVEL CANE CHARACTERISTICS/TERMINOLOGY

Straight canes with metal tips are used in SDCT. These canes offer tactile feedback through vibrations rising up the shaft to the handle regarding the terrain or when objects are encountered. In addition, the metal tip offers auditory information to the user. Working from the top of the cane and continuing to the bottom, the following characteristics and terminology will help with understanding why the straight cane is the superior option for students and consumers.

SDCT CANE CHARACTERISTICS/TERMINOLOGY

Terminology	Definition
Strap or Chain Attached to the Handle	The strap (or chain) attached to the handle is used to hang the cane when not in use. Although it has been shown in pictures of children's story books (Best, 2015), the strap is NOT to be placed around the wrist when the cane is being used. This can be harmful to the user if the cane becomes tangled in another person's legs, stuck on a step, or shut in the door of a bus (Kalinowski, 2013). Rather, some people will attach a key chain to the strap as a way to personalize the cane and/or for identification purposes (especially when around other people who use long white canes.)
Cane Handle	The handle is cylinder-shaped which makes it easy to grasp, especially for very young children.

Terminology	Definition
Cane Shaft	The cane shaft is the length of the cane between the cane handle and the cane tip. It is hollow in the center and often made of fiberglass or carbon fiber to permit ultimate tactile feedback to the user. The light weight helps with longevity. For young children, the light weight is not overwhelming to manage.
The Cane Length	The length of the cane depends on the height of the individual. The National Federation of the Blind offers canes as small as 25 inches long. The length of the cane needs to be increased as the child grows—from toes to nose… or somewhere between the chin and the nose. For faster walkers, a longer cane may be warranted. For Infants and Toddlers: It is understandable that many adults (and some mobility instructors) feel that since infants and toddlers may not be walking, there is no reason to get them a cane. However, this is the wrong assumption. Rather, children at this age can be introduced to holding a cylinder shaped toy, which will lead to holding the cane as they get older.
Cane Tip	This is the part of the cane that touches the ground. Structured Discovery Cane Travel uses a metal cane tip, which offers many advantages. First, it offers auditory information (through echolocation) about the surrounding environment such as: 1) where a building is located; 2) if there is an automobile nearby; 3) if the area is open or enclosed; and 4) if the traveler is approaching the building or walking away from it. Tactually, the metal tip helps with 5) identifying floors/grounds such as grass vs. sidewalk, carpet vs. tile, rough tile in the produce section vs. smoother surfaces in other areas in grocery store.
Cane Color: White	The color of the cane is white. It is understandable that children would enjoy decorating their canes with stickers and/or duct tape for special occasions. However, keep in mind that the cane must mostly be white for safety reasons. In the 1930s, the Lions Club International adopted the white cane to enhance its visibility to motorists (Foundation Fighting Blindness, n.d.). Nowadays, canes are made with reflective materials.
Cane Color: Red	The red at the bottom of the cane can be confusing in some countries. In America, reflective red tape used to be added to the bottom of the cane shaft to enhance visibility to motorists. Now canes are made with white reflective materials, so the red tape is no longer necessary. However, in some countries red is still used in the form of stripes (or just one strip on the bottom of the shaft) to identify the user as deafblind (https://deafblind.org.uk/deafblind-awareness-red-and-white-canes/).
Identification Canes	Identification canes are not working canes with working tips. According to Ambutech (2020), identification canes are simply used to identify the person as being visually impaired or blind; they are not to be used as a mobility tool. Straight identification canes are not available, rather canes that can be folded into as many as five sections (Ambutech, 2020). Furthermore, identification canes are not used in Structured Discovery Cane Travel, for using such a cane for mobility purposes is impractical.

Terminology	Definition
Straight (ridged) canes vs. folding or telescoping canes 	**Differences between Folding and Telescoping Canes**

Folding Canes	**Telescoping Canes**
Folding canes can fold into two or more sections with an elastic band. 	Telescoping canes can have up to eight sections which can collapse into the handle like an antenna.

Advantages	
Folding or Telescoping Canes	**Straight Canes**
1. Easy to store when tandem biking, motorcycle riding, canoeing, or being involved in other compact sports or activities.	1. The light weight increases longevity for extended walking opportunities
2. Can be used as a back-up on trips because they can be stored in suitcases or backpacks.	2. Provides accurate tactual information about the terrain.
3. Extra-long canes can be stowed in extremely small compact automobiles.	3. Readily available in an instant.
4. Easier to store when not in use at school functions such as dances or sports.	4. When using a human guide, the cane is still available immediately, as needed. Thus, the cane still promotes independence and, if used properly, is still protecting the user from running into objects.
5. Although not recommended, it can help a blind person to be discreet regarding their visual impairment.	5. In restaurants or student centers, straight canes are easily stored along the floorboard or in the corner so that contaminated tips are not placed on tabletops where food may be in close proximity.
6. Although not recommended, when using a human guide, it can be folded up.	6. Instantly identifies the user as an individual with a visual impairment and is a symbol of independence.

Disadvantages	
Folding or Telescoping Canes	**Straight Canes**
1. Can be *hidden* as a way to avoid being identified as having a visual impairment (Best, 2015).	1. Straight canes cannot be discreet or "hidden."
2. When folded or collapsed, it is not easily accessible when needed in an instant (i.e., walking down stairs).	2. Although the long white cane is a symbol of independence, for many the cane identifies the user as an individual with a visual impairment. To some people, this identification is a considered a disadvantage.
3. Folded or collapsed canes encourage storage on table tops; thus, the tip of the cane which may be contaminated could be in close proximity to food.	3. Extra-long, straight rigid canes are sometimes difficult to store in small automobiles.
4. Too easily carried folded or closed rather than being used when traveling with a human guide (Best, 2015). Thus, consumers become dependent on their guide rather than being independent and protecting themselves from running into objects.	4. Rigid canes can be difficult to take on tandem bikes, but they can lie on the floor in a canoe.
	5. Straight canes are difficult to store in some restaurants when the table is in the center of the room or when the table is round with a center base and legs extending outward.
5. Over time, the telescoping cane will not stay ridged when opened and will collapse when in use such as when it encounters a curb or sidewalk crack. For this reason, a telescoping cane is not ideal for extended walking opportunities.	6. When not used correctly, they can trip other people when traveling in a crowd.
	7. Long canes can be cumbersome in small spaces.

More Disadvantage of Folding Canes

In addition to the above:
1. Folding canes are heavier than straight canes which can hinder long distance travel.
2. The elastic cord that runs through the middle of the cane can stretch over time, rendering the cane unusable.
3. The elastic cord can break after prolonged use.
4. Cold weather can cause the cane to stick, so opening and closing it can be difficult or impossible.
5. Some children (and adults, for that matter) do not practice safety when opening their cane in congested areas.

CANE BASICS

Beginning students learn Cane Basics as their first lesson as this is the primary tool consumers use for life. Cane Basics is the only Sequential Learning (SL) component of the SDCT curriculum because these skills are necessary to use in future lessons to advance the understanding of concepts and skills (Moss & Brookhart, 2012). Cane Basics consists of two grips: Pencil grip and the Open Palm Grip of which the ladder uses the Extended Technique. Also, Cane Basics includes Cane Etiquette. Keep in mind that students do not linger on perfecting Cane Basics before moving forward because "it does not take tremendous motor control to hold a cane….The cane is still acting as a bumper and a probe out in front of the child while not requiring a significant amount of motor control or muscle development" (Pogrund & Rosen, 1989, p. 432). Perfection will occur while traveling to destinations which are meaningful to them through intrinsic motivation.

CANE BASICS

NOTE: Structured Discovery Cane Travel utilizes a long, straight, ridged cane with a cylinder-shaped handle and a metal tip.

Technique	How	When to Use
Pencil Grip …helps to prevent the cane from going under obstacles such as tables and chairs.	1. Hold the cane as if it were a giant pencil and you are using it to write in the sand at your feet. Your hand may be either on the shaft of the cane just below the handle or at the lower part of the handle. 2. The cane is upright in front and center of the body with the cane tip slightly extended outward. 3. The elbow is bent and the hand is slightly forward. NOTE: If holding the cane like a giant pencil is a difficult concept to grasp, try holding the cane like a fork or spoon. Another option is to hold the cane with a fist.	• Traveling in narrow or congested spaces such as between school desks, theatre seats, lunchroom tables, through doorways, around peers. • Finding a clear place to sit on the floor. • Looking for an empty seat. • Standing in line. • Shore-lining. • Walking up or down stairs. NOTE: Ideally the hand is in the center of the body; however, often a person becomes relaxed and the hand simply favors the side of the body which holds the cane.
	For Toddlers	
	Young toddlers will not be able to hold the cane as if it were a giant pencil. Rather, they are more likely to hold the cane like a ski pole. This is quite acceptable at this age, and the pencil grip can be perfected when the child is older. Numbers 2 and 3 above still apply.	
Open Palm Grip …helps to avoid the cane from thrusting into the user's abdomen when the cane encounters an object.	**How** 1. Hold the cane extended from the center of the body whereby the handle is near (not touching) the navel and the cane tip is on the floor. 2. The palm of the hand is facing upward. 3. Fingers are wrapped around the cane handle, and the thumb points away from the body. Sometimes the index finger slips forward. 4. Movement of the cane is created through the wrist while the hand is stationary near the navel. If necessary, the hand may be used instead of using the wrist.	**When to Use** • In open areas • With the Extended Technique • With Two-Point Touch • With Touch & Slide • When Shore-lining Image from: https://www.nfb.org/images/nfb/ publications /fr/fr27/2/fr270213.htm

	For Toddlers
	Toddlers can still hold the cane extended out from their body. However, they are more inclined to favor the side of the body which is holding the cane. They will need reminders to move their hand to the center of their body so that the handle is near (not touching) the navel and the cane tip is on the floor. Although it is important that the palm of the hand is facing upward, young toddlers struggle with this. Therefore, young toddlers may focus on arcing their cane as wide as their shoulders. (See cane arc.)
Cane Etiquette—When Not in Use	At times, the cane will not be needed but will need to be nearby for easy and quick retrieval. The user must be in charge of their own cane. Thus, it is never recommended to give the cane to another person to store. (Parents are an exception for young children.) Here are some situations when the cane is not in use and what is recommended: • When standing still—the cane needs to be held upright. • At restaurants—the cane can be propped in a nearby corner, placed along a nearby floorboard or stored under the table. Never place the cane on the table! • In automobiles—the cane can easily slide between the seat and the door. It is not recommended to store the cane in the trunk of a car because it will not be easily accessible in case of an emergency. Nor is it recommended to lay the cane on the floor parallel to the seat between the front and back seats, where it may be stepped on and broken.
	For Toddlers
	Adults will need to model cane etiquette for their toddlers. For young toddlers, verbalize what is happening to the cane (i.e., *Let's put the cane along the floorboard or in the corner while we eat. While we stand here, let's keep the cane up and down.*) As the toddler gets older, instead of doing for the child, ask the child what needs to be done (i.e., *When standing still, where is the best place for your cane? Where do you think you need to put your cane while we are eating? Did you put your cane in the correct place in the car?*)

CANE MECHANICS

By using the cane to facilitate movement, students are more likely to be interested in their environment and are willing to explore it (Pogrund & Rosen, 1989). Students shift quickly from extrinsic to intrinsic feedback in Cane Mechanics where skills are progressively refined (Mettler, 1995) through problem-solving activities to master self-initiated correction procedures and internal error-detection mechanisms. Here, instructors assist students through adaptation to master "the physical mechanics of cane travel to the cognitive skills which undergird it" (Mettler, 1995, p. 15). Remember, environments are dynamic so "no matter how well orientated a child is or how accurately a child uses basic skills in other environments, he or she will inevitably trip over something or bump into something unexpectedly in the ever-changing world" (Pogrund & Rosen, 1989, p. 432).

Extended Technique ...helps to travel quickly and confidently in open spaces.	How	When to Use
	1. Hold the cane using the open palm grip. 2. The cane is extended from the front and center of the body (but not touching) the navel. 3. The cane tip is arced to the right and left as wide as the student's shoulders. (See Two-Point Touch, Touch & Slide, Shore-lining.)	• Often used with the open palm grip. • Used when traveling in *open spaces* that are typically clear of obstacles such as hallways, sidewalks, parking lots. • Used when crossing streets. • Used when Shore-lining.
	For Toddlers	
	This is where toddlers will excel. Basically, they are moving the cane tip to the right and left of their body. However, they will not be perfect and will need reminders to use their cane correctly.	

Cane Arc or Arcing the Long white cane ...provides information that the area in front of the body is clear of objects.	*Arcing the cane* is utilized at every walking opportunity. It is done when using the Open Palm Grip/Extended Technique or the Pencil Grip. When walking with the cane, the cane tip needs to go to the right and left as wide as the shoulders of the user. Thus, the cane sweeps in front of the body, providing information to the user either that the area in front of the body is clear of obstacles or that objects are within the travel path. If the individual has limited wrist mobility, the hand may be used to arc the cane to the right and left of the body. NOTE: Ideally the hand is in the center of the body; however, often a person becomes relaxed (especially on long walks) and the arm drops, favoring that side of the body. When this happens, a right-handed person may not correctly arc the cane to the left and vice versa for the left-handed person.

Height of Cane Arc	When arcing the cane, the tip needs to be only a half inch off the floor. If the cane tip is arced too high, the user may not easily detect subtle drop-offs.

Walk-in-Step ...provides *continuous* information that the area in front of the body is clear of objects	Walk-in-step is probably the most difficult task with the long white cane. It is not a technique that is perfected immediately and requires many reminders for beginners and plenty of practice. Walking-in-step with the open-palm grip/extended technique is used when walking in open spaces. This method is performed as follows: 1. Stand with the cane extended in front of the body while using the open palm technique. 2. Place the right foot forward and arc the cane tip in front of the left foot. Some people may prefer to begin with their left foot forward. If this is the case, then simply arc the cane tip to the front of the right foot. 3. When the next step is taken, move the cane tip in front of the opposite foot. Thus, place the cane tip in front of the opposite foot that is forward. For example, when the left foot moves forward, the cane tip needs to be moved to the right side of the body and vice versa. With the next step, the right foot moves forward and the cane tip returns to the left side of the body. NOTE: Moving the cane back and forth while walking is called the *arcing* the cane (See *Cane Arc*). 4. Repeat steps two and three over and over again. (By the way, this is also known as "Kick the Cane Game" because it is as if the user is kicking the cane tip back and forth with each step forward.) Walking-in-step with the pencil grip is used when walking in narrow or confined areas. This is done the same as the extended technique (described above), except the cane tip is closer to the body.

	For Young Children
	Please keep in mind that young children do not have the coordination required for this technique and therefore, it is not a priority until they are older. Also, it is difficult to determine at what particular age children can perfect this skill because every child develops at their own pace. Having and using the cane as a tool for mobility can be an early goal for young children, and as they get older the ultimate goal is to have the skill to walk-in-step.
Two-Point Touch …helps to create auditory (and perhaps tactile) feedback in various locations.	The Two-Point Touch technique uses the open palm grip/extended technique while walking-in-step. 1. When arcing the cane, the tip of the cane needs to be about a half inch from the ground. 2. The tip does not touch the ground until it reaches the furthest area to the right and left of the body. At this time, it needs to only briefly touch the ground. 3. When the cane tip touches the ground at the right and left of the body, it will provide auditory or tactile information. Auditory information may be an echo. (See Shore-lining.) Two-Point touch is used in conjunction with and for the same reasons as the Extended Technique and Shore-lining.
Touch & Slide …helps to provide tactile information regarding the terrain and locate peripheral landmarks that are best found using tactile methods.	The *Touch & Slide* technique uses the open palm grip/extended technique while walking-in-step and seeking a landmark. 1. When arcing the cane, the tip of the cane needs to be about a half inch from the ground. 2. The tip does not touch the ground until it reaches the furthest area to the right and left of the body. At this time, it needs to touch the ground and the student keeps the cane briefly on the ground while the body is still in motion. The time the tip is on the ground is slightly longer than with the two-point touch techniques listed above. 3. When the cane tip is on the ground, it can be moved either slightly forward or slightly outward, depending on the approximate location of the desired searched item. NOTE: The touch & slide technique will slow a person's speed of travel and may cause the cane to get caught in cracks.

	How	**When to Use**
Constant Contact …helps to locate small, hard to detect, landmarks that are best found using tactile (and sometimes auditory) methods.	The Constant Contact technique often uses the open palm trip/extended technique while walking-in-step. However, some people use this technique while using the pencil grip, as well. The Constant Contact technique involves the cane tip arcing left and right but never leaves the ground as it is arced to the right and left. NOTE: The constant contact technique will slow a person's speed of travel and may cause the cane to get caught in cracks.	• When searching for tactile landmarks which are fine in detail such as blended sidewalk at an intersection. • In school hallways or hospitals, as a means not to disrupt surrounding areas and/or where echolocation is not necessary. • On carpeted areas where echolocation is less likely to occur or not needed. • When following a tactile crease or texture change in a department store, food court, crack in the sidewalk, etc.

One technique used to maintain orientation is the method of following a **shoreline** which is following an edge of something such as a building, curb, sidewalk, or carpet. It can also be a or tactile surface such as a sidewalk crack. Auditory methods can also be used for shore-lining such as echolocation or traffic.

Shore-lining	How	When to Use

...helps when searching for tactile landmarks or items.	This technique uses the open palm grip/extended technique or the pencil grip while walking-in-step.
	1. Arc the cane left and right.
	2. Determine at which side of the body the searched item will be located.
	3. Position the body parallel to the side where the landmark is expected to be.
	4. When the cane arcs on the side of the body where the searched landmark is expected, use either:
	  a. the Two-Point Touch technique, or
	  b. the Touch & Slide technique
	  c. Touch the wall then raise the cane tip slightly and extend the cane tip further to explore the above the landmark (i.e., stairs going upward)
		Shore-lining is used when searching for:
		• connecting hallways
		• connecting sidewalks
		• doorways
		• stairs
		• ...or other landmarks (i.e., water fountain, trashcan, bush, curb cut, etc.)
		NOTE: Shore-lining may cause the cane to get caught in cracks or tall grass.
		WARNING: There are times when Shore-lining is not recommended. This includes when there are many twists and turns embedded within the tactile shoreline so that it may cause more confusion than it is worth.

CANE MECHANICS—ADVANCED MOVEMENTS	
Walking Up Stairs	When this technique is done correctly, the user will not make imaginary steps at the top of landings. To walk upstairs: 1. Use the Pencil Grip to hold the cane just below the handle of the cane. 2. Raise the arm slightly so that the cane tip is about ¼ to ½ inch above the first step; that is, the step which the traveler is about to place the foot on. 3. Move the cane to the left and right to ensure the step is void of objects. 4. Slightly place pressure on the cane so that the cane tip is against the front side of the second step. This will inform the user that another step is ahead. 5. Without moving the arm, step onto the first step. The cane will move with the body and will swing forward. This will cause the cane tip to tap against the front side of the third step. 6. Repeat this process until the top landing is reached. 7. When there are no more steps, the cane will simply 8. swing slightly forward without hitting any more steps. This informs the user that the top landing has been reached and prevents taking an imaginary step.

Walking Down Stairs	When this technique is done correctly, the user will not make imaginary steps at the bottom of landings. Trusting the cane to locate the stairs will decrease the need to use the foot to do so. To walk down stairs: 1. Hold the cane with the Pencil Grip at the upper side of the cane handle. 2. Place the cane tip on the step below the landing; that is, the step which the traveler is about to place the foot on. 3. Move the cane to the left and right to ensure the step is void of objects. 4. Slide the cane tip away from the body. 5. When the body moves forward to step down, allow the cane tip to slide ahead to the next step. As the cane reaches the edge of the step, it will drop down to the next step. 6. As it drops down, it informs the user there is another step. 7. Repeat this process until the bottom landing. 8. When there are no more steps, the cane will simply slide forward without a drop down. Sometimes the cane will rise, causing the hand to lower on the cane handle. This informs the user that the bottom landing has arrived.
Standing in Line	When standing in line: 1. Hold the cane using the Pencil Grip just below the handle. 2. Either listen for the person ahead to move forward or hold the cane tip just off the ground (about ¼ or ½ inch high) and touch the outer side of the shoe of the person standing ahead. 3. As that person moves forward, the cane tip will slightly swing inward. 4. When the cane swings inward, a small step can be taken forward AFTER checking to make sure the person has moved. To check this assumption, arc the cane to the right and left to ensure the area is clear.
Walking in Line	When walking in line: 1. Hold the cane using the Pencil Grip. 2. Arc the cane left and right to ensure the area is clear. 3. Follow the person in front and pay attention to the environment. 4. When the cane encounters the person ahead in line, slow down or stop, if necessary. 5. Follow the guideline for Standing in Line until it is time to proceed forward. Note: Some Preschool classrooms may use a line rope where children hold on to a loop as they walk. Children still use their canes one hand while holding on to the loop with the other.

Walking Backward with the Cane	How	When to Use
	The cane needs to always be between the body and the direction of travel, even if the person is walking backward. 1. Relax the dominant hand down the side of the body. 2. Hold the cane handle with the fingers and thumb wrapped around the cane. 3. Have the cane tip behind the body. 4. Arc the cane tip to the left and right as wide as the shoulder. Keep in mind that the cane needs to be extended further across the back of the body to the opposite side of the hand holding the cane. 5. Walking-in-Step, Two-Point-Touch, or Constant Contact is necessary. Shore-lining can be used as well.	• This is mostly a fun activity. • A person may wish to use this technique when walking in the direction of heavy winds. 

CANE MAINTENANCE	
How to Replace a Metal Cane Tip	To Replace a metal cane tip: 1. Put a drop or two of water in the black rubber cup of the new cane tip. (In an emergency, use hand sanitizer or saliva.) 2. Place the new cane tip on a hard surface on the ground with the metal down and the black rubber cup upward. 3. Lay the cane on the floor with the screwhead of the old tip resting on top of the black rubber cup of the new cane tip. 4. For a right-handed person, place the left foot directly on top of the resting cane tip so the ball of the foot is on top of the new metal tip. (If the user is left handed, do the opposite.) 5. Reach down and lift the cane upward while continuing to apply gentle pressure on the ball of the foot. As this is done, the screw of the cane bottom will be inserted into the black rubber cup. NOTE: the cane tip may slide away from the foot during this process. 6. Slowly slide the foot off the tip as the cane is lifted upward. Be sure not to bend the cane too much during this process. 7. Once the cane is straight up, twist and press the cane downward to help get the screw securely inside the rubber cup. 8. Turn the cane upside down. Wiggle and turn the new cane tip to ensure the new tip is securely on the cane.
Where to Order a New Cane	At the time of this printing, individuals who are blind or visually impaired may obtain a free cane, every six months, by going to**: • https://www.nfb.org/programs-services/free-white-cane-program • Email address: freecane@nfb.org • Phone number: 410-659-9314

** Before ordering a cane, be sure to read The Cane Length to ensure the correct length is ordered.

Date Cane Was Ordered	Length of Cane Ordered	Date Cane Was Received

CHAPTER 7

O&M FOR BABIES AND TODDLERS

It is no wonder that parents are a child's first teacher because from birth to graduation, 85% of the child's time is spent outside the school setting (The Parent Institute, 1998). That means parents are children's most influential teacher (The Parent Institute, 1998) therefore, they have the great responsibility and privilege to oversee their child's mobility education. Often, parents do not expect a baby to be walking at six months, yet the baby wears socks with rubber grips. This same proactive approach comes into play when placing a cane into the hands of a baby or toddler who is blind or visually impaired. Canes encourages movement because some mobility activities happen before the child takes that first step. Caregivers will be referred to as *parents* throughout this text.

To be an independent traveler, it is vital for the child to be: (1) introduced to the cane as soon as possible; (2) encouraged to use the cane when walking or maneuvering about *within* the home; and (3) strongly encouraged to use the cane at every walking opportunity *outside* the home. These lay the foundation for cane acceptance as a tool for life. At this age, parents need to securely support this philosophy because when canes are introduced at a very young age, it is more likely that the child will be a successful traveler as an adult (Martinez, 2007). Therefore, positive attitudes regarding blindness and the essential tool (the long white cane) begin with the parents whereby "independent travel and movement infiltrates every aspect of life" (Martinez, 2007, p. 8). Ultimately, "promoting motor development in young children with visual impairments leads to a higher probability of success in developing mobility skills, social skills and daily living skills, as well as improved health and fitness" (Strickling & Pogrund, 2002, p. 288).

BABY'S FIRST CANE

The Structured Discovery Cane Travel curriculum begins with the cane that the child will most likely use for life; that is, a long cane with a *cylinder-shaped handle*. For young children, canes with cylinder handles permit their small hands to grasp them securely. At this time, the National Federation of the Blind

The ABCs of Structured Discovery Cane Travel for Children, pages 51–58.

(NFB) provides canes as short as 25 inches, free of charge, at https://nfb.org/free-cane-program. The NFB canes are lightweight, which encourages easy movement, and the metal cane tip offers auditory feedback.

Chamberlain and Mackenstadt (2018) recommend not waiting until children begin walking before providing them with a cane. Since "toys are natural teachers" (Dodge et al., 1998, p. 18), very young children may be introduced to the cane as if it were a toy.

> **PARENT "TO DO" LIST:**
> **1. Order a Free Cane for the Child.**

They can learn new skills through exploration; cause and effect. Children tap the cane tip on objects and hear the various sounds it makes. They may also use it as a tool to find nearby objects, etc. However, if the child is reluctant to hold the cane, a similar tubular item such as a toy rattle or maraca, would suffice.

PUSH TOYS VS. PRE-CANES

If a cane is not available as soon as one would like, many children, blind and sighted, enjoy playing with push toys (i.e., toys that are pushed by toddlers and often make fun sounds such as child-sized lawnmowers). Push toys are excellent because they (1) build strength; (2) are age- and stage-appropriate; (3) build confidence; and (4) encourage balance strength. Most important, push toys explore the surface ahead and inform the user whether or not the path is clear of obstacles. Pogrund and Rosen (1989) state although push toys protect "the child from more of the environment than is necessary" they "do not provide the child with the tactual and auditory feedback useful in identifying various textures and obstacles in the environment" (p. 432).

Keep in mind that push toys are not pre-canes. Rather, *pre-canes* and/or *wearable mobility devices* generally categorized as Alternative Mobility Devices (AMDs) are often made out of PBC pipe and are heavy and cumbersome. Such devices do "not encourage the exploration of surfaces and the development of self-directed active discovery" (Castellano, 2017). Furthermore, such devices encourage passivity, thereby delaying the development of critical cane skills (Castellano, 2017).

Any type of mobility AMD "implies that the structure and function of the device fits into some continuum of progression for using travel tools" and that "once the child has mastered this device, the cane would be the next step" (Cutter, 2001). Note that the SDCT curriculum does not support the use of pre-canes, just as pre-pencils are not offered before pencils. That is, actual "canes" need to be introduced at the very beginning. Cutter (2001) states when children receive canes as young as 20 months, they were successful in engaging higher levels of technical skill and prehension that, over time, were equivalent to adult levels. He adds, barriers to independent travel are delayed or interrupted when AMDs are introduced prior to the cane. That approach causes the young child to first learn the pre-cane device, then learn the mobility tool used for life. However, the SDCT curriculum avoids that unnecessary pre-cane step.

Keep in mind that the cane is NOT the tool of last resort, yet introduction to pre-canes implies this as well as sends the message that the child is not ready for a cane. Structured Discovery Cane Travel instructors appreciate students of all ages are capable of learning for themselves (Koestler, 2004) with guidance. Therefore, the SDCT curriculum supports the simple design of the cylinder-handled white cane to encourage opportunities for movement since the cane is light-weight and provides auditory feedback which AMDs do not (Cutter, 2001). In addition, Cutter (2001) states the use of the long white cane promotes a positive, can-do attitude which facilitates movement for children better than any other tool.

EDUCATIONAL TEAM

Believe it or not, even for babies as young as six months, the next step for parents is to contact their school district to inform them that a child with a visual impairment will be entering their educational system. This "referral" is brought to the attention of the coordinator of the Early Childhood Special Education (ECSE) Team. The coordinator of the ECSE team will contact the parent (or whoever made the referral) then a meeting will be arranged and assessments may be conducted—all free of charge.

> **2. Make a referral to the school district.**

A **Teacher of Students with Visual Impairments** (i.e., Teacher of Blind Students or Teacher of the Visually Impaired) and an Orientation & Mobility Instructor (i.e., Cane Travel Teacher or Mobility Teacher) will also be members of the ECSE team.

EXPLORE & PLAY WITH THE CANE

It is important to take advantage of teachable moments as real-life opportunities to demonstrate how the cane is utilized as a tool. For example, students may use the cane to search for items under the bed or retrieve a ball from behind a hutch. These types of activities demonstrate acceptance of the cane not only for mobility purposes, but also as a tool; a tool such as silverware for eating or a broom for sweeping.

The child will follow the lead of the adult so it is important for everyone who comes in contact with the child to have a positive attitude regarding the cane and its functions. Frankly and simply, parents need to encourage the child to use the cane even if the child does so incorrectly. The child is considered successful even if the cane is dragged behind while walking, for the child is indicating that the cane is a wanted, valuable possession. Consider this as *scribbling with the cane* because many young children have not developed the dexterity to hold the cane correctly according to Chamberlain and Mackenstadt (2018). They add, at this early stage of development, children are simply using a method to move about their environment that meets their needs, just as children scribble before developing the ability to print.

In addition, consider it a positive sign if the child waves the cane in the air, for that is a method of exploring the environment beyond what is directly within reach. This action demonstrates their awareness that something is "out there" and is actually age- and stage-appropriate. Actions speaks louder than word, in this case, especially when a child is too young to know the words to express. Of course, eventually the child will need to comprehend that the cane tip needs to be lowered to the ground while searching around. As the child matures, the ability to manage the cane will become more finely defined.

Play is an integral component in the academic environment as it enhances cognitive development and problem-solving skills (Ginsburg, 2007). When students have the opportunity of independent (aka: undirected) child-driven, first-hand experience through exploration with the long white cane, they learn self-advocacy and decision-making skills. This play helps to create mental mapping skills about their everchanging environment. In addition, students enhance their gross motor skills by utilizing their whole

> **3. As the child grows, order a longer cane. (Measurement needs to be from the toes to the nose.)**

body, including their senses, and this is an essential component of learning how to maneuver safely with confidence (Family Lives, n.d.; Wells, 2008). Furthermore, this independent gross-motor activity helps students to strengthen their navigating skills (i.e., grassy banks, ditches, snow banks, slopes, etc.). Ultimately, students "who experience increasing challenges in their play are safer than those who have been protected from them" (Tovey, n.d., p. 11).

TEACHING CANES FOR PARENTS

Toddlers strive to be like their role models, who are often their parents. Mobility instructors who are blind will use their personal cane as a tool to demonstrate positive cane travel techniques to students. Sighted mobility instructors often utilize a *Teaching Cane* as an educational strategy for the same reasons. The teaching cane can be used to demonstrate a variety of skills such as tapping the tip to listen to various sounds.

> **4. Obtain a Teaching Cane. (Size: from toes to nose.)**

Parents may use teaching canes whereby the child holds the shaft of the adult cane to feel the movements (Thorpe, 2007). "This modeling technique allows the parent to play a vital role in helping the child to develop early movement and exploration," states Thorpe (2007, par. 10). In addition, the teaching cane helps to instill normalcy whereby when introduced to the cane early, having a cane becomes natural. That is, when there is a teaching cane, the child's potential fears may diminish while their confidence and trust levels in the cane increase due to the parental judgment (Thorpe, 2007). Keep in mind that parents of young children, who will most likely be the ones using a teaching cane, will need education regarding Cane Basics (See Chapter 6) so they can assist their child, effectively. When caretakers know the basics, they can identify when the child is not using the cane correctly and they can provide reinforcement when the child is. Parents using teaching canes actually assist the mobility instructor because they are able to monitor the child outside of the mobility lesson, which offers support to the child and instills correct cane mechanics. For more information regarding the teaching cane, contact your NOMC instructor or the National Organization for Parents of Blind Children through the National Federation of the Blind at http://www.nopbc.org or connect via Facebook: https://www.facebook.com/nopbc

HUMAN GUIDE FOR PRESCHOOL CHILDREN

Often, for safety reasons, it is common for both blind and sighted young children to hold the hand of their parent or other adult when walking from one location to another and is considered age- and stage-appropriate. *Human guide* is not the same as a child holding the hand of their parent,

> **5. Encourage independent cane travel.**

teacher or guardian. Rather, human guide is a method used when a person with a visual impairment holds the arm of another (just above the elbow) while being led to a specific location. Considering the height of a child compared to an adult, at this age the child will most likely hold the hand, rather than the arm just above the elbow of the other person. However, children use the human guide method with peers when holding hands may not be appropriate. Often the human guide method of travel is used when the individual with visual impairment 1) does not utilize or wish to utilize the cane for mobility, 2) does not have the self-confidence to do it independently, or 3) has a guide who holds low expectations regarding the child's mobility skills and therefore thinks the child needs assistance. Keep in mind that mental mapping skills cannot develop through constantly traveling with a human guide. Rather, the child will become dependent on others to go to specific locations even when that targeted area is within the same room. (See Chapter 11.)

BUILDING EXPERIENCE

With maturity and practice, mobility skills are gradually refined and improved, which leads to developing increased independence (Willoghby & Duffy, 1992). In the SDCT curriculum, teachable moments are paramount. Students

> **6. Be aware of and allow time for teachable moments.**

need to be encouraged to use their cane to encounter and/or find objects of interest. For example, a young child may find an obstacle with the cane while in the playground. Willoghby and Duffy (1992) states this is a great opportunity to examine the obstacle and perhaps play on it, if appropriate. This is a teachable moment that is meaningful to the child and encourages cane use so that the child will be more inclined to use the cane to encounter and explore additional interesting targets. Thus, this lesson addresses the child's needs. Considering the child's limited attention span, after the fun with the discovery, the lesson may continue to locate the next "obstacle."

VERBALIZE, VERBALIZE, VERBALIZE

"Say out loud what you are doing" suggests Dodge and Heroman (1999). Verbalization helps children to: (1) comprehend cause and effect; that sound provides information about their environment and what is happening around them; (2) obtain a head start on building connections for language; (3) provides opportunities educate them on how things work; (4) provides opportunities for them to ask questions (Dodge, & Heroman, 1999; Family Lives, n.d.). Although they may not comprehend what is being said in the beginning, their brains are "building the connection for language" (Dodge, & Heroman, 1999, p. 20) as well as beginning development of O&M skills.

7. Verbalize what is happening.

PARENT "TO DO" LIST:

1. Order a free cane for the child.
2. Make a referral to the school district.
3. As the child grows, order a longer cane. (Measurement needs to be from the toes to the nose.)
4. Obtain a Teaching Cane. (Size: from toes to nose.)
5. Encourage independent cane travel.
6. Be aware of and allow time for teachable moments.
7. Verbalize what is happening.

O&M ACTIVITIES FOR BABIES TO PRESCHOOLERS

When children are able to independently make discoveries through mobility, mental mapping begins to develop. Dodge and Heroman (1999) state "the brain connections that control movement are formed during the first four years of life" which helps prepare children to learn (p. 31). They add that learning basic motor skills, such as crawling, walking and reaching, is easiest during these early years. Here are some activities to help children develop mobility skills:

Level/Skills	O&M Activities for Babies to Preschoolers	Remember...
INFANTS	• Simply treat the cane as the child's toy. • Place the cane handle in the child's hand and repeat at least 2 or 3 times daily. • This introduction to the cane does not need to be prolonged because infants have short attention spans. • Don't become discouraged if the child does not grasp the cane.	At this stage, there is no right or wrong way. Be positive.
SENSO-RY	• Bring awareness to environmental sounds such as front door opening/closing, water turned on/off, refrigerator sounds, toast popping up, etc.). • Bring awareness to echolocation by tapping the metal cane tip in various locations. (NOTE: Echolocation is created with metal tips.) • Bring awareness to olfactory senses (i.e., smells of food, different rooms in the house, outside, etc.). • Bring awareness to kinesthetic senses such as movement and position of parts of the body. • Bring awareness to tactile senses with the cane (i.e., by rubbing the cane tip on the carpet or tile), and with movement (i.e., bringing awareness of body temperature by moving from a warm home to cooler outside or vice versa). • Encourage the child to tap the cane tip on different textures to retrieve auditory information with or without assistance. • The child may tap the cane behind the body and may or may not turn toward sound.	Verbalize actions so children comprehend that movement creates noise (information) Consider the child as "scribbling" with the cane just as a child learning to write—a beginner scribbles before being able to print.
CHILD HOLD-ING THE CANE	• The child may begin to hold the cane—when reminded. • Encourage the child to tap the cane on the floor or carpet to help develop auditory feedback. • Be aware that the child is exploring and may overly swing the cane so be mindful of nearby children. • Discourage playing with the cane in confined areas such as the crib or pack-n-play. • The child may use constant contact on different services with or without assistance to listen to various sounds the cane makes.	Parents utilize the *Teaching Cane* to model Cane Basics
STAND-ING AND CRUIS-ING	• As with sighted children, generally offer physical support when they start standing or walking. • Continue to be mindful that the child may swing the cane too widely. • Children's attention span is short, so vary the activities. • Strategically place the cane where it can be discovered by the child and/or place the cane just beyond reach to encourage the child to crawl (i.e., crawl) to it. • Encourage positive interactions with the cane.	

Level/Skills	O&M Activities for Babies to Preschoolers	Remember…
START-ING TO WALK and FIRST STEPS	• Give the child opportunities to hold the cane even if the child is being carried or is riding in a stroller, as this connects movement with the cane. • Use an elastic strap to attach the cane to the stroller for easy retrieval and to prevent loss. • Be aware the child may consider the cane as simply a toy and that is OK. • Compliment the sound the child makes when the cane taps the floor, wall or (yes) furniture. Repeat. • Encourage moving the cane tip left and right on the floor. • Practice walking with the cane several times a day while respecting their short attention span. • Begin using directional terms.	Parents utilize the *Teaching Cane* to demonstrate desired cane habits. Toddlers need to their canes.
	• Right from left: "I'm washing your right hand." "I'm washing your left foot." • Front from back: "Your tummy is in front of you." "The cat is behind us." • Top from bottom: "This is the top of your head." "This is your bottom lip." • Provide physical support behind the child as the child holds the cane and with each step, encourage the child to move the cane left and right. • The child may need some assistance holding the cane and walking at the same time, so be mindful not to squeeze the child's hand too tightly. • While walking and exploring, be excited about the different sounds the cane makes as it taps the floor or ground. • Assist the child to walk to and from the car with the cane when going on trips. • Take short walks with the cane within the neighborhood. • Encourage play with the cane. • Encourage the child to identify obstacles in the path of travel and move around them. • Encourage the child to locate interesting sounds to reinforce their desire to travel. • Encourage utilization of auditory landmarks for orientation and movement (i.e., "I hear the refrigerator turning on—it is behind us." "I heard the front door shut—it is in front of us.")	People usually grab their wallets, glasses, or purses as they leave their home; parents of blind or visually impaired toddlers need to grab their child's cane. Encourage the child to use the cane at walking opportunities outside the home environment. Be patient. Stay positive!

PRESCHOOL SUGGESTIONS
"A growing body of anecdotal evidence from the O&M field demonstrates that early cane instruction can produce extremely positive results for the preschool blind child" (Pogrund & Rosen, 1989, p. 438).

- Encourage the child to be as independent as possible at all times.
- Place the same high expectations on a blind child as is on a sighted child.
- Consider alternative ways of completing the same task.
- Think "tactual"—not visual. (It does not have to be pretty.)
- Verbalize, verbalize, verbalize—what is happening and/or what is about to happen.
- Attend Play Dates or Open Houses at the preschool or schedule an appointment to explore the school and classroom.
- Encourage the child to remember to get and use the cane without reminders. Perhaps say, "Are you forgetting something?" rather than saying, "Do you have your cane?"
- Assist the child to walk independently with the cane to and from the car/bus.
- Assist the child to hold the cane to go up and down bus steps until it can be done independently.
- To help develop mental mapping skills, provide opportunities for the child to make discoveries through their own mobility.
- To avoid dependency on others, *discourage traveling human guide.*
- Continue to use interesting sounds to encourage the child to walk to targeted locations of interest.
- The child will begin to utilize auditory and tactile landmarks for orientation with independent practice.
- At school, practice storing the cane on the floor at or very near work stations or floor activities.
- At school, encourage the child to walk to various targeted locations within the school (i.e., classroom, main office, nurse's office, principal's office, gym, lunch room, library, playground, bus.)

PRE-SCHOOL O&M

An important strategy to promote independent O&M in the preschool and kindergarten classrooms is by incorporating tactile adaptations. For example, if the classroom floor is tile, a carpet runner may be used in front of the door for the student to feel with the cane where to line up. Also, large area rugs or furniture can be strategically placed to mark off centers or help create a shore line to follow to reach a targeted area.

If the classroom is carpeted, two strips of Velcro (back-to-back) may be placed on the rug to help with navigation in open areas, line up at the door or create borders around learning centers. The Velcro may be moved or removed as needed. Make note of floor transitions such as carpet to tile as tactile borders or landmarks for shore-lining. Rubber mats or carpet samples may help identify the child's group time or "sit-spot." Below are some additional Preschool Suggestions.

CHAPTER 8

O&M FOR OLDER STUDENTS

Some older students fear using a cane in front of their peers. However, by doing so, the cane informs others that the user has a visual impairment which removes other labels such as *clumsy* or *awkward* (Pogrund & Rosen, 1989). As students begin each school year, often it is the O&M instructor who is the initial contact person between the students' family and the educational establishment. This is because the student often receives mobility training prior to the first day of school in order to begin building mental mapping skills and self-confidence through traveling independently with their cane in new environments. With practice and as students mature, their mobility skills will gradually be refined and improved leading to increased independence (Willoghby & Duffy, 1992). This will also lead to not needing the O&M lesson prior to the beginning of school. As the students progress through the educational system, they can begin to travel *independently* within, around, and beyond the school grounds as they utilize their cane in various locations while encountering teachable moments which are meaningful to them.

TRAVELING INDEPENDENTLY

Traveling independently means that the student is traveling without holding the hand or arm of another person, unless in special circumstances (i.e., a fire drill). It does not mean the student is traveling *alone*. Rather, the student is learning how to use the cane as a tool to encourage independence. As skills increase, students need to be expected to independently locate common school destinations such as their locker, lunchroom, gym, classrooms, main office, and nurse's office. Although this locating is done

> Independent travel does not mean the child is traveling alone.

independently, their mobility instructor is often nearby while students perform these tasks. Overall, students' O&M goals include high expectations with the understanding that they are to travel independently, when appropriate, equal to their peers.

INDIVIDUAL EDUCATION PLAN

The *Individual Education Planning* (IEP) Team includes both parents, if possible, school staff members (i.e., principal or vice principal, classroom teacher, special education teacher, and paraprofessional), Orientation and Mobility (O&M) Instructor, and the Teacher of the Visually Impaired (TVI) (i.e., Teacher of Students with Visual Impairments, Teacher of Blind Students). Parents may invite anyone else to the meeting who they feel will contribute to the welfare of the student, and this may include a staff member of the state's Vocational Rehabilitation Agency for the Blind. The main goal of the IEP is to ensure that everyone is working on the same goals for the student, and this includes O&M expectations.

> **Coordinate with the IEP team to ensure the child has and uses the long white cane at all times.**

Sometimes the number of members at the IEP team meeting can be overwhelming and confusing. Also, parents can be confused regarding the difference between a Teacher of the Visually Impaired (TVI) and the Orientation & Mobility Instructor (O&M). They often get the two roles confused and/or think the positions overlap. Basically, the TVI is a certified teacher who focuses on teaching the Braille code, classroom accommodations, computer technology, and Independent Living Skills. In addition, these individuals complete Functional Vision Assessments (FVA) and National Reading Media Assessments (NRMA). These are requirements on the Individual Education Plan (IEP) in order for students to receive services from the school district. The FVA is used to determine how students see best within the classroom setting and offers recommendations as to how to help students perform at their highest potential with the vision they have, or it suggests that students use Braille and the alternative skills of blindness. The TVI will also do FVAs on students with no vision. (By the way, *Vision Teachers* is an old term that needs to be discarded because these teachers *do not teach vision*. Just like Deaf and Hard-of-Hearing teachers do not teach hearing) The O&M instructor teaches mobility with the long white cane. This position requires a Master's Degree and is separate from the TVI certification. Some college programs offer dual certifications in both TVI and O&M. Most often, however, these services are offered by two people. The main thing to remember is that only a certified O&M instructor is qualified to teach O&M, just as only a TVI is certified to teach Braille.

> **Only certified Orientation and Mobility instructors are qualified to teach O&M.**

Young children do not usually understand the IEP, nor do they have the attention span to stay engaged in the discussion, so they often do not attend the meeting. However, by about 2nd grade, the child needs to be present as well as participate in the meeting in order to comprehend that everyone at the meeting is working together on their behalf. This informs the child that the same high expectations apply to him in all areas of the school, including having and using the cane. Also, if the student attends the meetings, while progressing through the educational system, they will be able to contribute to the IEP regarding accommodations, needs, and desires within the students' educational quest.

As the child gets older, IEP mobility goals will most likely involve O&M lessons off campus which needs to be approved by the parent. This is because O&M involves specialized instruction which addresses the child's need to learn the specific skills and techniques necessary to travel safe and effective within the community. A Consent for O&M Instruction will need to be signed by the parent and included with the IEP. An example can be found in the appendix.

ADDITIONAL COMMENTS/ANSWERS

Some parents are apprehensive about the cane, especially when they have to constantly remind a child to take their cane, in particular when the child has some remaining vision or is new to blindness. Here are some thoughts and responses parents have expressed:

- *My child is not blind enough to need the cane:* If the doctor said the child is "legally blind," or has a degenerative visual condition, then, yes, the child needs the cane. Children with degenerative conditions will benefit from exposure and practice with the cane for future utilization. Furthermore, if the child is unable to read the menus posted behind the fast-food counters, or recognize familiar faces without people speaking first, bumps into people or objects, or hesitates when walking or running, then the child is visually impaired enough to benefit from using a cane for mobility purposes.

- *My child is able to take my arm and I can be the human guide*: This is true. You have the option to be your child's guide. (See Chapter 11.)

- *My child is simply going a short distance such as to the car or a neighbor's house so he does not need to take his cane*: One never knows when there is an emergency and the child will need to travel independently in unfamiliar territories. Remember, the cane is a tool—just as a hammer is a tool for a carpenter or a spatula is a tool for a cook. The cane needs to be accessible to the user at all times—in the car or at the neighbor's house. Wherever, whenever.

- *My child has been to that store or restaurant several times and knows the layout, so he does not need his cane there*: There could have been changes since the last visit. Perhaps there are different staff now or the building is currently under construction. Perhaps you are going at dinner time instead of lunch and now the lighting is lowered, causing decreased vision. All these factors can come into play and may hinder the child from developing confidence to travel independently. However, by using the cane, your child can be successful in any location, regardless of any changes that may have occurred.

- *The cane makes my child look blind*: The cane does not *make* anyone *look* blind. The cane makes blind individuals look *independent*. Without a long white cane, a blind person may bump into objects or people. This awkwardness may cause sighted people to develop misconceptions about the abilities of individuals who are blind. The cane is an identifier; it provides information to others that the user has a visual impairment. Simply put, if your child does not use the cane, your child may be putting him or herself in harm's way.

- *How much time is necessary for O&M lessons?* Time often varies per student because of individualized instruction. Understanding the short attention span of young students, lessons can be as few as 15 minutes. From preschool to middle school, the lessons can typically be from 30 to 60 minutes a week. In high school, usually the minutes are equal to the minutes for one class period or can be as long as 90 minutes.

The following article was first published in *Future Reflections*, Winter 2017, Volume *36*(1).

Teachable Moments: How Parents of Blind and Visually Impaired Children Can Reinforce Lessons in Orientation and Mobility

by Merry-Noel Chamberlain

It is often said that parents are a child's first teachers. This idea holds true whether the child is blind or sighted. Before a child begins to walk, parents, grand-parents, and older siblings provide physical support to help her or him build strength and balance. When the time is right, these helpers support the child during those first shaky steps.

Children who are blind or visually impaired get the same assistance as sighted children do when they learn to walk. In addition, they generally receive formal training from a certified instructor of O&M (O&M), either at home or in a daycare or school setting. I am an O&M instructor and the parent of a blind child, my daughter Ashleah. I have been teaching O&M to Ashleah since she became my daughter at the age of eight.

In most cases, children of school age receive their O&M instruction in and around the school building. Ashleah receives much of her O&M instruction in the community, and mainly it occurs during teachable moments. A teachable moment is an opportunity that happens spontaneously. Such instruction is highly beneficial, since the action takes place within real-life situations.

When the O&M instructor is constrained by time and location, many teachable moments are lost. As a parent, I have discovered that I can use teachable moments to help my daughter gain valuable skills in orientation. On the other hand, I have sometimes put on my O&M instructor hat within the school setting to teach Ashleah. When she was in middle school, I provided instruction a week before the beginning of the school year, a practice I continue now that she is in high school. Ashleah and I visit her school and walk to all of her classes in the order of her daily schedule. Each year I instruct her less and less as her mental mapping skills improve. Despite my training in the field, I recognize that the person who helps orient a student to the school setting does not have to be an O&M professional.

In this article I suggest some possible teachable moments you can use to help your child gain O&M skills. First, let us define "orientation" and "mobility." Orientation is knowledge of where you are within a given space, such as a room, building, block, or city. Mobility involves the actual techniques used for movement. It includes how to hold the cane, how to arc the cane, and how to walk with the cane from one place to another. To become competent in mobility, one may need to turn to an O&M instructor. To build and enhance mobility skills, one can use teachable moments that occur outside formal lessons.

Mobility Basics

Your child has probably learned some basic mobility skills from his or her instructor. However, as a parent you may not be aware of the basics. The following list is not intended to be a complete set of instructions on how to use the long white cane. These are simply observations you may notice and suggestions to help jog your child's memory about solutions to become competent travelers.

- If your child is veering too much to the right or left, ask, "Are you extending the cane outward from the center of your body near your bellybutton?" By doing so, she will walk in a straighter line. The cane leads her from the centerline of her body.
- If your child veers to the left while holding the cane in his right hand, ask, "Are all your fingers wrapped around the cane shaft, including your index finger?" When the index finger is extended outward along the shaft, it can hinder the cane tip from extending far enough in that direction. The hand will be limited in moving far enough to the right. Thus, your child is not covering the right side of his body as well as the left. The same holds true if he holds the cane in his left hand and veers to the right.
- If your child is being jabbed in the abdomen by the cane handle when she approaches an up-curb or up-step, ask, "Is your wrist facing upward?" When the wrist faces upward, the cane handle will automatically move upward as the cane encounters an up-curb. The cane may poke your child in the stomach as it encounters an up-curb or up-step if the wrist is sideways.

- If your child seems to miss drop-offs or down steps, ask, "Are you keeping your cane low to the ground?" When the cane arc is too high (more than half an inch), it is difficult for her to detect small changes in the terrain.
- If your child seems to lunge forward with each step, ask, "Are you walking in step with your cane?" When a person walks in step, the cane sweeps for obstacles before the foot is placed in that location. When the child is walking, the cane tip needs to be opposite the extended foot. That is, when the cane tip is over on the left side of the body, the right foot is forward; then the cane tip swings over to the right side of the body and the left foot steps forward. This method clears the way so the traveler is aware that the area is free of obstacles before taking the next step.
- If your child bumps into doorframes, ask, "Are you arcing your cane as wide as your shoulders?" For best protection, the cane tip needs to move to the right and left of the body at shoulder width.

Instructional Strategies for Teachable Moments

1. Allow plenty of time for the teachable moment. This is not a time to be in a rush. Your child may need time to problem solve and to develop mental mapping skills.

2. Let your child make a mistake. If your child walks down the wrong aisle in the store, allow her to explore. She is building problem solving skills. As she explores, she gathers bits of knowledge that can be stored for future reference.

3. Problem-solving opportunities help individuals develop mental mapping skills. Mental mapping is the ability to create a map of an area within one's mind. Using the example above, while your child walks down the wrong aisle at the supermarket, she may discover the ice cream section, though she is not in need of ice cream at the time. (I have yet to meet a child who is not in need of ice cream.) She may make a mental note of where the ice cream is located. The very next time your family needs ice cream, she can be the one to retrieve it. This knowledge is a form of mental mapping.

4. During the teachable moment, walk quietly several feet behind your child. If you are in a store, you may even walk in the next aisle. If you are at a fast-food restaurant, you might sit at your table while your child goes up to the counter. You are there, but you are not directing your child's movements. You may step forward and assist if you feel your child truly needs your help because she appears to be seriously frustrated or confused. Again, it is best to give the child ample space and time to develop problem solving skills. Be far enough away so that she feels independent, but stay close enough to assist if needed. For safety reasons, be aware of your child's location at all times, just as you would with a sighted child.

   Incidentally, if you are a parent who also uses a cane for O&M, it is important to permit your child to focus on the auditory information from her own cane without being confused by the information projecting from yours. I often turn my cane upside down when I am monitoring my daughter. In this way, the steel tip does not strike the ground to create distracting sound and echoes. I learned this technique from a blind mobility instructor, and I use it when I monitor my students as well.

5. Instead of jumping in to help, offer some wait time. Wait time is the time you give your child to process the situation, determine a solution or hypothesis, create a plan, and carry out the plan to test the hypothesis. If he is successful, your child continues traveling to his destination. If not, he may need time to discover a different solution or hypothesis. If you jump in with the solution, he will not have the opportunity to process the situation himself. He may come to expect that someone always will be there to solve his O&M woes. When you provide wait time, he can build problem solving skills that may be transferred to other situations. Of course, please step in if you feel that your child is truly frustrated and needs your help. After all, you know your child best.

6. You may need to redirect people who want to be overly helpful. Often, they are not aware that your child is being monitored, or they simply want to do a good deed. It is your decision if you want your child to ask for or accept assistance. Personally, I think about the goal of the teachable moment. Is it to get from point A to point B? Is it to learn how to ask or receive help from others, perhaps in the form of information? For some of my students, asking for assistance from a pedestrian, customer, or store clerk is a scary experience. Practice in a safe situation can help the child overcome this fear.

Teachable Moments

Now that you have some basic mobility guidelines and some teachable moment strategies, you probably wonder how you can help your child with O&M. Here are some O&M teachable moments I have used with my daughter over the years. As I mentioned above, teachable moments are opportunities that occur spontaneously. They are very beneficial, since the action takes place within real=life situations. The more meaningful the activity, the more memorable the experience is to the child. Concrete memories can be retrieved and used later on.

As you read this list, you will probably say to yourself, "Yes, I've been in that situation," or "Yes, I can do that." Know that you are already on the right track. Have fun with these teachable moments!

Opportunities for Teachable Moments

Stores and Restaurants: Many stores and restaurants have similar floor plans, especially when they belong to a chain. For example, many Walmart, Target, Walgreen, McDonald, Burger King, or Cracker Barrel are laid out in the same way. If a person has been in one, it is not problematic to maneuver in another. Supermarkets also are quite similar in layout. The cash register is located near the entrance. Meat, baked goods, and dairy items are usually located around the perimeter of the store. The produce section is generally near the entrance, and customer service is near the front. When you are in this type of location, share this knowledge with your child.

Sidewalks: A perfectly straight sidewalk is an excellent place to practice walking in a straight line. If you are out walking and find such a sidewalk, challenge your child to walk ahead of you without touching the edges of the sidewalk. The faster she walks, the straighter.

Shorelines: If you are walking along a sidewalk with a curb or building on one side, ask your child to be the leader. Have him let you know when he approaches a door, another sidewalk, or the corner of a building. He can do this by using a technique called *Shore-lining*. When the child is Shore-lining, the cane touches the edge of the sidewalk, curb, or building each time the tip is on that side of the body. The child then follows this tactual line. Be sure the shoreline is fairly straight. Inset doorways, bike racks, or other irregularities can lead to frustration.

Fast Food: Perhaps you're at a fast-food restaurant, and your child wants some cherry pie. Hand him the money, give him some general directions to the counter, and send him on his way. Allow him to problem solve the path back to your table. If he really has a taste for pie, his motivation is likely to be strong.

Trash bins: When everyone has finished eating at a fast-food restaurant or food court, ask your child to take the tray and empty it in the trash. She may need some directions about where the trash bin is located.

Automatic or main doors: When you are about twenty feet from an automatic door or some other main door to a large store, step back and ask your child to locate the store entrance. Sometimes the opening and closing of the doors by other customers can be heard, making the task easy.

Cash registers: Just out of earshot of the dings of the cash register, ask your child to locate the checkout area. Next time, increase the distance when you give him this teachable moment opportunity. For an older child, ask her to locate the cash register all the way from the back of the store.

Shoe Section: Certain areas of department stores have their own unique smells. The shoe section is one of them. From a few yards away, ask your child to locate the shoe section. Then, to make the task a little more challenging, ask her to locate the section with her size shoes. She can do this by selecting a shoe and placing the sole next to her own. If the first shoe is too big, she can go up and down the aisle until she is successful.

Fruit and Vegetable Section: Ask your child to find a sweet apple. Once he finds the apple bins, it is simple to find the sweet apples because they have bigger bumps on the bottom. The ones that are smooth on the bottom can be sour.

Malls: When you walk in the mall, ask your child to identify stores that offer great olfactory stimulation. These include Starbucks, Bath and Body Works, etc.

Street Crossings: When you stand at a street corner with your child, ask him to tell you when it is safe to cross. He can determine when it is safe by listening to the direction and flow of the traffic.

Cardinal Directions: When you stand at an intersection, ask your child in which direction the automobiles are traveling. Try to use cardinal directions (north, south, east, and west) rather than right and left, though the latter are also important concepts for your child to know.

Restrooms: Eventually every child reaches the stage where he or she is ready to visit a public restroom unaccompanied by a parent. When an older child needs to go to the restroom, give him directions and be sure to review the return route. Whenever possible, use cardinal directions rather than simply saying right or left, as it can be confusing to reverse directions on the return trip. It can be difficult to remain behind, but let your child go alone. As he returns, provide some sound clues to help him find his way back.

Elementary School: When you visit your child's school, let your child be the leader. Ask her to show you where her classroom is located. Invite her to show you how to get to key locations in the school such as the front office, cafeteria, gym, and music and art classrooms.

Middle and High School: Go to school with your child before the first day of class and discover the locations of all the required classrooms. Ask your child to walk through his daily schedule, and point out some landmarks along the way. Landmarks are stationary items that can be used as reference points, such as water fountains, or differences in the texture of the floor. If the item can be moved, it is not a landmark.

Neighborhood: If you and your child are walking to the school or a friend's house, ask her to lead the way. Allow her to walk ahead, but instruct her to wait at corners, even if you are not crossing the street. Until it is appropriate for her age and skill level, do not permit her to cross the street without you.

Treats: Looking for a special treat at the store is a great way to motivate your child to explore and problem solve. Ask her to show you how to get to the bakery section, where free cookies are given away. Ask her to locate the dairy or ice cream section, which is usually at the back of the store. If your child wants a special item or two, have her go to customer service, and ask an employee to show her to the item she wants. Once she finds it, she can go through checkout and meet you at the front of the store. This activity may be too advanced for some teens, so you may wish to practice a time or two before you send your child to do it independently. Once your child can find and purchase items at the store without your help, you can drop her off and wait for her in the car. When she is done, honk the horn to provide a sound cue so she can return to your vehicle.

After the Teachable Moment

After a teachable moment, pat your child on the back for a job well done. It can be valuable to talk to him about the experience. Be sure to ask open-ended questions such as "What did you like or not like about what you did?" "How did you feel when you were done?" Be sure to praise success. If your child asked for assistance, praise him for knowing when and how to ask for help. If you stepped in to help without being asked, tell him why you did so.

Teachable moments lead to nuggets of knowledge you allow your child to discover. Each teachable moment is a gift your child can treasure and build upon, even though she might find the experience a bit frustrating at the time. ("What? You're making me work?") If your child can problem solve in one location when you are with her, she will most likely be able to problem solve in another location when you are not present.

For additional information, visit the National Organization of Parents of Blind Children at http://nopbc.org/. They offer *Future Reflections*, a quarterly magazine for parents and educators of blind children. See Appendix for additional articles.

Right: Two friends explore the paper eating lion at the zoo during O&M.

CHAPTER 9

ORIENTATION AND MOBILITY TRANSFORMATIONAL SKILLS

The Structured Discovery Cane Travel curriculum focuses on perfecting *Transformational Knowledge*, which is the ability to learn and master techniques within a plethora of settings during training through hands-on experiences and then transfer those skills post training to other settings. These hands-on, personalized experiences are intended for future retrieval. For young children, and/or English Language Learners (ELL), some concepts (or vocabulary) may be new to them so extra time may be necessary to address those individualized needs. For example, with the initial encounter and exposure to a *curb*, both the word and the concept of *curb* will need to be comprehended.

The *Orientation and Mobility Transformational Skills Checklist* is a compiled list of mobility transformational skills and although these recommended O&M skills are somewhat listed from simple to complex, this list is not to be used as a sequential learning curriculum whereby one skill must be mastered prior to the next. It is by no means intended to be a complete list to meet the plethora of environments students will encounter in O&M class or later throughout their lives. In the SDCT curriculum, skills are introduced as they are encountered during mobility lessons and therefore cannot be addressed in the order they are listed below. These real-life encounters, known also as teachable moments, are educational opportunities students engage in during novel encounters. Keep in mind that hands-on experiences ensure strong personal impacts that stimulate long-lasting concepts or memories (Hansen, 1998) for later retrieval and the ultimate goal of mobility instructors is to be phased out. In other words, as students acquire skills and comprehend of the necessity of independent travel, their need for ongoing O&M instruction vanishes (Mettler, 1995).

The *O&M Transformational Skills Checklist* is a *printable form* to help mobility instructors keep ongoing records of students' O&M transformational skills by checking off the tasks as they are mastered.

Remember all of the items compiled on this list will not pertain to all students; rather, this list simply proposes recommendations to help reduce possible splinter skills from occurring. Some students may need specific skills not included on this list so extra space is available at the end of each section and at the end of the form to add individualized transformational targeted skills.

Student's Name:		Date:
Name of Orientation & Mobility Instructor:		
School/Agency:		

	ORIENTATION AND MOBILITY TRANSFORMATIONAL SKILLS CHECKLIST	✓
CANE AWARE-NESS FOR BEGINNERS (i.e., toddlers or individuals with additional disabilities)	• Opens hand to grip cane with☐ or without☐ prompts. • Holds cane for 15☐, 30☐ seconds, 1☐, 2☐, 3☐, • 5☐, 10☐ minutes. • Retrieves cane with☐ or without☐ prompts when beginning to engage in travel. • Retrieves cane with☐ or without☐ prompts when exiting the home environment.	☐
SENSORY DEVELOP-MENT	• Taps the cane tip on different textures to retrieve auditory information with☐ or without☐ assistance. • Taps cane in front☐, behind☐ the body. • Turns head☐, body☐ toward environmental sounds. • Uses constant contact on different surfaces with☐ or without☐ assistance.	☐
SELF-PRO-PULSION, WALKING FOR BEGIN-NERS (i.e., toddlers or individuals with additional disabilities)	• Independently scoots☐, crawls☐ around on the floor, holding or pulling the cane. • Walks 3 steps with☐ or without☐ assistance while holding the cane. • Walks 3☐, 5☐, 10☐ feet, holding the cane in front of the body without tapping or walking-in-step. • Taps the cane tip with☐ or without☐ assistance on different textures within☐ or outside☐ the home environment. • Walks 3☐, 5☐, 10☐ feet while moving the cane in front of the body left and right. (Note: Does not need to be walking-in-step.) • Walks 3☐, 5☐, 10☐ feet, *tapping* the cane left and right in front of body☐. (Note: Not walking-in-step.) • When requested, stores cane in correct location☐. • Walks toward the direction of sounds☐. • Seems to be aware of echolocation with the cane☐ (i.e., turns head or body when metal cane tip makes different sounds). • Alternates feet when ascending☐ and descending☐ stairs. • Maneuvers about quickly within own home☐. • Maneuvers to favorite location within the home☐, yard☐ (i.e., swing, slide) with☐ or without☐ cane.	☐

	ORIENTATION AND MOBILITY TRANSFORMATIONAL SKILLS CHECKLIST	✓
IDENTI-FY CANE PARTS	• Able to identify: • Cane strap or chain—used to store the cane on a hook☐. (Warning: This is not to be wrapped around the wrist while walking as that may cause harm to the user.) • Cane handle☐. • Cane shaft☐. • Metal tip☐.	☐

KNOWL-EDGE OF CANE GRIPS	Pencil Grip helps to prevent the cane from going under obstacles such as tables and chairs and is used in enclosed areas, while standing, or walking in line. Very young children may use a fist-type grip similar to holding a ski pole.
	1. Holds cane as if it is a giant pencil☐ or fist☐.
	2. Uses Pencil Grip while ascending stairs☐ and curbs☐.
	3. Uses Pencil Grip while descending stairs☐ and curbs☐.
	4. Uses Pencil Grip while standing☐ among friends and walking☐ in a line.
	5. Knows when to use Pencil Grip with☐ or
	6. without☐ reminders.
	7. Able to change to Pencil Grip as needed, with☐ and without reminders☐ when walking.
	Open Palm/Extended Technique helps to prevent the cane from thrusting into the user's abdomen when the cane suddenly encounters an object (i.e., curb) and is used to travel quickly and confidently in open spaces.
	1. Holds cane with palm upward☐.
	2. Wraps all fingers around the cane with the thumb pointing to the cane tip☐.
	3. Holds hand in front, center of the body, near but not touching the navel☐.
	   • Knows when to use Open Palm/Extended Technique with☐ or without☐ reminders.
	   • Able to change to Open Palm/Extended Technique as needed, with☐ or without☐ reminders when walking.
		☐

WALKING POSTURE	While walking: • Keeps cane tip low☐. • Maintains good posture☐. • Keeps head up☐.	☐
BASIC CANE TECH-NIQUES	**Cane Arc** provides information that the area in front of the body is clear of objects. 1. Arcs cane tip about 1 inch high with☐ or without☐ reminders. 2. Arcs cane as wide as the shoulders by pivoting the wrist from the body midline position when using the open-palm technique with☐ or without☐ reminders.	☐

	ORIENTATION AND MOBILITY TRANSFORMATIONAL SKILLS CHECKLIST	✓
BASIC CANE TECH-NIQUES	**Walk-in-Step** provides information about obstacles within the path while walking. 1. Able to alternate cane and foot (When right foot is forward, the cane tip extends from the left side of the body and vice versa) when walking with☐ or without☐ reminders. 2. Walks-in-step using the Pencil Grip when traveling in narrow or confined areas with☐ or without☐ reminders. 3. Walks-in-step using the Open-Palm/Extended Technique when traveling in open spaces with☐ or without☐ reminders. 4. Able to correct when walking out of step with☐ or without☐ reminders. 5. Able to acknowledge when out of step☐. **Two-Point Touch** helps to create auditory (and perhaps tactile) feedback in various locations. 1. Walks-in-step and taps the cane to the far right and left as it is arced in front of the body with☐ or without☐ reminders. 2. Acknowledges echolocation brought about by the metal cane tip as it taps surfaces (i.e., when approaching enclosed areas, buildings, parked cars, etc.) with☐ or without☐ reminders. **Touch & Slide** helps to provide tactile information regarding the terrain or to locate landmarks that are best found using tactile methods. 1. Walks-in-step while tapping and sliding the cane outward as it is arced to the right and left of the body with☐ or without☐ reminders. 2. Able to detect textural changes☐, subtle drop-offs☐, and blended areas with☐ or without☐ reminders ahead of time. **Constant Contact** helps to locate small, hard-to-detect landmarks that are best found using tactile (and sometimes auditory) methods. 1. Uses constant contact technique with☐ or without☐ reminders. 2. Able to follow a row of Velcro or tape attached to carpet with☐ or without☐ reminders. **Shore-lining** helps when searching for tactile landmarks or items. 1. Uses shore-lining techniques with☐ or without☐ reminders. 2. Independently demonstrates Two-Point-Touch☐, Touch & Slide☐, or Constant Contact☐ to Shoreline walls☐, sidewalks☐, and cracks☐. 3. Shorelines a curb while walking in the street☐. 4. Walks on the grass and shorelines the curb☐. 5. Self-corrects when veering away from shoreline☐. A) Utilizes sound for shore-lining (i.e., uses echolocation off a building or the sound of traffic when walking in a parking lot) ☐.	☐
CANE ETI-QUETTE	• Keeps the cane upright when not in motion (i.e., when standing in the hallway; not walking☐, waiting to cross streets☐, standing in lines☐) with☐ or without☐ reminders. • Stores cane nearby when not in use (i.e., on the floor☐ or propped in the corner☐) with☐ or without☐ reminders. • Stores cane correctly in automobiles (i.e., along the floor between the door and the seat, from front to back) with☐ or without☐ reminders.	☐

	ORIENTATION AND MOBILITY TRANSFORMATIONAL SKILLS CHECKLIST	✓
LEFT AND RIGHT	• Able to lift left foot☐, right foot☐, left hand☐, right hand☐ upon request. • Able to turn body left☐ and right☐ upon request. • Able to veer left☐ and right☐ upon request.	☐
LAND-MARKS	• Utilizes☐ and identifies☐ inside landmarks (i.e., terrain☐ or acoustic☐ changes, specific offices☐, classrooms☐, water fountain☐, or hand sanitizer stands☐.) • Utilizes☐ and identifies☐ various sounds inside☐, outside☐. • Utilizes☐ and identifies☐ floor changes (i.e., carpet☐, tile☐). • Utilizes☐ and identifies☐ outside landmarks (i.e., terrain☐ or acoustic☐ changes, noticeable • cracks in sidewalks☐, fence☐, driveways☐, sidewalks☐, playground equipment☐). • Able to determine the difference between sidewalks and driveways (i.e., slope☐, width☐).	☐
CARDINAL DIREC-TIONS	• Within a building, when given *north*, is able to identify cardinal directions: south☐, east☐, west☐, northeast☐, southeast☐, northwest☐, southwest☐, and back to north☐. • While outside, uses environmental clues to identify cardinal directions (north☐, south☐, east☐, west☐, northeast☐, southeast☐, northwest☐ southwest☐). • Names streets that run northbound/southbound☐, eastbound/westbound☐ within own neighborhood☐, around school grounds☐, and main streets downtown☐.	☐
SELF-PRO-PULSION, MOBILITY	• Locates obstacles with cane and goes around them☐. • Walks toward sounds☐; follows someone who makes sounds ahead via talking☐ or walking☐. • Demonstrates efficiency with Cane Basics☐. • Successfully walks, without veering, 10☐, 25☐, 50☐ feet in open areas. • Demonstrates the ability to independently navigate school or campus☐, using proper cane technique☐, going to☐ and from☐ various locations (i.e., restroom☐, cafeteria☐, or office☐.) • Uses the cane to locate the door knob☐. • Locates door☐, opens☐ and closes☐ after going through. • Holds door open for person walking through behind and announces door is on the right or left☐. • Demonstrates cane skills most appropriate to the travel demands indoors☐, outdoors☐, familiar☐ and unfamiliar☐ areas. • Independently explores classroom☐. • Travels to targeted locations within the classroom☐. • Travels to desired locations that involve 1☐, 2☐ or 3☐ turns within a building. • Able to walk up☐ turn-around☐ and walk down☐ a sidewalk that is about 50 feet long without shore-lining☐ or is able to self-correct when veering☐. • Able to locate and identify an intersecting sidewalk☐.	

	ORIENTATION AND MOBILITY TRANSFORMATIONAL SKILLS CHECKLIST	✓
SELF-PRO-PULSION, MOBILITY	• Able to cross a driveway from one sidewalk to another without veering ☐ and is able to self-correct ☐ if veering occurs. • Travels around own block or school campus block with ☐ or without ☐ assistance which involves no street crossings. • Travels around unfamiliar block with minimal assistance ☐ or independently ☐ which involves no street crossings (i.e., city park block). • Travels around unfamiliar block with minimal assistance ☐ or independently ☐ which involves driveways ☐ or alleys ☐. • Travels to desired locations that involve 1 ☐, 3 ☐, 5 ☐, 7 ☐, 10 ☐ blocks (i.e., travel from school to home). • Travels independently to specific locations using problem solving techniques ☐. • Uses alternative techniques to locate desired landmarks ☐. • Adjusts line of travel when the cane contacts obstacles in the pathway ☐. • Takes cane to designated locations outside comfort zones ☐. • Uses the cane correctly outside of O&M class on ☐ and off ☐ campus. • Uses cane when going out with family ☐ and friends ☐. • Demonstrates cardinal directions ☐, self-monitoring ☐, mental mapping ☐ techniques, various sound ☐ and tactile ☐ cues to complete independent routes to unfamiliar locations.	☐

O&M VOCABU-LARY	Ascending ☐ Backward ☐ Block ☐ Cane ☐ Cane tip ☐ Camber ☐ Cane handle ☐ Carpet ☐ Corner ☐ Curb ☐ Door ☐ Descending ☐ Distance ☐ Far ☐ Forward ☐	Go ☐ Intersection ☐ Landmark(s) ☐ Left ☐ Mobility ☐ Near ☐ Parallel ☐ Perpendicular ☐ Ramp ☐ Right ☐ Sidewalk ☐ Stairs ☐ Street ☐ Stop ☐ Sun cues ☐	Tile ☐ Time ☐ Travel ☐ Veer ☐ Walk ☐ Cardinal Directions North ☐ South ☐ East ☐ West ☐ Northeast ☐ Southeast ☐ Northwest ☐ Southwest ☐	

Space for Additional Vocabulary	☐ ☐ ☐	☐ ☐ ☐	☐ ☐ ☐	

LETTER LAYOUTS	• Understands mobility movement using print letters: L ☐, U ☐, or Zigzag ☐. • Understands intersection (streets and hallway) layouts using symbols or letters: + ☐, T ☐, Y ☐, X ☐, I ☐. (Note: "I" = approaching a street from the middle of the block such as a school crosswalk, or crossing a hallway from one room to another directly across.)	☐

	ORIENTATION AND MOBILITY TRANSFORMATIONAL SKILLS CHECKLIST	✓
STREET CROSSING	• Verbally acknowledges upcoming streets☐ intersections☐, and alleys☐ using environmental clues (i.e., traffic sound☐.) • Acknowledges intersections☐, streets☐, school crosswalks☐ has been reached by identifying descending sidewalks☐, curbs☐ or texture changes☐. • Motions to drivers to move on for various reasons☐ (i.e., if not ready, not intending to cross, environment too loud, or does not feel it is safe to cross the street). • Identifies parallel☐ and perpendicular traffic☐. • Analyzes traffic flow: 2-way☐, 4-way☐. • Analyzes intersections: +☐, T☐, Y☐, I☐, X☐. • Analyzes intersections: controlled☐, uncontrolled☐, crosswalk☐, roundabout☐. • Aligns to cross streets using environmental (auditory☐, tactile☐) clues. • Able to describe intersections☐ and indicate direction of traffic☐ and light changes☐ while standing at the curb. • Able to identify when it is safe to cross controlled ☐, uncontrolled☐ intersections. • Maintains line of travel when crossing street and corrects if veering☐. • Exhibits the necessary skills to cross streets safely and accurately at school crosswalks☐. • Completes street crossing and immediately steps off street at an intersection☐. • Able to identify when a truncated dome (i.e., wheelchair ramp) is encountered☐. • Maintains intended line of travel after crossing streets☐. • Comprehends *camber* (arch in the road)☐. • Recognizes when streets are being crossed. That is, does not unintentionally cross a street☐. • Demonstrates the confidence and skill to independently and safely cross a four-lane road at a controlled intersection☐. • Demonstrates the confidence and skill to independently cross a two-lane street at a noncontrolled intersection☐. • Demonstrates the skills to negotiate complex controlled intersections independently within the community☐.	☐
NUMBERING SYS-TEMS	• Comprehends the numbering system inside buildings (doors☐, offices☐) and outside (homes☐, businesses☐). • Understands the city/town's block numbering system☐. (Note: typically, each block contains numbers 1–99, 100–199, 200–299, etc., with odd-numbered addresses found on one side of the street and even-numbered addresses on the other side.) • Able to independently travel to specific addresses☐.	☐

	ORIENTATION AND MOBILITY TRANSFORMATIONAL SKILLS CHECKLIST	✓
CAFETERIA OR FOOD COURT	• Able to manage tray in line to retrieve meal☐. • Able to manage tray with food around tables☐ while seeking empty seat☐. • Able to manage dirty tray☐ to locate trashcan☐ or tray-wash area☐. • When bringing own lunch, able to locate empty seat☐ and trashcan☐ afterwards. • Able to locate targeted food vender to purchase meal☐ and able to locate seat afterward☐. • Able to locate trashcan to empty tray☐.	☐
COMMUNI-TY TRAVEL	• Understands *near*☐.and *far*☐. • Knows home address☐ and phone number ☐. • Knows how to provide directions to home☐ and can provide nearby landmarks ☐, home or building characteristics ☐ (i.e., color, bushes). • Demonstrates the ability to enter various businesses and locate targeted areas (i.e., customer service☐, restroom☐, elevator☐, specific merchandise ☐.) • Demonstrates ability to travel to various community locations using problem-solving skills and proper cane travel techniques: • Store or business on city/town's main street☐. • Fast Food Restaurant☐. • Dine-in Restaurant☐. • Grocery Store☐. • Department Store☐. • Post Office☐. • Bank☐. • Travels within local businesses and makes 5 purchases 1☐, 2☐, 3☐, 4☐, 5☐ (Note: Does not include traveling to). • Demonstrates comprehension of addressing systems by locating businesses in their local community☐ and in another town☐. • Manages personal items when traveling☐ (i.e., backpack, books, Brailler, or shopping bags). • Travels to 6 downtown destinations (2 addresses ☐, 2 named businesses☐, and 2 personal address or business☐). • Recognizes particular downtown streets by defining characteristics, such as the direction-bound☐, one-way☐, two-way☐, residential☐, business☐, semi-business☐, busy☐, slow☐, steady☐, or dead-end☐, and other landmarks or characteristics upon request☐. • Travels to targeted areas by creating own travel routes that require negotiation of residential☐ and business travel situations☐ (including intersections☐). • Able to successfully complete 1☐, 2☐, drop-routes with less than 3 requests for assistance from the public☐. • Appropriately solicits assistance from the general public using safety awareness☐ (i.e., knowing when and with whom to share personal information.). • Appropriately accepts☐ or declines☐ assistance from the public☐. • Able to solicit rides☐ (i.e., from family members, friends, neighbors). • Able to solicit a human guide, if necessary☐. • Politely refuses unwanted assistance☐ or guides☐.	☐

	ORIENTATION AND MOBILITY TRANSFORMATIONAL SKILLS CHECKLIST	✓
OTHER O&M SKILLS	• Identifies a door☐ or doorway☐. • Navigates through doorways by opening☐ and closing☐ the door). • Navigates elevators: • Locates call button☐. • Finds desired floor button☐. • Checks floor number (just inside the elevator doorframe) before exiting☐. • Navigates escalator: • Locates entrance☐. • Locates moving handrail to determine☐ and confirm☐ the direction of escalator. • Uses cane to locate the beginning of the moving stairs☐. • Quickly steps on the escalator with confidence and places the cane tip on the step ahead of the body☐. • Prepares to exit when the cane rises or lowers☐. • Exits the escalator with confidence and quickly moves out of the way☐. • Navigates moving sidewalks: • Locates entrance☐. • Locates moving handrail to determine☐ or confirm the direction of the sidewalk☐. • Uses cane to locate the beginning of the moving sidewalk☐. • Steps quickly on moving sidewalk with confidence and puts cane in front of the body☐. • Prepares to exit moving sidewalk when cane moves toward the body☐. • Exits sidewalk quickly with confidence and moves out of the way☐. • Uses upper-hand protective technique when walking under low-clearance objects such as tree branches☐. • Self-corrects when veering☐. • Uses cane to retrieve dropped items or items under furniture☐. • Walks backward using the cane behind the body☐. • Locates empty seat in a classroom or meeting hall with minimal assistance☐.	☐
CANE MAINTENANCE and STORAGE	• Protects cane by storing it nearby when not in use☐ (i.e., on the floor or propped in the corner). • Protects cane by storing it correctly in the automobile☐. • Secures cane correctly on a school bus☐. • Holds cane up and down while on a public bus☐. • Able to replace cane tip in controlled area (i.e., school or home)☐and while on travel routes☐. • Knowledgeable of where to purchase or obtain replacement canes☐and cane tips☐.	☐

ORIENTATION AND MOBILITY TRANSFORMATIONAL SKILLS CHECKLIST	✓
PROBLEM SOLVING SKILLS	• Uses auditory☐, olfactory☐, and terrain☐ cues to orient self outside of own home☐ or in the community☐. • Interprets echoes made by the cane tip when passing an open door☐, parked car☐, or side hallway☐. • Travels to a specified location using problem-solving techniques within the school building or campus: 1☐, 2☐, 3☐, 4☐, 5☐ times. • Demonstrates problem-solving skills to independently navigate to residence☐ and businesses☐. • When brought to unknown locations, successfully travels to specified destinations using problem-solving techniques: 1☐, 2☐, 3☐, 4☐, 5☐ times. • Demonstrates problem-solving skills by successfully locating 1☐, 2☐, 3☐, 4☐, 5☐ particular landmarks. • Knows the safe way to request assistance from the general public☐ (i.e., does not reveal personal information). • Successfully completes drop-offs (more than 5 blocks away) and returns to specified home-base using problem-solving skills: 1☐, 2☐, 3☐, 4☐, 5☐ • Able to provide verbal directions to others☐. • Performs complex routes in a variety of settings☐. • Able to identify travel needs (i.e., bus☐, automobile☐, pick up☐ and drop off☐) to meet personal☐ or vocational☐ goals.	☐
INCLEMENT WEATHER	• Digs cane tip into snow and pushes it forward while walking to contact the ground underneath☐. • Uses Pencil-Grip to stab down into the snow to feel the surface underneath☐. • Moves head covering aside to unmuffle environmental sounds☐. • Uses cane to locate landmarks above deep, packed or frozen snow surface☐. • Relies on taller landmarks (i.e., bushes, fences, benches, large rocks) when traveling through snow☐. • Uses upper body protective technique to detect low, heavy snow-covered tree branches☐. • Uses cane to probe snowbank to determine height and width or seek path☐. • Uses constant contact so metal cane tip can detect icy patches☐ (i.e., cane glides over ice). • Walks on grass beside icy sidewalk to avoid slipping☐. • Compensates arc of cane on windy days to avoid veering☐.	☐
PUBLIC TRANSPORTATION	• Identifies common public transportation options ☐ (i.e., Intra-city and inter-city bus travel, Taxi, cab, Uber, Handi-ride, Air Travel, Subway, Light Rail.). • Obtains information regarding time and location options from appropriate local sources of public transportation☐ (i.e. local bus system). • Utilizes public transportation (i.e. local bus system) to travel to targeted locations: Locates bus stop☐, asks driver the bus number before entering☐, informs driver of targeted bus stop to exit☐, sits near the front of the bus to hear driver and to remind driver to announce stops☐ and exits the bus at the correct location☐.	☐

	ORIENTATION AND MOBILITY TRANSFORMATIONAL SKILLS CHECKLIST	✓
MOBILITY APPS (Trudelle & Jones, 2020)	• Utilizes Orientation Verification☐ (i.e., Microsoft Soundscape, Blindsquare, "Hey Siri"). • Explores and Contacts Points of Interest☐ (i.e., Apple Maps, Google Maps,). • Uses Live Callouts☐ (i.e., Soundscape, Blindsquare). • Finds turn-by-turn directions☐ (i.e., Apple Maps, Google Maps). • Uses route planning☐ (i.e., Moovit, Transit App, Google Maps, Apple Maps).	☐
RURAL TRAVEL	• Able to shoreline dirt driveway or road☐. • Able to cross a dirt intersection☐. • Successfully follows rock path to desired location☐. • Able to determine cardinal directions while standing in a field☐.	☐
		☐
		☐
		☐
		☐
		☐

(Chamberlain, 2017, 2017b; Moskowitz, 2007; NMSBVI Orientation & Mobility Inventory, 2012; Willoghby & Duffy, 1992)

CHAPTER 10

TEACHING ORIENTATION & MOBILITY TO STUDENTS WITH VISUAL IMPAIRMENTS AND ADDITIONAL DISABILITIES

For all students, "the goal of O&M is to facilitate an individual's independence to the greatest degree possible" (Pogrund & Rosen, 1989, p. 435). Students with additional disabilities benefit the best when instructors use the SDCT curriculum. The following article, was first published in *Future Reflections*, Winter 2018, Volume 37(1).

Teaching Orientation & Mobility to Students with Visual Impairments and Additional Disabilities

by Merry-Noel Chamberlain, NOMC, and Denise Mackenstadt, NOMC

Orientation and Mobility (O&M) instructors are encountering increasing numbers of students with significant additional disabilities. These students present a variety of behavioral and physical differences, and they may have extensive individual needs for which instructors have not been prepared during their professional training (Olmstead, 2005). O&M instructors need to be open to creativity, discovery, and sometimes failure before their students can succeed. In this article we share some of our experiences in the hope that other O&M

instructors may find them helpful. Many of these ideas may also be helpful to parents as they encourage their children to move and explore at home or in the community.

Preparation

When a student is referred for O&M instruction, the instructor may perform an O&M evaluation. The evaluation will determine whether the student qualifies for instruction in the use of the long white cane. Usually the O&M instructor begins by examining the student's eye report from a qualified ophthalmologist. In some cases, it is difficult for an ophthalmologist to do a complete eye exam because the child may be uncooperative or may lack the ability to understand verbal requests. Nevertheless, some information is better than none at all. Next the instructor observes the student at home, in the classroom, or on the playground. Is the child stationary or active? Does he or she depend on family, friends, and/or staff members in order to move from one place to another? Observation may reveal that the child has difficulty moving from brightly lighted environments to darkened areas or has trouble with depth perception on stairs.

> For blind children, as for all children, the freedom to move, to be self-amused, and experience the joy of movement is fundamental to being human.
> —Joe Cutter (2007)

Based on the student's diagnosis and performance during observations, the instructor may request an audiology report. Hearing difficulties may hinder the student's success with Orientation and Mobility. It is wise to rule out this possibility or, if necessary, include it in the lesson planning process.

Students

When blind students have additional disabilities such as hearing loss, autism, developmental delays, cortical visual impairment (CVI), behavior disorders, or physical impairments, the O&M instructor needs to devise some unique instructional methods. Unfortunately, some educators believe that students with severe academic delays cannot benefit from mainstream educational programs, including O&M instruction. In reality, a student with severe struggles in the classroom may be a capable cane traveler. On the other hand, a student who is successful in a mainstream educational setting may have significant challenges with spatial orientation, body awareness, or directionality. Instructors need to be aware of their own biases about students with additional disabilities.

Instructors typically follow a general checklist of O&M skills necessary for safe travel in a variety of settings. Yet lessons cannot be copied from a curriculum or instruction manual because each student is unique and the terrain varies widely. When it comes to students with additional needs, O&M instructors must draw upon their creativity, their previous experience, and the expertise of others. The O&M instructor obtains the greatest success by keeping the student involved and by incorporating the student's interests into the lessons. It is valuable to keep the following ideas in mind.

Self-discovery is powerful. The student is more likely to remember an action when he discovers it through experience than when he is simply told about it (Hallowell, 2011). For example, say a student walks too far as he searches for the classroom door. By doing so, he finds a row of lockers with his cane. He explores farther down the hallway and finds the water fountain. At that point he hears the distinctive squeak of the classroom door. He turns back toward the sound and enters the classroom. The next time he searches for the door and encounters the lockers, he is more likely to correct his mistake. For some students with additional disabilities, this self-discovery process may take several tries. It may even turn into a game, with the student purposely passing the classroom to get a drink of water.

Allow the student to use the dominant hand. The dominant hand can be determined through observation and interviews with parents or teachers. It is the norm to place the cane in the student's right hand, just as it is almost automatic to place a pencil in the child's right hand. Note which hand is dominant and try placing the cane in that hand. For instance, one nonverbal student had a tendency to hold her cane in front of her body as she walked down a hallway, but then would switch and drag the cane behind her. An instructor noted that she did this when her cane was in her right hand and happened to swing into an open doorway. When the student was encouraged to hold her cane in her left hand, this tendency disappeared.

Points to Keep in Mind

These points and strategies may be helpful in working with students who have additional challenges.

Wait time: Some students, such as those with cortical visual impairment (CVI), may need extra time to process their surroundings along with the instruction. This can be referred to as "wait time." Repeating the instruction may actually hinder the student from moving forward in the lesson. Each time the instruction is verbalized to the student, she may need to wind back to the beginning of her processing. The wait time between the instructor's request and the student's action needs to be extended.

Communication methods: The student's communication methods may not be self-evident. Some students communicate happy and sad feelings by emitting high- or low-pitched screams, singing slow or fast tunes, rocking back and forth, or swinging out to attack. Some students show acceptance of a person by clinging or smiling, and ignore or avoid a person to demonstrate displeasure. Such actions can speak more loudly than words. Both the student and the instructor may experience frustration while the instructor learns how the student communicates through trial and error.

The student's tolerance level: Many students are unaware of their own tolerance level or are unable to express when they have reached their maximum. Instructors need to respect the student's actions and may need to respond quickly when there is a hint of frustration. For some students, a grain of frustration can quickly turn into a sandstorm, while for others a grain is simply a grain. If a student appears to be upset at the beginning of the lesson, it may simply be emotional carryover from the previous task. The classroom teacher may need to de-escalate the situation before the O&M lesson can begin. When frustration occurs during the O&M lesson because the student's maximum tolerance level has been reached, the instructor may need to pause the lesson so the student can take a break.

The student's behaviors: If the student intentionally drops the cane, the instructor needs to wait for him to pick it up. Sometimes the instructor may need to roll the cane closer so he knows where it is. If the instructor collects the cane and assists the student to the targeted destination via human guide, the student will expect that service every time he drops the cane. If "wait-time" is allowed, the duration of the unwanted behavior will decrease.

Be aware that dropping the cane or sitting on the floor during a lesson may be the student's way to communicate that he needs a break. Prolonged sitting on the floor may also be a behavior issue. It may be advisable to consult with the classroom teacher. A "behavior plan" may be necessary.

Reassurance and praise: Verbally reminding the student that she is not alone and that assistance is available may not always be successful, due to the student's cognitive or comprehension level. On the other hand, focusing on her success by offering a pat on the back or verbal praise using voice inflection may be quite rewarding for her. However, for some students, too much praise has the opposite effect. Overabundant praise quickly becomes meaningless. It is important to encourage the student to do as much as she can do herself, even if it means beginning with small steps.

The student's goals: Take time to be a part of the student's world. In some cases, the instructor can get to know the student's needs and motivations only through observation. If the student likes to sit in a special seat next to the CD player, he will be motivated to return to that spot. He may be frustrated when asked to walk to a location away from that spot, but he may work quickly to return to the spot he prefers. Effective lessons may begin at a location away from his favorite seat and focus on returning. Maybe the student has a special fondness for one of the cafeteria workers. The instructor might teach him the way to the cafeteria so he can turn in the classroom lunch count.

The student's preferred method of travel: Does the student tend to reach out for someone's arm as soon as she stands up? It may be that human guide technique is the only travel method she has been taught. This does not mean that she cannot benefit from O&M instruction. She may do well when she is taught the skills and expectations of independent travel.

Lesson Planning

The ultimate goal of an O&M instructor is to phase out the need for instruction as the student acquires the skills and understanding necessary for independent travel (Mettler, 1995). In order for this to happen, lessons based on the checklist must be adapted for the individual student. Instructors must have a full toolbox of individualized techniques. Time and time again, O&M instructors need to devise new plans and strategies. Here are some examples of adaptations for O&M instructors working with students with additional disabilities.

Have flexible lesson plans and allow for "teachable moments." During one lesson a student was walking on the sidewalk in front of the school. Along came a blind gentleman from the neighborhood who was using his long white cane. With guidance from the O&M instructor, the student and the gentleman had a short conversation, and the student learned that other people also use canes.

Keep the lesson successful. Even the best lesson plans may be interrupted due to unforeseen circumstances such as sudden hallway congestion, wet floors, or a fire drill. Sometimes the best lesson involves using a human guide through the difficult area and then continuing to the original goal. Treat tackling unforeseen circumstances as a separate lesson.

Realize that what works in one location may not work in another. A student may be very successful in walking straight down a hallway, but may have difficulties walking straight across a pedestrian bridge. Sounds, wind, or slopes in the terrain may create distractions that impair performance in a particular location.

Be sensitive to unfamiliar sounds. Since some students have difficulty with communication, they may not know how to express their fears. For example, one student with severe cognitive delays traveled quite successfully in familiar areas. However, one day while she was traveling in the community, some construction noise appeared to make her uncomfortable. She expressed her fear by making loud noises and sitting down on the sidewalk. She would walk only when she held a staff member's arm. Once past the construction site, she was able to walk independently again.

Realize that lesson plans may need to be altered—often.

Realize that lesson plans may need to be repeated—often.

Remember that lessons and instruction techniques may need to be adjusted—often.

Allow for choices. Have a few lesson goals on hand and let the student select from those choices. When a student selects the lesson goal, he often feels more in control and will perform with greater enthusiasm. Choice does not mean the student will never have to do the other lessons. It just means he does not have to do those lessons on that particular day.

Don't be afraid to abandon the lesson. Sometimes it may be best to end the lesson when unexpected problems arise. If this happens, explain to the student as well as possible why the lesson has ended. "Johnny, we need to go back to class now because it's raining very hard."

Allow the student to "scribble" with the cane. Many students don't have the dexterity to hold the cane correctly. We say that a student "scribbles" with the cane when she holds it incorrectly, as defined in the textbooks. The goal of instruction is for the student to use the cane to move about in her environment, and she may need to find her own best method. With time and gentle instruction, the student may accept encouragement to use the cane properly.

Allow the student to push the cane. Pushing the cane may not be ideal, but with time and encouragement he may begin to use it properly, especially after he has lightly bumped into a doorframe or two.

Allow the student to use the cane upside down if preferred. If she holds the cane this way to provide a reaction from the instructor and does not succeed, she will stop. If she likes the feel of the tactual flexibility better, she will continue. She may just be experimenting. Give her time, and she may correct herself. Remember that the student may know best. If she tends to do better when the cane is upside down, who is that hurting? She is walking independently, which is the ultimate goal.

Exploration

Don't wait until the student can walk before giving her a cane. Sometimes students don't realize there is anything "out there," so they have no reason to venture beyond arm's reach. A child who has not yet begun to walk can benefit from sitting and exploring her surroundings with a cane.

If the student is reluctant to hold the cane, give him something else to hold. For small children, try a push toy or paper towel roll. For older students, start with the top handle of a cane, but not the whole cane. The student may realize that the towel roll or cane handle finds things just beyond the reach of his hand. From here move to a wrapping paper tube or drumstick, then to the long white cane.

Allow plenty of time for the student to explore with the cane. When a student receives his first cane, he often will explore all around him, including the ceiling! Getting your first cane is like putting on your first pair of glasses. Allow students (especially those who are hearing impaired) to touch the ceiling with the cane or gently tap the walls above waist level. This is an opportunity for them to learn about their surroundings. It is fine to allow "ceiling time" at the beginning of a lesson, followed by instruction time with the cane tip on the ground. "Ceiling time" helps the student become aware of the environment, but it may put other students in harm's way. It is advisable to keep spectators at a safe distance!

Show the student other uses for the cane. The cane can be more than a walking tool. The instructor may encourage the student to use her cane to explore the height of the ceiling or the depth of a hole. The cane even can be used to measure a piece of furniture or to retrieve lost items from under the couch.

Be aware of weather conditions, even when working inside. Some students are very much affected by sensory changes. One student may do well on calm weather days, but he may resist completing a lesson when it is windy.

Be aware of the student's preferred environment. If a student feels comfortable only in his work station, move a necessary work item a few inches away so he has to reach for it or even take a step. Innovation is necessary when working with students who are severely affected by change.

Remember that what works for one student may not work for another. The instructor needs to find ways to motivate each particular student. Without motivation there is no success. One student who enjoyed going down the slide was motivated to work on her O&M skills in order to walk to the playground. Extra slide time was her reward.

Try reversing roles so that the student is the teacher and the instructor is the student. When the student provides the lesson, the instructor may learn why she is struggling in a particular area.

Remember to have fun. Students enjoy going to places of special interest. Mobility instruction provides a break in their regular routine.

Build trust with the student. If you promise something to a student, follow through.

Teamwork

With your guidance, allow the parent to be the teacher. When the parent has fears about letting the child use the cane, the instructor needs to teach the parent. Invite the parent to tag along on travel lessons. The parent will come to understand the basic O&M concepts, goals, techniques, and teaching methods (Castellano, 2010).

Maintain communication with the team. When you include the team, all team members can assist. Team members include parents, teachers of students with visual impairments (TVIs), occupational and physical therapists, classroom and special education teachers, and doctors. Everyone who works with or lives with the child can help, if only by supplying empty paper-towel tubes.

Teaching Children Who Are Deaf-blind

There are varying degrees of visual impairments, and there are many degrees and types of hearing impairment as well. A person may fall anywhere on the range from being hard of hearing to profoundly deaf. He may have frequency loss in the high or low range. Any level of hearing impairment can create a hindrance to the independent traveler, and it may lead to some anxiety for the instructor.

Communication with a deaf-blind student may involve signing hand-in-hand, signing within a close range or, for students with tunnel vision, signing at a distance, but bringing the signs in close to the body. A student with severe to profound hearing loss may communicate using American Sign Language (ASL). Unless the instructor knows ASL, he or she may need to work with an interpreter or intervener.

An intervener is trained to work with individuals who are deaf-blind, whereas an interpreter is trained to work with individuals who are only hearing-impaired or deaf. The intervener may provide intervention designed for a specific individual. He or she may assist the individual with access to environmental information that is otherwise unavailable or incomplete (SKI-HI, 2010). By developing a trusting relationship with the deaf-blind person, the intervener may also assist with social and emotional concerns (SKI-HI, 2010).

Unlike interpreters, interveners may not interpret word-for-word. For example, if the student is unable to understand the instruction or concept, the intervener is trained to step in and change the wording in order to convey the meaning. When working with an intervener, it is imperative for the instructor to feel that the intervener is conveying the O&M concept in its entirety.

Here Are Some Recommendations:

Meet ahead of time with the interpreter/intervener to review special O&M terminology. Not all vocabulary words have established signs. The instructor needs to review the O&M terms with the intervener to create a sign to represent such terms. The instructor can teach the interpreter/intervener pre-established specialized signs such as extended grip, pencil grip, open-palm, shoreline, or walking-in-step.

Ask the interpreter/intervener to refrain from acting as the instructor. This can be a touchy subject. The student may be totally dependent on the intervener, and the intervener may be totally protective of the student. However, for safety reasons, it is imperative that the student not turn to the interpreter/intervener for instructional guidance outside their realm of expertise.

Establish when it is permissible for the intervener to provide information to the student outside the O&M lesson. The intervener may sign to the student "actions" or "activities" surrounding the student's environment. It isn't advisable for the intervener to disrupt the lesson to provide irrelevant and possibly confusing information.

Prepare for the use of sleep-shades. Some instructors may be apprehensive to have a hearing-impaired student wear a pair of sleep-shades. Sleep-shade training can be successful if the instructor and student establish an agreed-upon sign that allows the student to stop the lesson and ask a question or for the instructor to provide additional instruction. Perhaps the instructor may slightly tap the student's sleep-shades or give three squeezes to the student's hand. Such a sign can give the student permission to lift his shades for visual communication. The student may begin to sign or tap his own sleep-shades to request permission to remove them.

Know the escape code. If the lesson needs to be terminated immediately in the case of an event such as a fire or tornado drill, the instructor or interpreter/intervener draws an X on the student's back with a finger. Using the human guide technique, she quickly leads the student. Ideally the evacuation plan can be explained and practiced ahead of time. The student can be assured that an explanation of the situation will be given once he is in a safe location.

Adjust the length of the lesson as needed. The student will need additional time to adjust to wearing sleep-shades. Keep in mind that the student has depended on his remaining vision to gather information that his hearing does not provide. It is best for the instructor to begin lessons in an area that is very familiar to the student. The student will need time to gather the courage to leave his comfort zone and to trust the information a long white cane can offer.

Consider contact to be the student's lifeline. At the beginning, the student may want to maintain constant contact with the interpreter/intervener or the instructor. Contact can be maintained by holding the hand that is not grasping the cane. As the student's confidence builds, contact can be maintained by placing a hand on the student's upper arm, shoulder, or back. Later still the instructor may simply walk at a close distance and touch the student if she appears to be upset.

Allow additional time for problem solving. The student may become easily frustrated and may need an occasional break. The instructor may let the student remove the sleep-shades and discuss possible problem-solving strategies. When the student is ready to return to the lesson and the sleep-shades are back in place, the instructor needs to assist the student back to the spot where she became frustrated in order to continue with the lesson. In some circumstances, the lesson may need to be abandoned for the time being.

Allow time for the student to touch with the hands items found by the cane. Keep in mind that the student may not be able to determine what something is based on the sound the cane makes when tapping the object. If the cane touches a trashcan, the student may use her free hand to follow the shaft of the cane down to the object.

The student may prefer to slide rather than tap the cane across the terrain. If he is unable to use echolocation, he may gain more information about the ground or floor by sliding the tip of the cane. If the student has been using a marshmallow cane tip, the instructor may recommend a metal tip instead. Metal cane tips provide more tactual information about the terrain. The tip will glide smoothly over icy areas and provide vibrations on sidewalks. It is also easier to tell the difference between carpet and tile with a metal cane tip.

When crossing a street, the student may need to depend on the instructor for the "go-ahead." The instructor can monitor the crossing itself to supplement the student's ability to determine parallel traffic.

Whenever possible, instruction needs to emphasize the student's other senses. Smells can indicate leather stores, restaurants, or hair salons. The feel of a breeze may suggest an alley, and a puff of heat on a cold day may suggest that the student is passing a doorway.

Instructional routes need to include tangible, unchanging landmarks. Cement posts or bus shelters, changes in sidewalk or flooring material, elevators, or stairs are clear and consistent landmarks.

Canes with Crutches or Wheelchairs

Often students with physical disabilities use crutches, walkers, support canes, or wheelchairs in addition to their long white canes. These students have the potential to move independently, and they can benefit fully from O&M instruction.

Specialized wheelchairs are designed for the needs of a specific user. It is important for the instructor to be familiar with the characteristics of each wheelchair and to assess what adaptations will be appropriate for the student. Here are some suggestions for O&M instruction with students who use wheelchairs:

Use a longer cane than is typically needed. The front of the wheelchair has an extension for the user's feet. A longer cane will allow the student to detect what is in front of him when he sweeps it back and forth.

When a student is unable to move the wheelchair independently, she can still use a cane. Even though the wheelchair user is being pushed, the cane will allow her to experience environmental cues such as slopes, openings, and changes in surface or terrain.

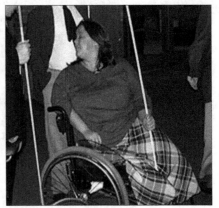

The user of a manual wheelchair can sweep the cane to the left and right before moving forward a couple of feet. The wheelchair moves only after the user has swept the cane to clear the area in front. Students who use motorized wheelchairs need to estimate speed in proportion to their ability to sweep the cane to cover the area ahead of them. The sweep of the cane needs to be in sync with the movement of the wheelchair whereby the wheelchair is not moving faster than the cane.

Attach "curb feelers" to the wheelchair. These can be attached to the wheelchair on either side to help the student know when the chair is close to a wall or a row of lockers. Curb feelers are typically used for automobiles so drivers do not rub their tires against the curb (Wiener, 2010).

Attach a shorter children's cane to the back of the wheelchair to identify the student as someone with a visual impairment. Because not all wheelchairs are alike, it is advisable to place the cane in the best location for optimal visibility.

Attach a pocket to the wheelchair so the student can store a telescoping or folding cane. The cane needs to be within easy reach for the student to find open spaces such as doorways.

Here are some adaptations for instruction with students who use crutches:

The student needs to hold the cane loosely, using the index and middle fingers. While she walks, the cane will be extended forward in either the right or left hand as the user has his/her hands on the crutches. Between each step, the user will need to sweep the cane across the terrain to make sure the area is clear and smooth before moving forward.

Use one of the crutches as the cane. Although this is not the ideal method, it is successful for slow walkers and in smaller spaces. This technique is done by the student sweeping the crutch in front of his body the width of his shoulders, then using the crutch to take a step forward.

Attach a children's long white cane to the crutch to identify the student as someone with a visual impairment.

If the student only needs one crutch, the long white cane can be used with the other hand.

Communication

Deaf-blindness is only one of many disabilities that affect a student's communication. Some students use electronic communication devices such as the DynaVox or Augmentative Alternative Communication Device. The student's educational team may provide vital communication information. In many cases, it is up to the O&M instructor to unlock the student's communication around independent travel.

Here Are Some Communication Tips:

In the beginning, communication may be nonexistent due to the student's fear of strangers or unfamiliar situations. The O&M instructor may interact with the student by sitting next to her. The student may acknowledge the instructor's presence through her actions. The instructor may then imitate the student's actions and add some actions of her own. If the student imitates the instructor's actions, the odds are good that she will learn O&M.

Even the student's smallest reaction is a form of communication. The student may push or turn away from the instructor. She may frown, sit down, scream, hug, or stand very close. Through these behaviors she expresses likes, dislikes, understanding, or uncertainty. It is important to express verbally to the student that her actions have been received and understood. "That noise tells me you don't want to hold your cane in your right hand." "I hear you screaming, and that tells me that you don't want to go outside today." Explain to the student what you expect of her, even if she isn't able to answer in words.

Sometimes asking is more successful than telling the student what to do. "Johnny, do you want to walk to the playground today?" Wait for his response.

Give choices where the student's action is the answer. "Stephanie, if you want to play in the ball pit, stand up." "Steven, take my hand if you want me to show you how to get to the water fountain."

Observe or video the student in other situations or with other staff members. Sometimes a student's behavior varies, depending on the situation or the people around him, and this information will be helpful to know.

Greet the student as you greet others. Students who may not be able to communicate expressively, may still be able to receive communication without difficulty. Through tone and inflection, they may be able to tell when someone is expressing praise or speaking in a derogatory manner.

Be sure that you and everyone working with the student use consistent terminology. If you have been saying, "Arc your cane from left to right," don't switch and say, "Sweep your cane from left to right."

Ask the student if it is okay for you to see him again. If he agrees, great! If not, tell him when you will be back. If you can't make it, send a note or call him directly. Often when a student knows the instructor is coming back, he is more willing to work at each lesson.

Be honest. "I'm sorry we need to do this today. I know you would much rather play on the computer. But this is something the school wants us to work on so you can be independent."

Explain the goal of the lesson, and ask the student if it is something he would like to do. Sometimes a student can't choose the lesson because of the Individual Education Plan (IEP) goal. "Johnny, it's nice out today, and we need to walk to the flagpole. Would you like to do that?" Rephrase the question if you think the student didn't understand. "Johnny, the sun is shining today. Shall we walk to the flagpole?" If the student cannot answer verbally, suggest an action. "Johnny, if you want to walk to the flagpole, stand up."

Tactile or Object Communication Systems

Individuals learn to communicate from the concrete to the abstract. At first infants know they are going to be fed when the bottle reaches their lips. Later the infant will hear her parent say, "We are going to feed you." Still later, the infant will be able to understand feeding time by hearing the preparation of the bottle with the pouring and filling sounds. Similarly, students who are nonverbal need a way for you to communicate needs and expectations. A student may be handed a cane to communicate that it is O&M time. Later a portion of the cane can be handed to the student indicating O&M time. Later yet, a cane tip can be handed to the student. Even more abstract would be to hand a card with the cane tip attached and the name identified in Braille and large print. In the end, only a verbal prompt "it is O&M time" will be used. This is how to take a single act from the concrete to the abstract.

High Expectations

High expectations are truly individualized. The O&M instructor must always be aware of what the next step needs to be to accomplish the level of independence the student needs to achieve. The instructor must never be satisfied with just what is expected of the student today, but must focus on the achievements available for the student in the future. The O&M instructor must:

Never underestimate the student's capabilities. . . EVER! One of us worked with a student who didn't seem interested in walking on his own. Often, he would simply sit down on the ground. Former instructors thought that the student would not benefit from a cane because he was not walking anyway. However, when he was given a cane and some lessons, he began walking . . . everywhere!

Build upon a simple goal. Perhaps the goal for the student is simply to walk from one classroom to another. Take a look at the route. Is there more than one way to travel? Is there an opportunity to take stairs, use a different hallway, or even go outside? How about counting the doors between the classrooms? Could the student walk in the middle of the hallway without shore-lining? The opportunities of the simple route are numerous.

Have high expectations, but be realistic. Adjust high expectations for students with multiple impairments: not all students have the same capabilities. What may be obtainable for one student may not be reachable for another. Whereas one student's goal might be to walk from one classroom to another, another student's goal may be to walk from his classroom to the lunchroom and carry his tray to the table.

Assess Success

For some students, success may be difficult to assess on charts because progress may be drastically slow. It is vitally important to:

Acknowledge even baby steps as successful. Consider a student who never walks without holding on to the arm of another. The lesson may begin by sitting at a table in a familiar area and perhaps playing a game. Have a desired item nearby but just beyond reach (away from the table). Allow the student to independently take a small step to retrieve the desired item. At a later date, place a desired item a little farther away and encourage the student to walk farther and farther.

Document, document, document! Sometimes it is difficult to see the progress unless one is able to step back and look at the big picture.

Use a timer. Perhaps the student needs to travel from one classroom to another without deviating and he often becomes distracted by the noise of other children in the hallway. Measure his success by documenting the length of time it takes him to reach the classroom each day. Even the smallest improvement is a success!

Conclusion

When it comes to teaching O&M to students with additional disabilities, instructors are constantly learning from their students and their students' families and teachers. They also learn from their colleagues through collaboration and consultation. The O&M instructor draws upon previous experience with other students who may or may not have the same set of additional disabilities. The list above is simply a place to start. It is merely one drawer of a toolbox for O&M instructors to fill as they gain experience. Each new student with multiple disabilities comes to the O&M instructor as an empty page ready, and sometimes longing, to be filled with independent travel skills.

References

Cassin, B., & M. Rubin. (2001) *Dictionary of eye terminology* (4th ed.). Triad Communications, Inc.

Castellano, C. (2010). *Getting ready for college begins in third grade.* Information Age Publishing, Inc.

Cutter, J. (2007). *Independent movement and travel in blind children: A promotion model.* Information Age Publishing, Inc.

Fazzi, D., & B. Petersmeyer. (2001). *Imagining the possibilities: Creative approaches to orientation and mobility instruction for persons who are visually impaired.* AFB Press.

Hallowell, E. (2011). *Shine: Using brain science to get the best from your people.* Harvard Business School Publishing.

Mettler, M. (1995). *Cognitive learning theory and cane travel instruction: A new paradigm* (2nd ed.). Nebraska Commission for the Blind and Visually Impaired.

Olmstead, J. (2005). *Itinerant teaching: Tricks of the trade for teachers of students with visual impairments.* AFB Press.

SKI-HI Institute. (2010). *Deafblindness and the role of the intervener in educational settings.* http://intervener. org/wp-content/uploads/2011/05/Deafblindness-and-the-Role-of-the-Intervener.pdf

Smithe, M. & Levack, N. (1998). *Teaching students with visual and multiple impairments: A resource guide,* (2nd ed.).* Texas School for the Blind and Visually Impaired.

Wiener, W. (2010). *Foundations of orientation & mobility.* AFB Press.

NOTES

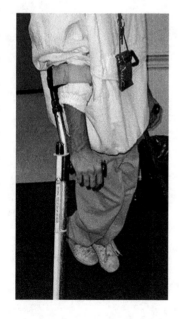

CHAPTER 11

GUIDE TECHNIQUE

The long white cane instills independence and is the tool consumers use for mobility to locate obstacles and landmarks. On the other hand, traveling with *human guide* (i.e., **sighted guide**) assistance is an alternative often used to avoid obstacles (Long & Giudice, 2010; Williams, Hurst, & Kane, 2013), or, in some cases to increase speed to get to targeted destinations. Students learn when it is necessary to seek a human guide (or accept assistance) and when or how to politely decline assistance (Hudson, 1997). Human guide is a simple technique whereby a leader guides a consumer, who holds the arm of the leader, as they walk from one location to another, and this technique takes only a few minutes to learn (American Foundation for the Blind [AFB], 2018b; Ensing, 2016; Pogrund & Griffin-Shirley, 2018; Saltzman, 1978). Cutter (2001b) adds, the primary lesson students *actually* learn when being guided is merely how to mimic the physical movements of the guide rather than perfecting their own mobility skills. Actually, to travel with or without a guide has been a debate among O&M instructors (Blasch et al., 1997; Soong et al., 2000). One performance study of 14 consumers (ages 55 to 89), found no significant differences as to which produced better mobility performance (Soong et al., 2000). Furthermore, this study revealed consumers demonstrated quicker walking speeds when traveling independently (Soong et al., 2000).

At times, adults may consider it convenient for students to travel with a guide (Ensing, 2016; LaGrow & Weessies, 1994) rather than maneuvering independently, especially for novice travelers who may take longer to reach desired locations. In the educational environment, for example, students often utilize guides during fire or tornado drills to quickly transition to the required safe location. Often, this is due to the drill being timed and the school officials' concern for the safety of students with disabilities…any disabilities. For that reason, classroom teachers, paraprofessionals, and even peers, learn from the O&M instructor how to provide human guide technique. However, it needs to be remembered that peers are not to be held responsible for another student's safety during drills.

> **Peers are not responsible for another students' safety—ever!**

The ABCs of Structured Discovery Cane Travel for Children, pages 91–96.

Before we venture forward, let's be clear that there are various forms of *assumed* guiding. First, there is a difference between *guiding* and *holding the hand* of a young child. Simply holding hands is not traveling via a guide (AFB, 2018b). Parents and grandparents will hold the hands of their children—sighted or blind—just as teachers and paraprofessionals hold the hands of preschoolers and kindergarteners. Therefore, it is *not* considered walking with a guide when adults (i.e., parents, teachers) hold the hands of young children because this is age and stage appropriate. Second, in physical education class, a long tether may be used between two runners. This also is not considered traveling via a guide because the follower is not mimicking the physical movements of the guide. Rather, this is simply an alternative technique for running among several students, and the student is still responsible for his own safety. Third, short tethers attached to the follower's upper arm or wrist are not effective either since they, too, remove the ability of the follower to mimic the physical movements of the guide. Keep in mind that real mobility skills include the ability to maneuver independently, says Cutter (2001b).

HUMAN GUIDE TECHNIQUES

Girl Scouts and Boy Scouts earn Disability Awareness badges when they learn about performing good deeds by assisting people with disabilities (Wang, 2014). This caring awareness often extends into adulthood, whereby assisting a person with a disability is considered a good deed (Ferguson, 2001; Koestler, 2004; Tuttle & Tuttle, 1996). Therefore, when people with visual impairments appear in need of assistance, sometimes the general public will offer help. Some of the more common occasions when the public assume a guide may be needed include (1) a street crossing; (2) an emergency; (3) a crowded area; (4) a darkened restaurant; (5) an occasion when speed is of the essence (i.e., running to an airplane gate for take-off.); or (6) a child needs to go to the bathroom immediately.

When a guide is desired or necessary, it is important to know some basic steps. Vaughan (1993) states that the helper (or leader) is not to grab the arm of the follower (i.e., the person with the visual impairment). See Table 11.1 for a Breakdown of Duties and Responsibilities regarding Human Guide techniques. While doing so, remember consumers are the "instructors," unless, of course, the consumer is a young child. Keep in mind that experienced consumers are quite capable of providing directions/guidance to novice human guides (Foundation Fighting Blindness, n.d.). Also, although some members of the community (and professionals) may believe guides must be sighted (American Foundation for the Blind [AFB], 2018a; Ensing, 2016), others contend that any competent traveler may be a guide, regardless of visual acuity, so long as the guide (i.e., the leader) has better mobility skills (i.e., mental mapping skills) than the consumer (i.e., the follower) (Chamberlain, 2015). Also, "as hard as it sometimes is to find help when you need it, sometimes it is harder to get rid of help when you don't want it any more" (Bickford, 1993, p. 72).

HUMAN GUIDE FOR YOUNG CHILDREN

Sometimes parents, guardians or caretakers of young children find it difficult to limit the amount of human guide provided by others and this has been an ongoing concern with some O&M professionals. The problem arises because, since the early 1950s, human guide instruction is introduced or presented prior to cane travel techniques in the Sequential Learning O&M training manuals, pamphlets, and storybooks (Chamberlain, 2019; Crow & Herlich, 2012; Cutter, 2001b; Fazzi & Barlow, 2017; Flaherty et al., 1997; Halpern-Gold et al., 1988; Ho'opano, n.d.; LaGrow & Weessies, 1994; Pogrund & Griffin-Shirley, 2018; Pogrund et al., 1995; Salus

> Real mobility skills include the ability to maneuver independently, says Cutter (2001b).

TABLE 11.1.	Human Guide: Breakdown of Duties and Responsibilities	
	The Guide (i.e. The Leader)	**The Follower (i.e., The Consumer)**
1.	Acknowledge someone needs assistance (i.e., a guide).	Realize there is a need or a desire for assistance (i.e., a guide).
2.	Offer to be a guide either verbally or through actions if the follower is a friend (see #3).	Verbally seek a guide or, if the guide is a friend, use actions to indicate a guide is desired (see #3).
	NOTE: Human guide is NOT providing verbal directions without any physical contact.	
3.	Offer an arm to the follower verbally or through actions if the follower is a friend. This can be done by gently placing an elbow or arm on or near the student's arm as a way to make physical contact with the follower. If necessary, take a step closer to the follower.	Initiate physical contact with the guide by gauging the location of the guide's arm. This can be done by slowly reaching the back of the hand towards the guide to seek their arm. If necessary, take a step toward the guide. It is important not to have the palm facing outward to avoid touching others in areas that are inappropriate.
	NOTE: At times, the follower may put the hand on the guide's shoulder (AFB, 2018b) when the follower is much taller than the guide.	
4.	Naturally relax the arm or have it bent at the elbow.	Hold the guide's arm slightly above the elbow.
	NOTE: The guide does NOT take the arm of the consumer or walk behind the consumer while physically directing the consumer toward the targeted location. This technique removes the follower's independence.	
5.	Turn to face the desired direction of travel.	Follow the movements of the guide in order to face the desired direction of travel.
6.	Walk slightly ahead of the follower toward the desired location.	Walk slightly behind the guide for adequate reaction time.
	Both individuals walk at a comfortable pace whereby neither is pulling or pushing the other (Foundation Fighting Blindness, n.d.).	
	The guide is not in control of the follower. Rather, the guide is only leading the follower to the targeted destination.	If ever there are concerns with the guide so that the situation feels uncomfortable—LET GO OF THE GUIDE'S ARM! Remember, the follower is in control—not the guide.
	Pay attention! Although the follower may be using a cane, be mindful of objects (i.e., doorframes, tables) in front of the follower. If physical movement is not sufficient, verbal communication may be supplemented to help with pace changes, terrain or direction transitions (Tuttle, 1984) Bickford (1993), a consumer, states "the guide then needs only to locate and steer, not to investigate and govern" (p. 72).	Continue to use the cane when walking with a guide for it is not the guide's responsibility to protect the follower's body. Continue to arc the cane as wide as the shoulders to ensure the area is clear of obstacles. Note: It is a passive action to walk without a cane or to have one folded or carried (i.e., not in motion). Pay attention to the surroundings to maintain awareness in space and contribute to mental mapping skills.
	NOTE: It is the follower's choice to act upon any extrinsic information provided from the guide (Glasser, 1990).	

(continues)

TABLE 11.1.   Continued

	The Guide (i.e. The Leader)	The Follower (i.e., The Consumer)
	In narrow spaces, bend the arm behind the back.	When the guide's arm is bent behind the back, move behind the guide to travel through a narrow passage.
	When encountering areas of uncertainty (i.e., ascending or descending stairs, going up or down curbs), stop and inform the follower before proceeding.	When encountering areas of uncertainty, be kind to the guide for the guide, may be unsure how to proceed. Use this as an opportunity to educate the guide. Also, remember the guide is a volunteer and be respectful.
7.	Give a verbal cue that the destination has been reached, if the follower has not already come to that conclusion. Slightly move away from the follower or remove the follower's hand, if necessary.	When the destination has been reached, move slightly away from the guide and let go of the guide's arm. If necessary, physically rotate the arm outward to break the connection. Note: Do not abuse the guide's generosity.
8.	Don't linger, unless the follower is a friend and other activities are planned.	Thank the guide for their service or for volunteering.

University, n.d.; Scholl, 1986; Schwartz, 1987; Wainapel, 1989; White, 1991). When guide technique is the focus of the first several lessons, before introduction to the white cane (COMS Handbook, 2018; Salus University, n.d.), students subconsciously assume that safe travel is only possible if a guide is available (Chamberlain, 2015, 2019). Furthermore, this belief can hinder or even halt self-confidence development in independent travel post training, as discovered in Chamberlain's study (2019).

DANGERS OF HUMAN GUIDE DEPENDENCY

Although consumers have used canes (i.e., sticks) for independent mobility since the beginning of human history (Bryant, 2009; First Steps, n.d.; Foundation Fighting Blindness, n.d.; Kim & Wall Emerson, 2012; Roberts, 2009; Sauerburger & Bourquin, 2010; Williams, 1967), starting in the late 1960s, deciding when or if to obtain a guide has been a quandary for consumers (Leonard, 1968). By the early 2000s, researchers such as Omvig (2002) considers traveling with a guide to foster *learned dependency* (i.e., learned helplessness). That is, when students use human guide as their sole mode of travel, they can become extremely dependent on traveling with a guide (Tuttle, 1984). Therefore, traveling with a guide removes independence and sense of space (Ferguson, 2001; Pogrund & Griffin-Shirley, 2018) which are vitally needed for mental mapping development. Ferguson (2001) provided an example of learned dependency on guides by sharing a story of a woman whose doctor asked her to travel down a hallway. He states this woman admitted she could not walk down the hallway independently because she was used to walking with a guide and had been doing so for several years. Thus, when human guide is the sole mode of mobility, extreme dependency may occur, as well as decreased independence (Chamberlain, 2015; Ferguson, 2001; Pogrund & Griffin-Shirley, 2018; Tuttle, 1984).

The reason for this dependency is because traveling via a guide takes away independent movement. When students are physically involved and responsible for their own mobility, they learn through movement which includes multi-tasking while walking, whereby their brain develops spatial orientation via touching the environment with the cane (Deverell, 2011; Kaiser et al., 2018; Payne, 2002). Passively walking with a guide inactivates students' cognitive processes (attention, auditory and memory) which, according to Iskow (2010), are relied upon during rehabilitation training. While traveling, the mental ability to access cognitive maps, known as Mental Mapping Skills, is a higher level spatial ability which is necessary for successful independent mobility, and this skill is above simply memorizing sequential actions or landmarks (Long & Giudice, 2010).

As individuals become more and more dependent on traveling with a guide, their self-confidence decreases (Chamberlain, 2015, 2019; Ferguson, 2001). When students consistently travel with a guide, they create a dependency on the instructional setting, according to Mettler (1995), and "this dependency, in turn, impairs independent performance in real-world settings" (p. 2), post-training. Chamberlain's (2019) study supported Mettler (1995), demonstrating that lower self-confidence leads to less independent travel, fewer social interactions, and reduced employment possibilities. Her study also found that consumers who received cane instruction prior to guide instruction had higher self-confidence levels, post instruction, whereby they traveled farther and more often than those who always traveled with a guide.

While leading a consumer, guides often feel compelled to verbalize visual observations to the follower who is expected to maneuver through the environment using second-hand information, states Mettler (1995). He adds, students perceive that ongoing monitoring is required and such monitoring must be visual. This slows students' growth toward developing their own independent mobility. Furthermore, when students focus on extrinsic feedback (i.e., external verbal information), the utilization of intrinsic feedback necessary to development internal problem-solving techniques is impaired.

Being guided opens the door to dependency, says Castellano (2005), which is equivalent to being a passive passenger in an automobile. When human guide is used as a primary, quick, and convenient mode of travel, progress toward independent mobility decreases (Alan Beggs, 1992; Cutter, 2007). LaGrow and Weessies (1994) state that students who become dependent on traveling with a guide end up having rudimentary travel skills. Furthermore, Alan Beggs (1992) determined through a study that consumers who traveled with guides were "more susceptible to anxiety and loss of confidence on a journey, and had fewer means of coping with these problems" (abstract). A firm reliance on guide reinforcement or instruction can easily lead to overuse, adds Mettler (1995). The more one uses a guide, the more self-confidence decreases, whereby students "who are skeptical of their ability to exercise adequate control over their actions tend to undermine their efforts in situations that tax capabilities" (Bandura, 1982, p. 129). Thus, those who have better O&M skills only use guides on occasion, when it is necessary, or more convenient (LaGrow & Weessies, 1994).

ALTERNATIVES TO HUMAN GUIDE

Rather than focusing on human guide technique, the SDCT instructor encourages students to stay together in large crowds, just like everyone else. For example, sometimes groups or friends want to stick together at a zoo, theatre, concert or fair. Consumers use the same techniques as sighted individuals to maintain contact in a number of ways such as: 1) communicate with one another; 2) keep hold of the leader's elbow while snaking a path through a crowd; or, yes, 3) maybe even hold hands. Keep in mind that these options do not require specialized lessons to master.

INDIVIDUAL CHOICE

Overall, post-instruction, it is up to the consumer if and/or when they want to use a guide which is a decision that depends on the consumer and the situation. A study conducted by Williams et al. (2013), discovered that some consumers prefer to use a guide only in unfamiliar/new locations, because they feel uncomfortable asking strangers for guide assistance while others enjoy the opportunity to meet new people. Two navigation influences identified by Williams et al. (2013) include: (1) Scenario (characteristic and geographical location of travel); and (2) Personality (individual characteristics, and views regarding the cane, human guides or guide dogs). On the other hand, Vaughan and Omvig (2005) state that individuals who have the philosophy that they are capable independent travelers may use guides for occasional assistance, only if one is available and when it is more convenient, or they may absolutely refuse guide assistance.

Right: Ashleah and Noah at CampAbilities.

NOTES

_____

_____

_____

_____

_____

_____

_____

_____

_____

_____

_____

_____

2019

CHAPTER 12

CUSTODIAL AND INDEPENDENCE PARADIGMS

It is vitally important that parents, caretakers, guardians, teachers, etc., not over rely on guiding students, even though LaGrow and Weessies (1994) state the use of a guide for mobility is the most widely and socially acceptable method of travel. Some consumers, as well as students, get a sense of protection when using a guide, also it "requires few decisions on the part of the traveler" when the guide is in the lead (LaGrow & Weessies, 1994, p. 30) so that the follower can actually be a passive passenger, if desired. Depending on the circumstances, both students and consumers have used a human guide from time-to-time as a mobility option, demonstrating the decision to use or not to use a guide is simply an individual choice. Furthermore, sighted or blind, or most everyone has a toolbox of sorts to retrieve necessary equipment to complete a task and the same is true of using a guide. However, aside from being (1) a navigator, when overly used the guide can be considered as: (2) a custodian; (3) a protector of obstacles; and (4) a model of physical movements to mimic or duplicate (LaGrow & Weessies, 1994). Keep in mind that the first lesson in O&M sets the level of independent expectations placed on the student by the instructor. When beginning lessons focus on using a guide, students embark on the *Custodial Paradigm.* However, instruction in using a human guide is not emphasized in the Structured Discovery Cane Travel (SDCT) curriculum. Students begin with lessons focused on using the long white cane, directly entering the path toward the *Independence Paradigm.*

Silverman (2014) states that some accommodations may convey a negative message about the capabilities of those with visual impairments or blindness. When it comes to self-confidence, students need to be successful in independently performing mobility tasks because sometimes no one will be available to help (Silverman, 2014). The Bottom line is that overusing guides is an accommodation which will limit future independence based on how much the student utilizes and depends on the guide.

HISTORY OF THE CUSTODIAL PARADIGM

Before we venture forward, we must understand the history of the Custodial Paradigm and how it impacts the lives of children, still today. In the early days of O&M in the United States, the military mobility instructors were told their position would be custodial (Miyagawa, 1999). Perhaps this emphasis originated because of the birth of compassion and pity for those with visual impairments during the early Christian and Judaic periods (Ferguson, 2001; Koestler, 2004; Tuttle & Tuttle, 1996). Tuttle and Tuttle (1996) reports that consumers were thought incapable of contributing to society and therefore needed to be cared for by those more fortunate. This negative philosophy was embraced by many Vocational Rehabilitation programs, which in turn hinders opportunities for gainful employment for consumers (Omvig, 2002). In addition, this negative philosophy has been and continues to be seen in literature, including children's literature, which often portrays blind individuals as unhappy, helpless, or pitiful (Blasch et al., 1997). For example, one children's book narrator states, "It was my first week in Jodi's class. She knew who I was, but I hadn't talked to her yet. I thought she might be a little weird because she couldn't see" (Schwartz, 1987, p. 2). Individuals with visual impairments have been stigmatized and because of this, they may elicit predictable negative reactions from their peers, the public, or even family members, leading to a harmful impact on the child and their O&M performance (Blasch et al., 1997). Consumers often wish themselves to be seen not as a burden, but as a contributing member of society (Kelley, 2004). Unfortunately, many consumers and rehabilitation professionals alike still "only see the disability, not the person" (Kelley, 2004, p. 8).

CUSTODIAL PARADIGM

When things are done for the student (such as guiding them) rather than expecting things from the student (such as traveling independently), they enter the Custodial Paradigm. Often, this philanthropy belief glorifies the guide and diminishes the student (Lumadi et al., 2012), making it difficult for students to detach from the custodial stigma. It may be challenging not to conform to the custodial influences, attitudes, and beliefs which have been operating in society for many years because "the justification for much of what we know and believe, our values and our feelings, depends on the context—biographical, historical, cultural—in which, they are embedded" (Mezirow, 2000, p. 3). Thus, students "often experience negative attitudes from teachers and employers who doubt their abilities and potential" due to deep-rooted, internalized beliefs (Lumadi et al., 2012, p. 302; Rowland & Bell, 2012). When thinking about students, consider consumers who often state that their main concern is to see themselves "and be seen by others as *normal* . . . when making choices about where to go, and when and how to do so" (Bell & Nicolle, 2015, abstract; Vaughan, 1993).

> When beginning lessons focus on using a guide, students embark on the Custodial Paradigm.

Novice students, who are overly dependent on using a guide, may demonstrate or express feelings of helplessness and reliance on the assistance of others. When the first several lessons in mobility focus on traveling with a guide (particularly one who is sighted) students may have minimal expectations and be cemented into dependency (LaGrow & Weessies, 1994). Thus, students who are faced with crippling dynamic forces will be left vulnerable, with a lowered sense of self-competence, self-worth and self-confidence (Tuttle & Tuttle, 1996). Therefore, attempting to transition from guide dependency to traveling independently with the long white cane may be difficult for some students, leading some to even reject this transition because, frankly, traveling with a guide is much easier.

In the Custodial Paradigm, O&M instructors preview targeted locations or review a map to create a sequential step-by-step route to help students create a mental representation of the landscape prior to performing the mobility lesson state Guerreiro, et al. (2017). They add that this sequential method includes points of interest (POIs) located along the route. Keep in mind that this information is often from the point-of-view of a "fully-sighted mindset about the world, or what those instructors imagine, to the extent that their dominant visually-grounded assumptions will permit, what a nonvisual orientation to the world might be" (Mettler, 1995, p. 31). The Custodial Paradigm continues with verbal route information including event sequence schemas and/or scripts (i.e., *when you leave the classroom, you will need to turn to your right and walk four steps to the water fountain*) intended to "guide the way in which we experience, feel, understand, judge, and act upon particular situations" (Mezirow, 1991, p. 48). Keep in mind that these schemas only bring attention to what the custodian considers is relevant. Two custodians may perceive the same route differently, or they may offer opposite explanations using their own individualized perceptions and values, all the while considering their own observation is accurate (Sullo, 2007), thereby relaying completely different information to students. In actuality, even when they receive information second-hand, students will gather their own information through their senses and will comprehend and interpret it based on their personal experiences and/or prior knowledge (i.e., Transformational Knowledge), then evaluate it based on their own personal values (Sullo, 2007).

IN THE SCHOOL SYSTEM

It is inescapable that school personnel will represent the society around to some degree. However, their philosophy may be transformed through education via observable examples, for actions speak louder than words. When students walk with confidence, others comprehend that individuals with visual impairments can be independent travelers. Morais et al. (1997) state that educators need to hold positive attitudes regarding the capabilities of students, and Tuttle and Tuttle (1996) add that students' performance will mirror their self-confidence as well as how they believe others perceive them. Williams et al. (2013), state that individuals with visual impairments who have low self-confidence in their O&M skills and abilities or accept the assumption that traveling with a guide is the safest method often return for additional training from their mobility instructor or rehabilitation agency whenever they face a new travel obstacle such as a change in residence or employment, closure of a grocery store or bus stop, etc.

INDEPENDENCE PARADIGM

When students learn to travel without a guide, the opportunities to travel independently are endless, not limited to only traveling at certain times or only traveling to certain locations. These individuals enter the Independence Paradigm and a great example of an individual who lives within the Independence Paradigm is Mr. Tony Giles. He has independently traveled to over 120 countries, as reported by the British Broadcasting Company (BBC) News (2017), and states the big-

> **When lessons begin with the long white cane, students embark on the Independence Paradigm.**

gest challenge he faces is having too many people hinder him from traveling independently. Giles reports when he travels without a guide, he is able to interact with more people and adds:

> if I travel with someone, particularly someone sighted, they would be doing all the work, they would be doing all the guiding, and I wouldn't get to touch as many things, and find as many things, as I do by myself (British Broadcasting Company [BBC], 2017)

Students can learn from consumers like Mr. Giles that these who have higher self-confidence and problem-solving abilities travel independently farther from their home base than their counterparts who do not, as proven in Chamberlain's (2019) study. Another consumer example is Omvig (2002), a blind gentleman within the Independence Paradigm who relocated to six various locations (Chicago, New York City, Baltimore, Washington, D.C., Tucson, and Anchorage) states, after receiving SDCT training, he never had to receive additional O&M training. As he looked back, Omvig (2002) added that by learning through a structured discovery curriculum, he was able to develop the skills and confidence to travel alone in big cities and those skills gave him the ability to travel independently in other locations.

The SDCT curriculum utilizes *transformational learning* as the fundamental skill necessary for O&M problem-solving, which directs students toward the Independent Paradigm. Students use transformational learning to help handle unpredictable situations, and this process changes their frame of reference through their own interpretation of their experiences (Mezirow, 2000). Transformational learning helps them to direct and guide their actions and empowers them to determine reasonable and acceptable rationales for their decisions (Mezirow, 2000). Take, for example, a letter written by Everett Gravel (2006) to his former SDCT instructor: "I'm unafraid to venture out on my own now, even when traveling in a new city…[I] can be dropped off anywhere, not even knowing exactly where, and still find the location where I need to go" (p. 24–25). The confidence expressed by Mr. Gravel represents the ultimate goal of the Independence Paradigm.

PARADIGM PARALYSIS

As stated in Chapter 11, Girl Scouts and Boy Scouts earn Disability Awareness badges where they learn about performing good deeds by assisting people with disabilities (Wang, 2014). This birth of comparison and pity towards people who are blind often extends into adulthood whereby assisting people with disabilities are considered *good deeds* (Ferguson, 2001; Koestler, 2004; Tuttle & Tuttle, 1996). Actually, in rehabilitation, the custodial philosophy can be traced back to the 1940s where the O&M instructors at Hines (Veterans Administration) were told their position was a custodial one (Miyagawa, 1999) and this is evident in *A Veterans Administration Medical Film* (1952, 1952b). This compassionate, yet negative, paradigm paralysis is still prevalent in many Vocational Rehabilitation agencies today.

The SDCT curriculum breaks away from the Custodial Paradigm and leads students toward the Independence Paradigm. Students need not be stuck in a paradigm paralysis so long as their parents, instructors, school staff, and basically every person who has any influence have and hold high expectations and believe that the student can and will become an independent traveler. Keep in mind that a **Paradigm Paralysis** is when there is a refusal or inability to see beyond the current way of thinking and this includes organizations that focus on what is supposed to work instead of programs that have proven to be successful (Smith & Rigby, 2015, p. XIV, 71, 73). Chamberlain's 2019 study proved that

when sighted guide instruction commences prior to introduction of the long white cane… self-confidence is hindered and leads consumers toward the Custodial Paradigm. However, when instruction of the long white cane and problem-solving is paramount (as in the SDCT curriculum); the foundation for ongoing successful O&M post-instruction is likely whereby consumers are led toward the Independence Paradigm (abstract).

NOTES

CHAPTER 13

PARAPROFESSIONALS

Paraprofessionals are extremely important IEP team members because they are often the individuals who work very closely with the students throughout their day. If the paraprofessionals are present during O&M lessons, they can assist students when the instructor is not immediately available. Furthermore, they may be able to provide valuable information regarding mobility concerns that the student may have. When paraprofessionals are in attendance during the mobility lesson, the student realizes the paraprofessional shares the same high level of independent expectations. When everyone imposes the same expectations, there is no room for passive behavior (i.e., the student going human guide or expecting the paraprofessional to carry materials).

WAYS TO STEP BACK FOR TYPICALLY DEVELOPING STUDENTS

Although it may feel good to assistance a student with a visual impairment, it may not always be in their best interest for you to do so. Sometimes your best action is to step back so the student may step forward to become as independent as possible. Ask yourself the following (Hudson, 1997):

1. Do you provide extra time for the student to complete a task? Although it may take a few more seconds for a student to learn a new skill, over time and with practice, this extra time will decrease. The student's self-confidence grows and the student becomes more independent.
2. Can you keep your hands off theirs? Although it might be tempting to take their hand to help them complete a task, provide verbal information or assistance instead of touch cues. However, if the student absolutely needs touch cues, use *hand-under-hand* to give the students more choices.
3. Can you step back and let the student make mistakes or get into trouble? Not only is letting the student face the consequences of making mistakes or getting into trouble, it is a teachable moment and a learning experience that will reinforce transformational knowledge that will last a lifetime... much longer than a warning or lecture.

The ABCs of Structured Discovery Cane Travel for Children, pages 103–109.

4. Are you in the helping profession for you or for the student? Acknowledge that the reason you are in this field is to help the student move forward, not to meet your own personal satisfaction.

5. Are you sitting too close to the student? The closer you are in proximity, the easier and quicker it is for the student to gain assistance. Although for some students, decreased distances is necessary. However, for others, it provides a great Orientation and Mobility opportunity if you are further away. For some, this distance may need to be done in baby steps. For example, if you've been within arm's reach, then move to just within earshot or if you've been within earshot, move across the room.

6. Are you providing visual information too fast? If you are playing a dice game and the student rolls a "good number," then hold back and let the student discover this rather than gasping with joy. By doing so, you are stealing his thunder. Your job may be to provide some information, but if the task is something that the student can do, then step back so that the student can do it.

7. Are you providing too much assistance? Keep in mind that too much assistance is short-term. Remember the proverb: if you give a fish, the person eats for a day; if you teach how to fish, the person can feed the village. Same goes for students. If you help too much, the student only gains splinter skills.

8. Do you provide too many answers while the student completes desk or homework? Remember, it is the teacher's responsibility to teach the student. This includes correcting the student's work. If the teacher does not know what the student does not know, then the teacher cannot help the student with any deficits. This is about the student's work…not yours.

9. Are you the student's answering machine? Students need to pay attention in class. If they miss instructions, they need to ask their teacher or peers general questions instead of relying on you.

10. Are you always the student's learning partner? If so, STOP! Students need to be partnered with their peers.

11. Are you the student's human guide? If so, STOP! If students and others become too dependent on you as the student's full-time human guide, their independent travel will be hindered. The student needs to maneuver from one point to another independently using their long white cane.

12. Do you step back whenever another person wants to help the student? If so, encourage the student to know when and how to decline assistance, especially when the task is something that the student can do independently. Sometimes, it is out of respect to accept the assistance while other times it is acceptable to decline the help. Also, perhaps the student would rather try to do the task without assistance.

13. Is the student depending on too many prompts? If there is a noticeable pause by the student before moving to the next step, then the answer is YES. If so, create a plan to phase out prompts.

14. Are you feeling that you are shirking your responsibilities when you step back? If so, DON'T! You are an example to others on what is necessary in order for the student to be more independent. Teach by example and, if necessary, tell the student and others that you are there to assist, as needed, but are confident that the student can do the task independently.

15. Do you find yourself helping the student too much? If so, get help by collaborating with other adults to help you break this habit. Everyone needs to agree to remind each other to step back.

16. Are you working as a team with the classroom teacher(s)? Collaborate or create a communication signal on if the student needs to respond directly to the classroom teacher or if the student is expected to problem solve before seeking assistance.

17. Are there any other ways you could step back? There is absolutely no way this list can answer all the questions to meet the individual needs of all the students. Each student is unique. The important thing to remember is to collaborate with the student's Individual Education Planning team to meet the needs of the student.

The following article addresses the many specialized duties of paraprofessionals working with students with visual impairments. It was first published in Future Reflections, Special Issue: Early Childhood Education, Winter 2018, Volume 37(3).

Helpful Hints for Paraprofessionals Working with Students Who Are Blind or Visually Impaired
by Merry-Noel Chamberlain

Sometimes students who are blind or visually impaired have one or two paraprofessionals available to assist them throughout the school day. These paraprofessionals seldom receive specific training in how to work with blind or visually-impaired students. Generally, paraprofessionals receive on-the-job training focused on the student's individual needs. Training varies widely from one school district to another, and it may be influenced by the supervising teacher and a variety of circumstances. This article offers some helpful hints for paraprofessionals working with students who are blind or visually impaired. As not all students have the same needs, it needs to be understood that these recommendations will not apply to every individual.

In some ways the duties of paraprofessionals working with blind or visually-impaired students are similar to those of all paraprofessionals who work with students one-on-one. Overall, the goal is to avoid promoting learned helplessness in the student. The aims of most paraprofessionals are:

- Assist the student without doing for the student.
- Encourage the student to be as independent as possible—equal to his or her peers.
- Be as invisible as possible to avoid becoming a wall between the student and his peers or teachers.
- Provide just the right amount of support for the student—not too much and not too little.
- Work as a team member with the classroom teacher or special education teacher to help the student reach her or his highest potential possible in the least invasive way possible.

Basic Duties

For the paraprofessional who works with a blind or visually-impaired student, the basic duties go well beyond those listed above. For best results, the first person the paraprofessional needs to turn to for guidance is the teacher of students with visual impairments (TVI). The TVI works directly with the student and knows best the individual student's nonvisual or low-vision needs. Although paraprofessionals work one-on-one with students, they are not teachers. They are supporters who reinforce what has been taught by the classroom teacher, TVI, or Orientation and Mobility (O&M) instructor.

In a sense, paraprofessionals are reporters. They relay information back to the TVI or O&M instructor, noting problem areas they have observed or upcoming events of which the TVI or O&M instructor may not be aware.

Paraprofessionals work closely with the TVI, the O&M instructor, and the classroom or special education teacher. Because of this close working relationship they have with the student, they are part of the team. They need to participate in the student's Individualized Education Plan (IEP) meetings. If the student attends his IEP meetings, he will be aware that the paraprofessional is current on all expectations and will support those expectations. The student will not be able to pull the wool over the eyes of the paraprofessional in order to avoid taking responsibility—not that children will ever attempt to do such a thing, mind you!

Here are some of the basic roles and duties of paraprofessionals who work with blind and visually-impaired students.

Reader

Paraprofessionals who work with blind or visually-impaired students serve as readers. In this case, a reader is not simply someone who reads printed materials such as textbooks, worksheets, or storybooks. Rather, the reader is a person who describes the environment to the student. This describing may include, but is not limited to, the following:

- Verbalizing overhead or board information/instructions, such as daily assignments on the board that are to be read as soon as the students enter the room.
- Verbalizing worksheets that have not been Brailled or enlarged.
- Verbalizing filmstrips or movies, especially any words that may appear on the screen but are not read aloud by the teacher or made clear via the film. This is especially important when the information is pertinent to the class instruction or to the film's storyline. For a better understanding of how to verbalize filmstrips or movies, watch a recent movie with the audio description option turned on, or go to a movie theater where descriptive audio headphones are available.
- Verbalizing actions during special presentations or lectures. The paraprofessional needs to describe actions that are pertinent to the program or presentation. Sometimes simply verbalizing the actions may not be enough for the student to comprehend what is happening. If this is the case, the paraprofessional may need to let the student touch her arms or hands as she goes through the actions to provide the student with a clear visualization. Such physical movement may be most necessary during P.E. classes or during music classes when physical movement accompanies a song.
- Verbalizing signs on the walls at the school.
- Verbalizing observations while on field trips.
- Verbalizing lunch options and describing where items are located on the salad bar.
- Verbalizing actions happening around the classroom, playground, or hallway.
- Verbalizing where friends are located on the playground or in the lunch room.
- Verbalizing (on occasion) the presence of power cords, hoses, or other obstacles that may temporarily be in the path.

Scribe

On occasion the classroom teacher may assign a project on short notice, without allowing time for the materials to be enlarged or transcribed into Braille. Perhaps she has decided on a teachable moment or a pop quiz. To ensure that the student doesn't miss out, the paraprofessional may not only be the reader but also serve as the scribe. A scribe is a person who does all of the writing. This writing could involve filling out a worksheet, completing a math journal, or completing an assignment on an inaccessible website. The paraprofessional needs to keep in mind that:

- This is the student's work.
- She needs to write down nothing but the answer the student dictates.
- She needs to avoid making comments, providing additional instruction, or offering prompts such as "Are you sure?" unless the team has determined beforehand that this can be done.

Here are some other helpful hints a paraprofessional may wish to keep in mind when serving as a scribe for a student:

- Ask the student if he is ready to go to the next question.
- If the student seems confused about what you have written down for him, ask, "Is that your final answer?"
- If time is available, review all the answers with the student.

If a paraprofessional is too helpful, a student may learn to accept unnecessary help from everyone around him, such as friends, family, office staff, acquaintances, and the general public. This behavior is known as learned helplessness. Keep in mind that the paraprofessional is not:

- The student's errand runner. For example, the paraprofessional need not volunteer to deliver the student's work to the teacher. The student must be responsible for the completed paper; he must turn in his assignment if that is the next step required of all students.
- The one to sign the student up for extracurricular activities. When requested by the student, the paraprofessional may write the student's name on the sign-up sheet, but the paraprofessional is not responsible for doing so when the student is not present.
- The one to remember the student's assignments and the dates when they are due.
- The one to carry the student's materials from one class to another, unless there are extenuating circumstances.
- The one to do anything that encourages learned helplessness.

Adapting Materials

Paraprofessionals working with students with visual impairments may be called upon to adapt materials, that is, to make them accessible for the student. Examples of such materials are worksheets, games, diagrams, pictures, and charts. Depending on the individual student's needs, they may be adapted in three ways: tactile, outlined, or enlarged.

Tactile: There are many ways to provide students with tactile access to materials. The paraprofessional can use puff-paint, foam stickers, raised-line graphing tape, raised-line drawing kits, or tactile graph paper. Braille labels or other items can be glued onto paper, game boards, or posters.

Outlining: For low-vision students, targeted areas on a worksheet may need to be accented with a bold black marker. The marker indicates the box where the student needs to write answers or the line the student needs to cut with scissors.

Enlargement: Enlarged materials need to be discussed with the TVI. The TVI will explain the percentage of enlargement needed and the size of the paper to be used. Some students need to have enlargements on 11x17-inch paper, while others prefer legal-size paper. The TVI or O&M instructor may be able to provide instructions on how the materials need to be adapted for the individual student.

Finding time to adapt materials can be a challenge for the paraprofessional. The availability of such time depends on the student's schedule. Unlike teachers, paraprofessionals are seldom given official planning periods. Time may be available while the student participates in activities that do not require the paraprofessional's direct involvement, or when the student is out of school due to illness or doctor's appointments.

Braille

Paraprofessionals working with students who are Braille readers or who are learning Braille need some general knowledge of the Braille code. Beginning paraprofessionals may learn alongside their young students or their students who are just starting to receive Braille instruction. However, most paraprofessionals learn Braille through correspondence courses in order to keep ahead of their students. It is extremely important that the paraprofessional's Braille skills surpass the student's level. The TVI may provide the paraprofessional with information on available Braille correspondence courses.

Some paraprofessionals wonder why they need to know Braille since they are not the ones who teach it. Knowledge of Braille is important for several reasons:

- Paraprofessionals need to support the student who is learning Braille when the TVI is not present.
- The paraprofessional can help ensure that the student has the Braille volumes he needs for each class. For example, the student may be nearing the end of the second Braille volume of a math textbook. The paraprofessional can go to the storage room and collect the third volume of the math textbook so it is available for the student when he needs it.
- Once a paraprofessional learns Braille, she may be able to provide some simple transcription. She may be able to transcribe sentences from print into Braille or transcribe the student's completed Braille homework into print for the teacher.

- Some Braille materials entering the school may not include print labels, or the print copy somehow may have become detached from the Braille pages. With some knowledge of Braille, the paraprofessional may be able to sort things out.

Keep in mind that the paraprofessional (or even the TVI) who knows Braille is not considered a certified Braille transcriber.

There is more to Braille than simply learning the code. For example, Braille students need to:

- Have proper posture when reading Braille, with the paper positioned correctly on the desk. If the student is not sitting up straight when reading Braille or if the paper is not positioned correctly, the student can misread the Braille. If the page is tilted to the left, a 'k' could be read as a 'ch' contraction. The 'k' could be read as 'st' if the paper is tilted to the right.
- Have proper posture when writing Braille on a Perkins Brailler. If the Brailler is on a table that is too high or too low for the student, it will be difficult for the student to maintain his stamina in completing assignments, reading what he has written, or putting paper into or out of the Brailler.

Specialized Equipment

At times students with visual impairments use specialized equipment such as a closed-circuit magnification device, Perkins Brailler, or electronic notetaking device. The paraprofessional is not required to know everything about the student's specialized equipment. However, it is very helpful if he knows basic functions and problem-solving techniques.

Some students use the abacus for doing math or the slate and stylus for writing Braille. The paraprofessional may wish to learn more about this equipment, and the TVI can provide information about correspondence courses or online tutorials.

Orientation & Mobility (O&M)

The paraprofessional needs to observe the student's Orientation and Mobility lessons. This will give the paraprofessional insight as to how to assist the student when the O&M instructor is not present. The paraprofessional is not an O&M instructor, but he can support and reinforce the techniques the student has been taught. The paraprofessional can report to the O&M instructor when he notices problem areas for the student.

School staff and other students sometimes mistakenly assume that the paraprofessional is the blind student's personal human guide. The paraprofessional will learn the proper human guide technique, as there may be critical times when walking human guide is necessary. However, when given the proper skills, the student can become an independent traveler.

Orientation and Mobility involves much more than teaching a student to walk from Point A to Point B. O&M involves concepts including cardinal directions, posture and gait, walking in step, problem solving, and mental mapping skills. When a paraprofessional works closely with the O&M instructor, he learns these skills with the student and can reinforce them outside of O&M class.

Letting Go

This section is mainly pertinent to students who have been blind or visually impaired for quite some time and have considerable experience working with a paraprofessional. It is not relevant for newly blinded or visually impaired students.

When the student reaches high school, her need for a paraprofessional diminishes. The upper-level high school student needs to become less dependent on the paraprofessional since this person is not going to follow her to college and beyond. It is important to wean the student from her dependency. However, transition can be difficult because the paraprofessional still needs to be on hand in case the student truly needs the assistance of a scribe or a reader.

The paraprofessional needs to back away so the student can attempt to be as independent as possible. Basically, the paraprofessional is "on call." Sometimes it is difficult for other staff members and even administrators to understand this transitional process. They may see the paraprofessional sitting in the back of the classroom, seemingly unengaged. Some classroom teachers give the paraprofessional other duties during this fading-out period. Ultimately, the goal is for the student not to need a paraprofessional any longer.

The second semester of the student's junior year can be the transition time for students with visual impairments, for this is a great opportunity to help prepare them for college. When students go to college, they will often be required to hire their own readers/scribes, and their senior year is a great opportunity for them to practice using a reader/scribe via the available paraprofessional. Therefore, it is important for the paraprofessional to only be available to read or scribe when requested by the student. This process is, of course, overseen by the TVI and the classroom teachers to ensure that the student is completing work in a timely manner. This is not a time for the student to fail; rather it is a time for the TVI, classroom teacher, and paraprofessional to provide guidance to the student, then step back, monitor, and provide feedback to the student, as needed.

Final Notes

The relationship between the paraprofessional and the student needs to remain professional. Sometimes when a student spends the majority of his educational experience attached to one paraprofessional, the relationship can become too close. If that happens, the student may take liberties she may not otherwise attempt with someone else. In addition, the paraprofessional may do things automatically for the student instead of waiting for the student to take the proper initiative on her own. If a paraprofessional has had the opportunity to spend several years with one student, the two can create a strong bond. If the relationship has remained professional, in that the student is aware of the role of the paraprofessional, the relationship can be successful and enriching.

PART II

CHAPTER 14

MERRY-NOEL'S TREASURE TROVE OF O&M ACTIVITIES

The action of playing enhances brain development and provides students opportunities to engage and interact in the world while building skills which gives them a sense of their abilities and satisfaction (Family Lives, n.d.). Play cannot be underestimated for it is very powerful. It incorporates many skills such as adventure, cognition, collaboration, concentration, creativity, dexterity, emotional strength and growth, imagination, language development, physical development, and problem solving (Family Lives, n.d.; Ginsburg, 2007). When mobility lessons are incorporated with play, students are able to explore and master their world safely while conquering any travel fears they may have. During O&M educational games, students are able to develop new competencies leading to enhanced confidences and problem-solving abilities which will help them in future challenges. Furthermore, with or without adult assistance, areas of interests, creativity, and leadership abilities may also be discovered.

Orientation and Mobility instructors can be *educational* **Play Facilitators** to help students gains mobility skills. That is, Play Facilitators

inspires play, creates space and time for many kinds of playful activities, and adapts his or her role to match where children are as they take on new challenges. Skillful facilitators are able to spot opportunities to integrate learning goals in playful settings without disrupting children's engaged and playful endeavors (Jensen, Pyle, Zosh, Ebrahim, Zaragoza Scherman, Reunamo, Hamre, 2019, p. 5).

Play is the primary means of learning and work for young children (Wells, 2008) and there are many kinds of play such as guided play and games. Within guided play, students are "to achieve one or more learning goals within a play context" (Jensen, et al., 2019, p. 14). Instructor creates game context with embedded learning focuses which helps students to obtain higher gains than instruction or free play alone states Jensen, et al. (2019). Learning through game playing incorporates structure and offer choices.

O&M instructors often develop or utilize games (i.e., training materials) to match the mobility and developmental needs of their students. Children need toys and games that are accessible (meaning blind-friendly) and they need items around them that represent themselves, such as dolls with canes. Toy canes can be easily made with lollypop sticks and black electoral tape with thread for handles with silver puff-paint for tips. They may need toys that are tactile or make funny, interesting sounds. Here are some activities that focus on enhancing mobility skills. Please note that these activities are recommended to be done while the student is occluded.

LEFT AND RIGHT

Quoridor Jr. and Quoridor (Gigamic Games):

These games focus on strategic mapping skills to move from one side of the board to another. With Quoridor Jr. the focus can be on using general directions (left, right, forward, and backward), while with Quoridor (for more experienced students) students can use cardinal directions.

Object of the Game:

Move playing piece from one side of the board to the other using proper terminology.

Preparation:

1. Place Velcro on the squares and under the playing pieces to hinder them from tipping over.
2. Use tape, puff paint, or Braille to label the tops of the playing pieces for identification.
3. Place a clear sticker or puff paint on the front of the playing pieces to help with directional awareness.
4. No need to apply any tactile marks to the bushes.

How to Play:

1. Follow the game rules as stated.
2. Players must state the directions they are going—left, right, forward, back or cardinal directions.

Left-Straight-Right-Stop (LSRS)

This game is best when played within the school building. It focuses on mental mapping skills, decision making, and planning ahead. Working on cane techniques is an added bonus!

Object of the Game:

One person directs the other on where to go—somewhat like Simon Says. The goal is to return to home base by giving the instructions of turning left or right, walking straight or stopping.

How to Play:

1. Player One gives instructions to Player Two to turn *right,* or *left*, walk *straight* or *stop.* Player two complies. They venture to different directions and return to home-base.
2. When told to walk straight by Player One, Player Two walks straight until walking straight is impossible. If veering occurs, nothing is said. When Player Two reaches something with her cane (i.e., wall or people), she stops.
3. Player Two does not move until Player One gives the instruction to turn left or right. After Player Two receives the instruction, Player Two turns in the required direction but does not walk until Player One says to walk straight.
4. Player Two stops when told to do so by Player One.
5. Repeat.
6. Reverse roles.

Lesson:

O&M instructor introduces the student to the game. Mobility instructor and the student practice with the instructor (Player One) directing the student (Player Two) to a targeted location by playing the game as described above. For beginners, the location need not be far and sleep-shades need not be required. However, for more advanced students, the location could be at the opposite end of the school and sleep-shades required. Once at the targeted location, either a) reverse roles so the student then directs the instructor back to the student's classroom or b) treat it as if it were a drop-route and the student must problem solve the way back to the classroom.

Alternative for Advanced Students:

Player One (mobility instructor) uses human guide to take Player Two to a targeted destination. Player Two then problem solves the way back to the classroom.

Left Center Right (LCR) (adapted for class time)

This game requires at least three players. Tokens are either kept, placed in the center of the table, passed to the opponent on the right, or passed to the opponent to the left of the player.

Object of the Game:

Be the player with the fewer tokens by the end of class time (or according to the LCR rules) .

Preparation:

1. A box lid helps with keeping the dice from being rolled off the table.
2. A small cup helps with rolling the dice when player's with small hands.

How to Play:

This game is tactually friendly because the L, C, R, and dot, can be easily identifiable through tactile methods. However, dice can be marked with Braille, if necessary, on other versions of the game.

1. Players begin with three dice and a few tokens (the number of tokens can be determined by the teacher or as recommended by the game, depending on the time allotted for the game.)
2. Players roll the dice and follow the directions by either keeping a token, placing a token in the center of the table, or passing a token to the opponent on the right or left.
3. Players only roll the number of dice as they have tokens. Thus, for two tokens, roll two dice; one token, roll one die.

Alternative Ways to End the Game:

1. Follow the game rules for determining the winner.
2. Play until time is over and the one with the greatest number of tokens wins.

Alternative Ways to Play LCR:

1. Use Braille dice with the guide to the right and either counting tokens or coins.
2. All players begin with the same number of tokens or if using coins, all players begin with the same number of coins such as three pennies, three nickels, and three dimes. Use quarters for older players.
3. Players only roll the number of dice as they have tokens (or coins). Thus, for two tokens (or coins), roll two dice; one token (or coin), roll one die.
4. Winner is the player who has the most tokens (or the most "money") at the end of the time allotted for the game (or use the LCR rules.) Note: If using coins, a player may have the most coins but not the most money.

LCR with Braille Dice
1 = Rest
2 & 4 = left
3 & 5 = right
6 = Center

The Sock Game (Adapted)

This game focuses on right and left while developing tactile awareness.

Object of the Game:

Collect the most points (in the time allowed for the game) by being the fastest to pull out the desired object with the correct hand.

Preparation:

1. Purchase the Sock Game (or make your own). This game requires two long, large socks and a wide assortment of small, tactually identifiable random items (i.e., metal cane tip, quarter, dime, nickel, penny, toy automobile, Braille eraser, Braille dice, etc.). Each player needs one sock filled with the same items.
2. Object Cards: Using Braille or large print, make a 3×5 card for each object in the sock. Snip the top right side of the cards to help with orientation.
3. Left/Right Cards: Cut 3×5 cards in half. Create 25 "left" and 25 "right" cards in Braille or large print. Snip the right side of the cards to help with orientation.

How to Play:

1. One player draws an object card and another player draws a Left Right Card.

2. Players race to see who can reach their hand into the sock and retrieve the object the fastest.
3. The Player who is able to pull out the correct object with the current hand wins a point.

Alternative ways to play the game:
1. One player decides the object to be retrieved and another player decides which hand to use.

Right, Left, One, Two (R-L-1-2)

This is an activity that involves practicing many concepts: left and right; odd and even; Braille; Open-palm and Pencil grips, Extended cane technique; 90 degrees; and Cardinal directions.

Materials:

One shuffled deck of Braille cards, including the Jokers.

Rules:

1. **Even Numbered Cards:** Go Left (Helpful hint: Both Even and left have 4 letters—4 is an even number.)
2. **Odd Numbered Cards:** Go Right (Helpful hint: Both odd and right have an odd number of letters—5 is an odd number.)
3. **Jack:** Turn 180 degrees (i.e., Turn around.)
4. **Queen:** Instructor's Choice, using cardinal directions, if possible.
5. **King:** Student's Choice, using cardinal directions, if possible.
6. **Joker:** Up to two minutes to explore with the cane and, if desired, establish a different direction to face and travel. Use the rules as posted to the right.

Preparation:

Explain the rules to the student. The student is the KING, rather than the instructor because the student needs to be aware that he/she is in charge of their own mobility. Thus, students have locus of control.

Activity:
1. Have a starting point. Walk as straight as possible until an obstacle is encountered (i.e., desk, wall, door.)
2. Select a card and follow the rules of the card.
3. Repeat number 2 & 3 above until the game is over.

Optional:

Differences in the terrain (changes in carpet to tile, stairs) are optional opportunities to (1) select a new card or (2) continue walking.

Ending Options:
1. The path leads back to the starting point.
2. Student selects a targeted destination ahead of time and the path leads to that location.
3. Out of time.

CARDINAL DIRECTIONS

Tic-Tac-Toe Cardinal Direction Game (Adapted)

This version is played like the traditional game except with some cardinal direction.

Object of the Game:

Be the first player create three "X"s or "O"s in a row.

Materials:

Any tactile Tic-Tac-Toe game.

How to Play:

Play Tic-Tac-Toe as usual with the following new rules:

Northwest	North	Northeast
West	Equator	East
Southwest	South	Southeast

1. The location of the piece needs to be announced by the player as it is being placed on the board. If the location is not announced correctly, the player must remove the playing piece
2. In order to win, the individual claiming his/her victory must correctly announce the proper locations of all the playing pieces confirming the win.
3. Proper locations of playing pieces are as follows:

Blocks Within the School Building

If the school building has four hallways that resemble a city block, this layout can be used for several activities.

1. The student walks around the block and ends up in the same spot.
    – Discuss how this is similar to a typical city block.
    – Discuss the shape of the block.
2. Independently, using the shore-lining technique, the student walks around the block clockwise and counter clockwise.
3. The student explores the block using cardinal directions.
    – Which hallways run north-south?
    – Which hallways run east-west?
4. The student is able to independently go to the following locations on the block:
    – North, south, east, and west hallways.
    – Northwest corner, Northeast corner, Southwest corner, Southeast corner.
5. The student answers the following questions by using only the doors within the block:
    – How many doors in total are around the whole block and what technique did you use to find out? (shoreline)
    – Reverse direction and confirm the above answer.
    – How many doors are on the east/west hallway on the north side of the block?
    – How many doors are on the north/south hallway on the east side of the block?

–How many doors are on the east/west hallway on the south side of the block?

–How many doors are on the north/south hallway on the west side of the block?

Name That Spot

This game creates mental mapping skills by using cardinal directions and "right and left" prompts to mentally lead the student to various locations within the building. The goal is for the student to receive points to earn an award. If the student can Name That Spot by just hearing the directions, he gets a point. If the student is unable to Name That Spot, then he needs to actively follow the directions to get to that spot to earn the point. If, along the way, he figures it out and is able to Name That Spot, he earns the point. How many points he needs to earn and if he earns __ points to receive an award, is up to the mobility instructor. Here are two examples:

1.   Can you Name That Spot if… from where we are sitting, you exit the room… turn west and walk as far as you can go… turn north and take the first opening on the west… then, at the end of that hallway, you turn north… and then end up at the third door on your right?

2.   Can you Name That Spot if… from where we are sitting, you exit the room… turn east and take the first opening to the north… then take the first opening to the west… then take the first opening south… then take the first opening east and end up at the fourth door on your left?

Hide-'N-Go-Seek Cardinal Direction Game

This is a fun and educational game to play during those rainy, cold, or snowy days! This game helps the student review cardinal directions and incorporates opposites, such as the opposite of east is west… etc. This game is four players. Additional supplies are needed for more players, if necessary.

Object of the Game:
The first spider to reach his home-base wins!

Materials Needed for the Game:
The following American Printing House (APH) items can be obtained through Federal Quota funds.

1.   A Hundreds Gray Grid Board (#61-219-001) and Velcro Adhesive loop dots from The Hundreds Boards and Manipulatives kit

2.   One counting chip (square, triangle, circle, and star) that has Velcro on the back and conveniently comes in The Hundreds Boards and Manipulatives kit.

3.   APH Spider Tokens (set of four) (#61-133-025) to identify each player (or other tactually identifiable game pieces with Velcro, such as buttons, or coins).

4.   Talking GlowDice (1-07500-00) or one Braille die (61-131-045), depending on students' abilities.

Preparation:
1.   Place Velcro inside each of the squares.

2.   For two players—Sixteen 3X5 cards with the words *North*, *South*, *East* and *West* (four of each) in either large print or Braille (depending on students' needs). For three to four players—double the above.

How to Play the Game:
1.   The youngest player begins the game.

2. Arrange beginner students to sit on the south side of the room facing the north so the *compass rose* on the game board is easily transferrable to real life and future O&M lessons. If necessary—remove one set of the cardinal direction cards to place around the grid to help identify the compass rose for beginner students. Randomly remove a card and return it to the deck until all the cards have been returned. (This accommodation is not necessary for advanced students.)

3. Players select a spider token and a home-base (i.e., Counting chip: the square, triangle, circle, or star).

4. Players randomly place both their spider and home-base on the board.

5. For each turn, players roll one die (or press the button of the Talking GlowDice) to establish how many squares they may travel. Then, the player selects a cardinal direction card (pre-shuffled) which states which direction he must move his spider.

6. If the player lands on a square occupied by an opponent's Spider Token, he is to select an empty space to the north, south, east or west of the occupied square. However, he must announce his choice prior to placing his spider in that spot. If he announces the wrong cardinal direction, his spider is moved to a random corner of the grid by the player owning the occupied square.

7. If the player lands on the square occupied by an opponent's home-base, the player must move the home-base elsewhere on the grid.

8. If the player runs out of squares in the required direction, he is to move his spider to the end of the board and then move it in the opposite direction. Note: This game is a great opportunity to review cardinal directions—the opposite of east is west… etc.

9. The first spider to reach his home-base wins!

POSITIONING

School Bus or Automobile

Using a toy school bus or automobile, identify various concepts:

1. Where is the front and back of the bus?
2. How many wheels are on the bus?
3. Where does the driver sit?
4. What is a steering wheel and how is that different than the wheels on the bus? How do they work together?

School Bus with People

Using a toy school bus with toy people/students (i.e., Melissa & Doug School Bus Wooden Play Set):

1. The student lines up the people/students to enter the bus. Who is the leader?
2. The student "walks" each person/student on the bus and selects a seat. As this is done, the student verbalizes the actions (i.e., "Jane goes up the stairs using her cane, turns left, and finds a seat on the right.")

3. The student and instructor discuss where the cane is stored on the school bus. (Perhaps, the instructor asks where a cane can be best stored on a city bus.)

4. The students "walks" each person/student off the bus and verbalizes this action (i.e., "Billy walks to the front of the bus and turns right. He uses his cane to go down the steps and especially uses it to exit the bus because the curb could be too close or not close enough. Billy steps onto the sidewalk.")

SKILL DEVELOPMENT

Pencil-grip and Maneuvering Around Obstacles (i.e. desks/ tables/furniture) with Cardinal Directions

1. In different (empty) classrooms:
   – Locate north, south, east and west walls
   – Locate northeast, southeast, northwest, and southwest

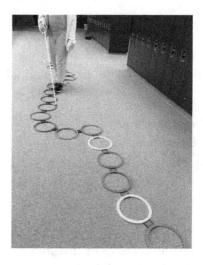

Pencil-grip with Constant Contact

Path of Rings:
1. Create a path of rings using *Milton Bradley Twister Hopscotch*.
2. The student begins at one end and walks to the other end and back without stepping off the rings.
3. Flip the path over and repeat.

Walking/Running without Veering

1. The student walk down the hallway without shore-lining—a sound cue (or person) may be needed as a beckon at the end of the hallway.
2. The student runs in the gym from end to end using a sound cue, much like the above.

Auditory/Echolocation Skills

1. Beachball Activity: (Put plenty of uncooked spaghetti into a beachball then break up the spaghetti.) A) The student kicks the ball down a quiet hallway; B) student locates the ball with the cane; C) repeat until student reaches the end of the hallway (or a predetermined end spot).

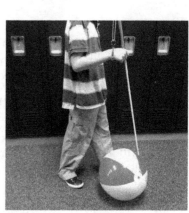

2. Tapping Activity: Walk to various locations in the school to hear what they sound like by tapping the metal tip of the cane in those settings (i.e., cafeteria, nurses' office, main office, principal's office, cafeteria kitchen, bathroom, main door, art room, music room, gym, computer lab, etc.). Be sure to discuss echolocation, carpet vs. tile.

3. Building Activity: The student and instructor begin several feet outside the main doors of the school facing the school. Walking toward the building, have the student announce when the building can be heard by the auditory sounds the metal tip is making before touching building with the cane.

Hide-n-Seek

Play Hide-n-Seek with *Silly Poopy's Hide & Seek* (sold by What do you Meme, LLC). Everyone loves a fun indoor or outdoor game of Hide-n-Seek. Silly Poopy's Hide & Seek © sings, talks, makes sounds, and whistles to help students find him. Once the button is pushed, the child has time to move away before the sound clues begin. This game offers skills of identifying sound locations which is necessary for O&M.

Note: Alternative is to us *JoJo & Friends Electronic Talking Hide 'Em and Find 'Em Easter Egg* (usually only available before Easter).

Address Numbering System (Beginners)

Understanding addresses can be confusing. This skill builder may help with understanding the numbering system for a typical street.

Materials:

One Mancala board (Folding Mancala boards help identify the middle of the block. Also, they can be used as two Braille cells, if desired, for other activities.)

Preparation:

1. Put a strip of textured paper lengthwise down the middle of the board to indicate where the street is located.
2. Create small flashcards with the following numbers on them: 100, 101, 102, 103, 104, 105, 106, 107, 108, 109. (Alternative: 0, 1, 2, 3, 4, 5, 6, 7, 8, 9)

Even #s	100	102	104	106	108	Odd #s
		Independence Avenue				
	101	103	105	107	109	

Activity:

1. Student separates the cards into two groups, even and odd, and places them in the storage areas located at the ends of the mancala board as shown in the diagram.
2. Student places the flashcards along Independence Avenue in numerical order with the odd numbers on one side and the even numbers on the other. NOTE: there will be one empty space on each side of the "street".

Extra numbers for skill building: Use the extra numbers below for practice. Mix the numbers and place them equally in the storage areas on the ends.

1.	200, 210, 230, 260, 270, 290, 201, 211, 231, 261, 271, 291	2.	220, 236, 242, 258, 276, 290, 225, 241, 255, 269, 281, 295
3.	326, 334, 338, 362, 372, 374, 329, 349, 363, 373, 381, 385	4.	400, 404, 408, 440, 464, 478, 407, 431, 445, 459, 473, 493
5.	502, 508, 522, 544, 566, 588, 507, 511, 533, 555, 577, 599	6.	606, 612, 630, 642, 664, 676, 601, 643, 663, 673, 679, 693
7.	720, 732, 748, 750, 774, 782, 705, 727, 749, 763, 779, 789	8.	812, 840, 858, 874, 876, 898, 827, 837, 853, 859, 877, 893

9.	920, 928, 930, 950, 958, 998, 905, 929, 935, 955, 983, 995	10.	1020, 1032, 1046, 1050, 1064, 1078, 1029, 1031, 1043, 1061, 1089, 1091
11.	2608, 2628, 2684, 2688, 2692, 2696, 2617, 2651, 2663, 2685, 2689, 2697		Idea: Create your own by searching maps online or using streets in the child's city/town.

Address Numbering System (Intermediate): Hallway Addresses

This activity also works on pencil-grip. It is best to find a hallway that will not disrupt other classes.

Materials:

Using the list of numbers above (or create different numbers), make address labels on 3X5 cards. Cut the top right corner to help with orientation.

Preparation:

Place ten chairs in the hallway—five on each side—facing each other.

Activities:

1. Repeat *Address Numbering System Activity* listed above using the chairs in the hallway instead of the Mancala board.
2. Use playing cards (remove the J, Q, K).
3. Increase the addresses and chairs, if desired.

Alternative:

Do the above activity except the student will place the cards on doors in the hallway.

Address Numbering System (Advanced)

This activity is for students who have a better concept of the address system but still need practice. Some students may need to have a few addresses already on the board to help them get started and/or they may need guidance. Also, due to class time or individual attention limitations, two or three class sessions may be necessary to complete this activity. There are a variety of solutions.

Materials:

1. A Hundreds Gray Grid Board (#61-219-001) and Velcro Adhesive dots from The Hundreds Boards and Manipulatives kit (American Printing House)
2. Velcro strips.
3. Four cups to help with organization of labels, if needed.

Preparation:

1. Place the Velcro strips (not included with Hundreds Board) on the board as shown to the right.
2. For every "**O**" in the diagram, place a Velcro dot on the board.

Address Labels		
96 For	96 Andy	388 L
97 For	97 Andy	389 L
98 For	98 Andy	422 L
99 For	99 Andy	423 L
100 For	100 Andy	488 L
101 For	103 Andy	489 L
102 For	104 Andy	522 L
103 For	105 Andy	523 L
106 For	106 Andy	388 M
107 For	107 Andy	389 M
108 For	108 Andy	424 M
109 For	109 Andy	427 M
200 For	202 Andy	458 M
201 For	203 Andy	469 M
202 For	204 Andy	531 M
203 For	205 Andy	534 M

3. Make Braille street labels (For Street, Andy Street, L St., M St.) and use Velcro to attach them to the board.
4. Make Braille address labels (as shown to the right) and apply Velcro on the back. Note: Omit number, letter, and capital Braille signs so the labels will fit the squares.
5. Snip off the top right corner of the address labels to help with orientation.
6. Mix or separate the labels according streets (depending on students' abilities).

Activity:

Students place the address numbers in their correct locations on the board.

Alternative:

Create your own streets and addresses using the board.

Address Numbering System (Advanced)

Hundreds Gray Grid Board (#61-219-001)

	O		O			O		O	
O	O		O	O	O	O		O	O
For Street									
O	O		O	O	O	O		O	O
	O	L	O			O	M	O	
	O	St.	O			O	St.	O	
O	O		O	O	O	O		O	O
Andy Street									
O	O		O	O	O	O		O	O
	O		O			O		O	

Possible Solutions:

	388		389			388		389	
96	98		100	102	106	108		200	202
For Street									
97	99		101	103	107	109		201	203
	422	L	423			424	M	427	
	488	St.	489			458	St.	469	
96	98		100	104	106	108		202	204
Andy Street									
97	99		103	105	107	109		203	205
	522		523			534		531	

	522		523			534		531	
202	200		108	106	102	100		98	96
For Street									
203	201		109	107	103	101		99	97
	488	L	489			427	M	469	
	422	St.	423			469	St.	427	
204	202		108	106	104	100		98	96
Andy Street									
205	203		109	107	105	103		99	97
	388		389			388		389	

NOTES

O&M TOOL HUNT

Dr. Merry-Noel Chamberlain, NOMC, TVI

This game is played like a typical scavenger hunt. Students independently collect the following items, which will need to be returned. Collection* of these items may be done over time. Store small items in the paper sack.

Items	Locations	✓	Discussion/Activities
Large paper sack*	Principal's office		1. Discuss the similarities and differences of the items (i.e., tools, made out of wood; from trees).
Sticky note	Main Office		
Hockey stick or bat: sticks used for games.	Gym		2. Discuss the history of the spoon; originally made out of wood; *Spoon* means *chip of wood* and has been documented as far back as Ancient Egypt (10,000–500 BC).
Paint brush: sticks used to create art.	Art room		
Ruler: sticks used for measurement.	Classroom #1		3. Discuss the relationship between the *pencil* and the *computer*.
Drum stick or baton: sticks used in music.	Music room		4. Discuss other stick/tools (i.e., walking cane, oar, toothpick)
Tongue depressor: sticks used for examinations.	Nurse's Office		5. Discuss the similarities & differences between *stick* and *cane*.
Pencil: sticks used to write.	Computer Lab		6. Why is a cane with a metal tip better than a stick for mobility?
Spoon: tools used for eating.	Cafeteria		7. Read Not a Stick, by Antoinette Portis.
Wooden spoon*: sticks used for mixing.	School kitchen		8. Discuss how the cane is "not a stick" but a valuable tool.
Broom: sticks used for sweeping.	Custodian		9. Discuss the history of the long white cane.
Yard stick: sticks used for measurement.	Classroom #2		10. Read The Giving Tree, by Shel Silverstein.
Books: Not a Stick, and/or The Giving Tree	Library		11. Discuss other ways wood can be used & how trees help the environment; habitats for animals/plants; food; shade, etc.
*Some items may need to be placed ahead of time. Some staff may need to be informed ahead of time, too			

O&M TOOL HUNT: HISTORY OF THE CANE AS A WOODEN TOOL
Dr. Merry-Noel Chamberlain, NOMC, TVI

Blind people have used a stick (i.e., a makeshift cane, of sorts) since the beginning of human history.[1,2,3,4,5,6,7] Actually, there was a British gentleman named Lieutenant James Holman (1786–1857), who used a walking stick with a metal tip.[5] Lieutenant Holman was a self-taught navigator who placed a metal tip on the end of his wooden stick to prevent it from splitting and considered this tool as "standard strolling equipment for gentlemen of the day."[5] Lieutenant Holman used the metallic sound of the stick as it hit various surfaces for detection of nearby objects such as walls and described this sound as a quick burst of noise.[5] Today, people who are blind use the metal tip for "echo-ranging cues and force-impact information" about the terrain[6] as well as a method to obtain auditory information regarding the surrounding environment. Therefore, "tap, tap, tap, [is] the sound of independence"[7] when a cane with a metal tip is used. After Holman was Mr. W. Hanks Levy, who in the 1870s expressed theories for cane use and design in England which are similar to those used today2 in the United States. Levy stated that it is extremely important that every blind person have the skills and ability to travel independently, that means walking without a guide.[2,8]

NOTES

[1]Bryant, E. (2009). My tree branch cane: How i became blind and then what. In Frye, D. (Ed.), Bridging the gap: Living with blindness and diabetes (3–6). Baltimore MD: The National Federation of the Blind.

[2]First Steps. (n.d.). Museum of the American Printing House for the Blind. Louisville, Kentucky.

[3]Foundation Fighting Blindness. (n.d.). Mobility & orientation packet. http://www.blindness.org/sites/default/files/pages/pdfs/Mobility-and-Orientation-Packet.pdf.

[4]Kim, D. S., Wall Emerson, R. (2012). Effect of cane length on drop-off detection performance. Journal of Visual Impairment & Blindness, 106(1), 31–35.

[5]Roberts, J. (2009). A sense of the world: How a blind man became history's greatest traveler. New York, NY: Harper Perennial.

[6]Sauerburger, D., Bourquin, E. (2010). Teaching the use of a long cane step by step: Suggestions for progressive methodical instruction. Journal of Visual Impairment and Blindness, 104(4), 203–214.

[7]Williams, R. (1967). Development of mobility programs which used canes as aids. Found in: Conference for Mobility Trainers and Technologists; Proceedings. Washington D.C.: Massachusetts Institute of Technology Faculty Club. Social and Rehabilitation Services.

[6]Pogrund, R. L., Griffin-Shirley, N. (2018). Partners in O&M: Supporting Orientation and Mobility for students who are visually impaired. New York, NY: American Foundation for the Blind Press.

[7]Winter, B. (2015). 10 fascinating facts about the white cane. Perkins School for the Blind. https://www.perkins.org/stories/10-fascinating-facts-about-the-white-cane

[8]Koestler, F. (1976). The unseen minority: A social history of blindness in the united states. New York, NY: American Foundation for the Blind.

O&M STORYBOOKS
Dr. Merry-Noel Chamberlain, NOMC, TVI

Book	Comprehension Questions	Assignment/ Discussion
*The True Story of Owin M.** (2011) By: Merry-Noel Chamberlain	*Found in PART THREE Pop Quiz (comprehension) questions are included within the book/chapters. **Owin M.'s Chair** "This chair belongs to Owin M. He left it here for a friend. Please don't take this chair away, for he'll come back another day and move it to a brand-new spot. (He likes to do that quite a lot!) Your long white cane can show you how to find the chair that's here right now."	1. Write a story on how you use your cane throughout your day. 2. Write a letter to Owin M. 3. Create an O&M song or poem. Teacher: Place the poem, *Owin M.'s Chair,* on a chair and move the chair around the school for the student to find.
*Flowers' Blooming*** (2011) By: Merry-Noel Chamberlain	** Found in PART FOUR What are some of the tools Sara uses in the story? (Cane, Braille notetaker, Braille watch.) Does Sara like to call her cane a stick? (No.) What is a Descriptive Video? (A narrator who describes the movie when no one is talking.) "Caw, Caw, Caw," means? (Three cars) Who is Flowers? (Royene; a character in the story.) What did Royene do at the All-School Talent Show? (She sang a song.) Why was this called, "Flowers' Blooming? (Royene overcame her fear and bloomed at the talent show.)	1. Perform the play for your school. 2. Walk to the local public library for a mobility lesson. 3. Volunteer at the school or public library to read stories in Braille (or over a few weekends read *Flowers Blooming*) to children. 4. Watch a Descriptive Video and discuss your experience.
The Night Search (1997) By: Kate Chamberlin, Jason and Nordic Publishers, Hollidaysburg, PA	Who is Crackers? (The family's dog.) Why did Heather feel that she did not need to take her cane with her when she took Crackers out? (She didn't think she needed it because she has been to the family camp before.) What did Heather smell and feel when walking to the pond? (She smelled damp and moldy pine trees and she felt cold mud over the top of her shoes.) Heather would not have to use her ___ if she had her ___. (hand, cane) Heather used her ___ to follow the edge of the road on her way to the pond. (foot) Why was it not a good idea for Heather to swing her hands back and forth, straight out in front of her when walking? (She hit a big rock with her hands.)	1. Listen to sounds outside and inside the house. Make a list of things you heard. 2. Make up an O&M song or poem. 3. In the story, Heather said her Mobility Instructor advised, "Use your long white cane to walk fast so you don't shuffle." Is there any outstanding advice your mobility instructor has said to you? If so, what?

Book	Comprehension Questions	Assignment/ Discussion
	Why did Heather's arms get tired? (She was holding her hands straight out in front of her and swinging them back and forth for a long time.)	
Why did Heather take off her hood? (So she could hear.) How did Heather know she was at the pond? (She could smell it.) How did Heather finally find Crackers? (She could hear the jangling sound of his collar.) What did Heather use as a mobility tool for walking back to the tent? (She used a long stick.) Name one thing that Heather used her cane-stick for on her way back to the tent: (Possible answers: • She moved it from side to side in front of her so she was able to find the big rock with it instead of hurting her hand. • She shore-lined the grassy edge of the road. • She used it to find the big mud puddle.)		
Keep Your Ear on the Ball (2007) By: Genevieve Petrillo, Tilbury House, Gardiner, ME TOOL: Put plenty of dried, uncooked spaghetti inside a blow-up beachball. Then, break the pasta and blow up the ball.	Did Davey use a cane at the beginning of the story? (No.) How did Davey explore the room? (He went around the room and touched everything.) How did Davey do everything the other students did? (He read in Braille and wrote using the Braillewriter.) What did Davey say to others to convey that he wanted to be independent? (He said "Thanks, but no thanks.") What tool could Davey use to help him to be more independent? (He could use the long white cane.) List two ways Davey's friends helped him play ball? Possible answers: • His friends stopped talking and stood still • Davey received a warning that the ball was coming. • Davey received verbal clues of where the bases were located. What did Amanda give Davey to wear at the end of the story? (A whistle)	Have you ever checked out a new area without using a cane? Do you think that was a good or bad idea? Why or why not? What are some "other" ways to explore new areas? How do you let others know you want to do something independently (without being rude)? Give examples of how your senses have helped you. What kind of sports do you enjoy and how are they accessible?

Book	Comprehension Questions	Assignment/ Discussion
The Blind Men and the Elephant (1992) Retold by Karen Blackstein, Scholastic Inc., New York, NY.	When did this story take place? (Long ago and far away.) How many blind men were in this story? (Six.) These men used their senses to hear the ___, feel the ___, smell and taste the ___. (flute, silk, food) What was the animal they went to check out and who owned it? (They went to check out an elephant that the Prince had.) NOTE: Describe that the pictures show that only the leader had a long stick that was being used as a cane. Name as many descriptions that you can of how the six blind men described the elephant. (Strong/wide wall, round snake, sharp spear, round/firm tree, fan, and long thin rope.) How did the blind men get home? (They rode the elephant home.)	Describe what your senses are and how you use them. How is Orientation and Mobility like putting several ideas together in order to understand something? What are some modern-day methods of travel? Why was it that the leader was the only one who used a cane? What does that tell you? Do you think blind people can lead other blind people? Why or why not?
Pedro and the Octopus (2018). By Deborah Kent, American Action Fund for Blind Children and Adults, Baltimore, MD	Dad says, "Listen to the ___, smell the salt in the ___." (waves, air) Pedro was not sure the ___ would be fun after Lena warned him to watch out for ___. (beach, octopi) What happened to Pedro's cane when he walked on the sand? (His cane poked holes in the sand.) What are some of the things Pedro found and put into his pail? (Smooth pebbles, a rough stone, clam shells, snail shells, a crab shell) What did the waves sound like? (RRRR-WHOOOOSH) What did the sand feel like? (Cool, smooth, and wet.) Did Pedro find an octopus? (No.) NOTE: Be sure to describe the picture of Pedro's cane on the shoreline while he is in the ocean.	1. Explore outside and collect treasures. 2. Walk barefoot in wet grass. 3. If possible, do a science project to determine if canes float or sink in a pool. 4. Do you think Pedro was brave to stay at the beach even though he wasn't sure he would like it? Why or why not? 5. What have you done that you were scared to do at first but ended up loving it? 6. Describe a time you were determined to do something and discuss the obstacles you faced.

Book	Comprehension Questions	Assignment/ Discussion
AND—Optional *The Great Googly Moogly* (2014) By: Courtney Dicmas, Child's Play Ltd., Auburn, ME	Who is the Great Googly Moogly? (The biggest fish of them all.) What did Stella dream about? (She wished for the Great Googly Moogly.) How determined was Stella to catch Googly Moogly? (She tried alternative ways; fly fishing and new bait.) Did Googly Moogly turn out to be as she had imagined him to be? (No.) Did Stella catch the Googly Moogly? (No.)	1. Compare and contrast these two stories. 2. Which story was more realistic and why?
Candy's Cane Top Dot Braille Institute, Los Angeles, CA	Who is Scooter? (Candy's cane) Why does Candy tap her cane on the ground in front of her? (She does this to know what is around her when she is walking.) Where does Candy put her cane when she is in her classroom? (She hangs it on a hook by the door.) How does Candy know exactly what day it is and what was on the schedule? (She uses a Braille calendar.) How does Candy find out who is at the table with her? (She asks.) Who is Ms. Beth? (Ms. Beth is Candy's O&M Instructor.) How can someone tell where the swings are located? (They squeak.) Where can the cane be stored when playing on the slide? (A trusted person can hold the cane, or it can be stored under the slide.) What kind of jokes does Candy like? (Knock-Knock.) From: www.specialcollection.org	1. What color is your cane? 2. Why are some canes red and white? 3. Why do canes need to be mostly white? 4. Is it a good idea to hang a cane by the classroom door? Why or why not? 5. Why is it okay to use the word "see" when talking to a blind person? 6. Does your cane have a name? If so, what? 7. What is your favorite knock-knock joke? 8. Make up a knock-knock joke and share it with a friend.

Book	Comprehension Questions	Assignment/ Discussion
My Favorite Place (1983) By Susan Sargent and Donna Aaron Wirt, Abingdon Press, Nashville, TN	How did the child know the road was curvy? (The child's body swayed in the car.) How did the child know they were getting closer to the ocean? (The child could hear the waves splashing against the rocks and the cry of the seagulls.) What could the child feel and smell when she got out of the car? (The child could feel the sun and the warm, soft sand on the feet and could smell salty ocean air.) Since people cannot "see" wind, how does the child know it is windy? (The wind could be felt on the body and flapping blanket could be heard.) What are some of the beach sounds the child heard? (People talking, yelling, laughing; a boat motor; a dog barking.) What are all the senses the child used at the beach? (Hearing, smelling, tasting and touching.) Was the child blind? (Yes.) Did the child use a cane? (No.) How did the child go from one location to another? (Held hands with parents.)	1. Name some locations you have gone to where you knew the location based on your senses. Describe those locations. 2. What are some of the ways people can tell when it is windy outside? 3. What are some of the sounds a person could hear at the following locations: 4. Mall 5. Airport 6. School 7. Grocery store 8. Do you think the child was independent? Why or why not? 9. What is human guide?
The Seeing Stick, (1977) Jane Yolen, Thomas Y. Crowell, New York	When did this story take place? In ancient times. Who was Hwei Ming? The emperor's daughter. Where did they live? Peking. What did the emperor do? He sent out a notice that is someone could help his daughter, that person would be rewarded. What did the old man take with him to the castle? A few possessions—a long walking stick, and his whittling knife. The sun rose hot on his right side and set cool on his left. Which direction did the old man travel? North The old man said the stick could ___. (see) What did the man do with the stick? Whittled pictures in it.	1. Did the old man help Hwei Ming see? If so, how? 2. Create a tactile map. 3. Create a tactile picture and <u>tell</u> a story about it. 4. Did you know that the old man was blind before the story told you? If so, how? 5. On your body, where would you feel the sun if you were walking south at 9:00 a.m.?

Book	Comprehension Questions	Assignment/ Discussion
See the Ocean (1994) Estelle Condra Hambleton-Hill Publishing	Where is Nellie going and with who? The beach with her parents and two brothers. Who was the scorekeeper? Nellie How did she keep score? In her head On this day, who said, "I see it!" referring to the ocean? Nellie. How? She smelled it. Nellie's mother said, "Though your sister's eyes are ___, she can see with her ___." (blind, mind) Activity: Use an abacus or the APH, Score Card Set (Catalog Number: 1-17001-00) to play a game of the student's choice. Compare mental math with using these tools to keep score.	1. Did you know Nellie was blind before it was revealed in the story? If so, how? 2. What are some places that are easily identified through aroma? 3. Describe an experience without actually revealing the event and have people guess what you described.
Abby Goes to the Farm (2013) Signature Book Printing	Note: Pictures need to be described (i.e., Abby carries a cane, safety pins are used to label clothes) Who is Fluffy? (Abby's guide dog.) Although Abby has Fluffy, she also carries a ___? (cane) On which side does Fluffy walk? (right) How does Abby manage her clothes? (Safety pins on her clothes.) How does Abby tell time? (Abby uses a talking watch.) What/who wakes Abby up in the mornings? (Her radio) How does Abby form pictures in her mind? (Her parents describe the places.) What does Abby use to learn about places and things? (She uses her other senses.) What does Abby like most at the farm? (She likes to ride the horse) **and why?**	1. How did you know Abby was blind? 2. What are other ways to manage or identify clothes? 3. Other than a talking watch, what are other ways to tell time? 4. Use senses on a farm then describe them in a paper to create a picture in some else's mind. 5. What do you like best on the farm? 6. If you've ever ridden an animal, what was it and how did it feel?

NOTES

_____

_____

_____

_____

_____

_____

_____

_____

_____

_____

_____

_____

_____

_____

_____

_____

_____

_____

_____

_____

_____

_____

THE RIGHT STORY FOR RUBY LEFT'S BIRTHDAY PARTY
Dr. Merry-Noel Chamberlain, NOMC, TVI

Goal: This lesson focuses on the concept of *left* and *right* while reading *The Right Story for Ruby Left's Birthday Party*.

Lesson options/ideas while listening to the story, *The Right Story for Ruby Left's Birthday Party*:

1. Students raise their left or right hand (or foot) whenever they hear the word *left* or *right* while listening to the story.
2. Students have two toys—one on their left side of the body and the other on their right side of the body. They pick up the toy on their left or on their right whenever they hear the word *left* or *right* while listening to the story.
3. While standing in a circle, students move one stuffed animal to the right or to the left whenever the word *right* or *left* is said in the story. The person who ends up with the stuffed animal is the winner.

Reading lesson:

Enlarge, Braille or use the print copy of the story that does not highlight the words *left* and *right*, for students circle the word *left* and place a square around the word *right*.

Game for two participants (or more) and a reader:

1. After selecting a reader, participants stand side-by-side with their back to a wall.
2. The reader of the story speaks aloud and does not pause when reading, as this will alert the participants that a step must be made.
3. As the story is read aloud, the participants step forward using the correct foot whenever they hear the word *left* or *right*. (i.e., When the word *right* is heard, the participant steps forward with the right foot.)
4. If a participant (#1) steps forward incorrectly and this action is caught by another participant (#2), then participant #1 must step back and then step forward using the correct foot and the other participant (#2) receives one bonus point.
5. At the end of the story, if done correctly, all participants will have arrived at the finish line at the same time. (25 lefts and 25 rights)
6. The winner is the person with the most bonus points. If no one has bonus points, everyone is a winner!

THE RIGHT STORY FOR RUBY LEFT'S BIRTHDAY PARTY
Dr. Merry-Noel Chamberlain, NOMC, TVI

I left my house and was on my way to Ruby Left's house. But I left Ruby's gift and the directions to her house at my home, right by the front door! I knew right away that I needed to have her gift and the right directions to Ruby Left's house. So, I turned left and left to make my way back to my house to pick up the right directions. Sure enough, there they were, right where I had left them, right next to the front door!

Finally, I was on the right track. I left my house by going right through the front door. Then, I turned right to get to the steps to get off my porch. I walked down the steps and then I turned left and walked to the end of the sidewalk. I had to turn left again and go down some more steps to get to my driveway. When I got to the driveway, I turned right and then right again to get on the right sidewalk to get to Ruby Left's house. I walked, and walked, and walked to get to the end of my block. Then I turned right again.

After many more rights and lefts, I was able to arrive right on time at Ruby Left's house. I set Ruby's birthday gift right next to the rest. More of Ruby's friends arrived and they sat right next to me. Mrs. Left made a list of everyone there and she was sure no one was left off her list. We then played many games. My favorite game is Left, Center, Right, and Ruby won! We all had so much fun!

Then Ruby opened her gifts which were all lined up. She started on the left and opened them one by one as she worked her way from the left to the right. But a couple of Ruby's friends said they left her gift at their house. Boy, was I happy I went back to get the right directions and to pick up Ruby Left's gift. Ruby was happy to receive the right gifts from her friends.

After we had cake and ice cream, Mrs. Left and Ruby gave everyone a party favor and thanked everyone for coming! Then it was the right time for everyone to leave. I left Ruby Left's house at exactly the right time because as soon as I got home, it started to rain! There is nothing left for me to tell you about going to Ruby's house except now I can't wait until the right day shows up on my calendar for my own birthday party!

Left—25 Right—25   Total: 50 points

THE RIGHT STORY FOR RUBY LEFT'S BIRTHDAY PARTY
Dr. Merry-Noel Chamberlain, NOMC, TVI

I left my house and was on my way to Ruby Left's house. But I left Ruby's gift and the directions to her house at my home, right by the front door! I knew right away that I needed to have her gift and the right directions to Ruby Left's house. So, I turned left and left to make my way back to my house to pick up the right directions. Sure enough, there they were, right where I had left them, right next to the front door!

Finally, I was on the right track. I left my house by going right through the front door. Then, I turned right to get to the steps to get off my porch. I walked down the steps and then I turned left and walked to the end of the sidewalk. I had to turn left again and go down some more steps to get to my driveway. When I got to the driveway, I turned right and then right again to get on the right sidewalk to get to Ruby Left's house. I walked, and walked, and walked to get to the end of my block. Then I turned right again.

After many more rights and lefts, I was able to arrive right on time at Ruby Left's house. I set Ruby's birthday gift right next to the rest. More of Ruby's friends arrived and they sat right next to me. Mrs. Left made a list of everyone there and she was sure no one was left off her list. We then played many games. My favorite game is Left, Center, Right, and Ruby won! We all had so much fun!

Then Ruby opened her gifts which were all lined up. She started on the left and opened them one by one as she worked her way from the left to the right. But a couple of Ruby's friends said they left her gift at their house. Boy, was I happy I went back to get the right directions and to pick up Ruby Left's gift. Ruby was happy to receive the right gifts from her friends.

After we had cake and ice cream, Mrs. Left and Ruby gave everyone a party favor and thanked everyone for coming! Then it was the right time for everyone to leave. I left Ruby Left's house at exactly the right time because as soon as I got home, it started to rain! There is nothing left for me to tell you about going to Ruby's house except now I can't wait until the right day shows up on my calendar for my own birthday party!

Left—25 Right—25   Total: 50 points

THE RIGHT STORY FOR RUBY LEFT'S BIRTHDAY PARTY—SCORE SHEET
Dr. Merry-Noel Chamberlain, NOMC, TVI

NAMES →	Left	Right	Left	Right	Left	Right	Left	Right
1								
2								
3								
4								
5								
6								
7								
8								
9								
10								
11								
12								
13								
14								
15								
16								
17								
18								
19								
20								
21								
22								
23								
24								
25								
TOTALS →								

Possible scores: Left—25 , Right—25   PERFECT SCORE: 50 points

ORIENTATION AND MOBILITY TRUE/FALSE GAME
Dr. Merry-Noel Chamberlain, NOMC, TVI

Use the following O&M questions for a simple True/False Game, test, or quiz. If desired, mobility instructors may wish to use these questions to open discussion ideas. Many questions came from the *50/50 O&M Game* on the following website: (http://www.pdrib.com/pages/omtfquestions.php).

Game Objective:
Score more points than the opponents.

Materials (Optional):
APH, Score Card Set (Catalog Number: 1-17001-00).

TRUE/FALSE QUESTIONS	ANSWERS
1. The cane needs to be used at every walking opportunity outside the home.	1. True! The cane is a tool that helps with mobility and safety.
2. When standing at the corner and waiting for a safe time to cross a street, the cane needs to be extended outward in front of the body.	2. False. The cane needs to be upright when standing at the corner to indicate the individual does not intend to cross the street, yet.
3. When standing in the lunch line, the cane needs to be held in the pencil grip and the tip of the cane is close to the body.	3. True. It is proper method in the lunch line to hold the cane in the pencil grip with the tip of the cane close to the body.
4. When walking, the cane tip needs to be moving from side to side, as wide as the shoulders.	4. True. Moving the cane as wide as the shoulders informs the user that the space is wide enough to proceed.
5. The cane tip is extended on the right side of the body when the left foot is forward while walking.	5. True. This is called walking-in-step. It ensures that the space is cleared for the foot to land on.
6. The cane must always move in the direction in which the person is traveling.	6. True. The cane must be in use between the body and direction of travel when moving forward, backward or even sideways.
7. It is impossible to walk backwards while using a cane.	7. False. The cane can be extended behind the body with the arm down to the side. The cane needs to be arcing back and forth as wide as the shoulder.
8. When walking forward, in an open space, keep the hand down against the side of the body with the cane extended forward.	8. False. The cane needs be extended forward with the hand in the center of the body, elbow bent and hand near the bellybutton.
9. When walking forward, one must extend the cane forward from the center of their body by the belly button.	9. True. This method will best ensure the safety of the user.
10. The pencil grip needs to be used when traveling in crowded areas.	10. True. The pencil grip needs to be used in crowded areas so that the cane does not trip someone who is not paying attention.

TRUE/FALSE QUESTIONS	ANSWERS
11. To store the cane in a car, lay it on the floor behind the front seat or wherever you can find a space.	11. False. The best place to store the cane is between the seat and the door. (Exception: cab or pickup truck.. Laying the cane on the floor may cause it to break by someone standing on it.
12. A guide dog user still needs to know how to use a cane.	12. True. A cane may be used if the guide dog becomes ill or if the guide dog is gone for a few days, such as in need of surgery.
13. The cane tip is extended on the right side of the body when the right foot is forward while walking.	13. False. When the cane is extended on the right side, the left foot needs to be forward while walking.
14. While standing and chatting with friends in the school hallway, the cane needs to be extended outward.	14. False. When standing and chatting, the cane needs to be upright. When it is extended, someone may trip over it.
15. When sitting at the lunch table, the cane may be stored on the floor under the table.	15. True. The cane is easily accessible in this location and no one will trip over it.
16. It is okay to loan your cane to a classmate so they won't get into trouble if they don't have theirs.	16. False. Never lend your cane to anyone. If you lend it, you will be without yours and that's not safe.
17. Knowing cardinal directions to travel from one place to another is necessary for every travel opportunity.	17. False. Although knowing cardinal directions is a great skill, it is not something that is needed for every travel event.
18. It is possible to run or jog with a long white cane.	18. True. Longer canes are needed for running or jogging…perhaps as tall as one's forehead.
19. The cane needs to be used at every walking opportunity outside of the home.	19. True! The use of a cane provides safety and independence.
20. A long white cane makes a person look blind.	20. False. The long white cane makes a person look independent.
21. A long white cane is a tool.	21. True. It is used to perform many functions.
22. A long white cane is a symbol of independence.	22. True. A person using a cane is able to perform many tasks without assistance.
23. When walking upstairs, the cane needs to be beside the body.	23. False. The cane needs to be held with the pencil grip and positioned upright in front of the body when walking upstairs. With slight pressure forward, the cane will tap the upper stair when walking upstairs.
24. Extend the cane outward, using open-palm, while walking in crowded areas.	24. False. The pencil grip is used in crowded areas. If the cane is extended outward, it may cause someone to trip, step on the cane and break it, or accidently kick it away.

TRUE/FALSE QUESTIONS	ANSWERS
25. While standing and chatting with friends in the school hallway, the cane needs to be upright.	25. True. Keeping the cane upright is proper cane etiquette.
26. It is not important to always know cardinal directions when traveling from one place to another.	26. True. One may simply be walking from one classroom to another across the hall.
27. A long white cane is not permitted on a plane or train.	27. False. A long white cane is permitted everywhere.
28. A guide dog user no longer needs a cane.	28. False. Some people use both a guide dog and a cane.
29. A cane can easily detect puddles.	29. False. It may pass over the puddle or not make enough sound for the puddle to be detected.
30. A cane can cause a lot of damage to an automobile when walking through a parking lot.	30. False. The cane is to find objects, such as automobiles in the parking lot. It will not dent a car or truck when used normally.
31. It is okay to tap your cane when walking.	31. True. It is recommended to tap your cane as wide as your shoulders while walking so the metal tip can create possible echoes.
32. It is okay to throw your cane up in the air.	32. False. If you toss your cane in the air, you might not find it again or it might hurt someone.
33. When going downstairs, the cane needs to be beside the body using open-palm technique.	33. False. The pencil grip is used and the tip of the cane needs to be on the first step lower when going downstairs.
34. It is okay to hold the cane outward with tip of the cane at waist level when walking.	34. False. This positioning is not safe for either the person holding the cane or someone standing in front of the person. Also, the cane will not be able to find objects on the ground or drop-offs.
35. When traveling upstairs, the pencil grip is used and the cane tip is two steps in front of the body.	35. True. This is the safest technique for climbing stairs.
36. When traveling downstairs, keep the cane tip one step in front of the body.	36. True. This method will allow you to detect if there is anything on the step you could trip on.
37. One keychain may be used to help identify a cane.	37. True. Many people use a personalized keychain to identify their cane.
38. Having five or more key chains on the cane for identification is a good idea.	38. False. Putting too many items on the cane can cause the cane handle to become heavy and cumbersome. The cane becomes unbalanced, causing difficulties in surface detection.

TRUE/FALSE QUESTIONS	ANSWERS
39. The cane tip is extended on the left side of the body when the left foot is forward while walking.	39. False. When the cane is extended on the left side of the body, the right foot is forward.
40. A long white cane is not a tool.	40. False. The cane is a tool used for independent travel.
41. Attaching balloons filled with helium on the cane is a good idea.	41. False. Dr. Chamberlain tried this once; the balloons kept hitting each other and making so much noise that she couldn't listen to the environment.
42. Not having a keychain on the cane is fine.	42. True. You may choose to use another method to identify your cane.
43. Walking forward and pulling the cane behind the body is all right on occasion.	43. False. The cane must always be between the body and direction of travel to ensure safety.
44. Walking forward and tapping the cane as wide as the shoulders is a proper technique.	44. True. This is an excellent way to travel.
45. Walking and carrying the cane under the arm is fine when you're tired.	45. False. If the cane is not in use, it is not serving its purpose for you.
46. Using the cane on the escalator is important.	46. True. Escalators can pose challenges, and the cane is an essential tool.
47. People in wheelchairs may use canes.	47. True. Some people in wheelchairs use canes regularly.
48. Children must be at least 10 years old to use a cane.	48. False. Babies and toddlers can get and use canes, too. They are beginners.
49. A long white cane is permitted on a plane or train.	49. True. These items are allowed and absolutely need to be brought along when traveling.
50. A 3-year-old can have a cane.	50. True. Young children need to have a cane as soon as possible. Some people get their first cane before they begin walking!
51. While standing in on elevator, one must hold the cane extended.	51. False. When in the elevator, hold the cane upright, to protect it.
52. When walking, it is okay to tap the cane from side to side.	52. True. This is the recommended technique for walking.
53. People can dance while using a cane.	53. True. Some people may lay it down next to the dance floor when dancing, while others bring it on the floor with them.
54. Individuals cannot take a cane onto a bus.	54. False. The cane is allowed and needs to be brought along.
55. It is okay to use human guide in an emergency.	55. True. But be sure to use the cane at the same time, if possible.

TRUE/FALSE QUESTIONS	ANSWERS
56. The emergency sign for a person who is deafblind is to draw an X on their back.	56. True. In the case of an emergency, draw X on the back of a person who is deafblind; this indicates there is an emergency. Then use the human guide technique to move from the situation and explain the emergency later.
57. The cane tip is extended on the left side of the body when the right foot is forward while walking.	57. True. This is the correct way to walk-in-step.
58. When using a human guide, it is important to still use and arc the cane.	58. True. Sometimes human guides forget they are guiding. Arcing the cane protects the body from running into objects.
59. Shore-lining is when the cane tip is used to follow the edge of a sidewalk, building, or other object with the tip of the cane.	59. True. This method allows you to proceed in a straight line, as if you were walking along a shore.
60. Cool blind people use canes.	60. True. All blind people who want to be independent use canes.
61. When moving, the cane needs to be moving also.	61. True. This is the proper technique for using a cane.
62. The cane can be used as a sword.	62. False. Using the cane in this way could be dangerous and result in breaking the cane.
63. The cane needs to be used at every walking opportunity outside the home.	63. True! The more the cane is used, the more one gains mastery and independence.
64. The cane can be used as a magic wand.	64. False. This is not a serious use for the cane and may be dangerous.
65. It is okay to let other people play with your cane.	65. False. Other people may damage the cane, and you would not be independent while they had it.
66. Only sighted people can teach Orientation and Mobility due to safety reasons.	66. False. Many blind and visually impaired people have successfully taught O&M.
67. The history of cane travel began over a thousand years ago in China.	67. True. Historians have found that cane travel began this far back in time.
68. The terms Orientation and Mobility and Cane travel mean the same thing.	68. True. These terms are often used synonymously.
69. Problem-solving is a technique needed for O&M.	69. True. Problem-solving is essential when one encounters unusual or unexpected circumstances when traveling.
70. Structured Discovery Cane Travel is a curriculum used by O&M instructors to encourage students to problem solve.	70. True. This curriculum is introduced very early by O&M instructors.

TRUE/FALSE QUESTIONS	ANSWERS
71. A person does not usually use a cane in their own home.	71. True. Individuals are most comfortable in their own home, usually know the layout of the furniture, and are able to travel independently without the cane.
72. It is okay to bang the cane from side to side.	72. False. Banging the cane on the ground causes the cane to break near the bottom of the cane.
73. It is okay to use a cane on the bus.	73. True. The cane is allowed and will be of use on the bus and after departing it.
74. When tapping the cane from side to side as wide as the shoulders, the cane needs to be low to the ground to help detect drop-offs.	74. True. If the cane is not low to the ground, drop-offs are harder to detect and may cause the traveler to unexpectedly step off the curb.
75. If the cane handle jabs the gut when walking, open-palm technique is probably not being used.	75. True. Using the open-palm technique will cause the cane handle to move upward when it encounters an object rather than into the abdomen.
76. On the city bus, the cane is held upright.	76. True. By holding the cane on a city bus, you maintain control of your cane.
77. When standing, the cane needs to be taller than the user's chin or as tall as the user's nose.	77. True. From toes to nose is the standard length of a cane. However, some people prefer taller canes.
78. The metal tip provides auditory feedback called echolocation.	78. True. Echolocation provides auditory information about the surrounding environment.
79. A cane cannot be used to travel during extreme weather conditions such as snow or ice.	79. False. The cane can dig into snow to help you feel the sidewalk, and the metal tip can identify ice because it glides easily over ice.
80. It is important to always carry a spare cane tip.	80. True. Sometimes carry two! Cane tips can and do break in inopportune times.
81. It is okay to carry the cane over the shoulders like a hobo stick.	81. False. If the cane is not being used correctly, it is not useful.
82. Playing games with the cane, such as batting, swinging, etc., is fine, especially if no one is around.	82. False. The cane is not a bat. It is a tool for mobility. Swinging the cane can cause it to hit something and get broken.
83. It is unsafe to use the cane in crowded areas.	83. False. The cane needs to be used at all times—especially in crowds!
84. Using a human guide is better than using a cane whenever a human guide is available.	84. False. Becoming overly dependent on human guides decreases independent travel skills.
85. Blind people can be human guides.	85. True. Blind people can guide another person especially when the guide has better mental mapping skills or knows exactly where to go.

TRUE/FALSE QUESTIONS	ANSWERS
86. Only blind people teach cane travel.	86. False. It is best to have a certified O&M instructor from which to learn O&M skills.
87. Once O&M training is completed, there is no need to remember or use the techniques learned.	87. False. The mobility skills learned in O&M are transformational whereby these skills can be used in other locations outside of class.
88. All O&M skills can be transferred outside the instructional setting.	88. True. By using problem-solving skills, generalizing, discovery, and prior experiences, O&M skills can be used outside the instructional setting.
89. If an individual has been to the same restaurant several times, bringing the cane to that restaurant is still recommended.	89. True. Changes are unpredictable. The cane needs to be accessible in case of an emergency.
90. Shore-lining is walking along the edge of the beach.	90. False but sometimes true! This is a trick question. A person can shoreline the water or the sound of the waves, but shore-lining isn't limited to the shore.
91. Cool blind people don't use canes.	91. Absolutely False. Cool blind people always use canes!
92. Canes will not break if shut in a car door.	92. False. Canes will absolutely break when shut in a car door. Be careful.
93. White Cane Law states that anyone carrying a long white cane has a right to equal access in public places.	93. True. In most states, drivers approaching pedestrians holding a predominantly white cane shall take all necessary precautions to avoid injury to such pedestrian or be liable for any damages.
94. Fiberglass canes cannot be straightened back if bent.	94. True. If overly bent, a fiberglass cane can break.
95. Metal cane tips provide echolocation and tactual feedback.	95. True. The metal tip creates echoes, and constant contact provides tactual information.
96. The cane needs to be used at every walking opportunity outside the home.	96. True! Whenever you leave the home, your cane needs to go with you.
97. It is okay to slide the cane (constant contact. from side to side.	97. True. Constant Contact helps to locate slight changes in the terrain.
98. Allowing someone to take your cane from you at any time is okay.	98. False. It is not okay for anyone to remove a cane from its owner.
99. In order to walk straighter, one needs to walk slow.	99. False. The slower you walk, the easier it is to veer off course.
100. When in the grocery store, one may lift the cane slightly off the ground and hold on to the cart as it is being pulled.	100. True. This technique is often used when shopping with a customer service employee.

TRUE/FALSE QUESTIONS	ANSWERS
101. Once a metal cane tip is worn out, the cane must be replaced.	101. False. Replacement cane tips are available.
102. One needs to walk slowly when crossing a street.	102. False. Walk quickly when crossing the street to avoid veering.
103. It is better to use your hand to trail a wall than shoreline with the cane.	103. False. Trailing the wall with the hand causes individuals to touch everything—even dirty surfaces. This practice can also cause you to knock things off the wall such as pictures or wall hangings.
104. If the cane touches someone when walking, there is no need to say, "Excuse me" because they should have seen a blind person approaching and moved out of the way.	104. False. It is polite to say "Excuse me" if your cane touches someone.
105. To store the cane in a car, slide it between the door and the seat.	105. True. This location protects your cane from getting stepped on and broken.
106. The cane needs to be as tall as the floor to one's forehead for jogging.	106. True. The faster you walk, the longer the cane needs to be so that you have plenty of reaction time when approaching an obstacle within the path.
107. It is important to know where your cane is at all times.	107. True. If you don't know where your cane is, your ability to travel independently is hindered.
108. Sleep-shades are used to help focus on alternative senses.	108. True. When you can focus on your other senses, you can be a better traveler.
109. One needs to hold the palm upward while extending the cane outward from the center of the body when traveling.	109. True. This is called open-palm technique and it prevents the cane handle from jabbing the user in the abdomen when the tip hits an obstacle.
110. Store the long white cane on the lap when sitting.	110. False. Place the cane on the floor, corner, or hold it up and down.
111. It is okay to put a folding or telescoping cane on the table when not in use.	111. False. The cane tip is dirty, so it would be unsanitary to put it on the table.
112. Old, broken canes make good plant stakes.	112. True. Old broken canes can support weak plants to help them grow stronger.
113. The long white cane can be used in the movie theatre.	113. True. Canes can be used in many places including movie theatres where the lights are dim.
114. Blind people can teach O&M.	114. True. It used to be that blind people could not get certified as O&M instructors but now they can.
115. Auditory information can be provided through echolocation with a metal cane tip.	115. True. Canes that are plastic do not provide echolocation to the user. They are unable to reflect sound off obstacles.

TRUE/FALSE QUESTIONS	ANSWERS
116. A cane is normally not taller than the person using it.	116. True. Normally canes are not taller than the user but some people do prefer taller canes.
117. While on the city bus, hold the cane upright.	117. True. Don't lay the cane on the floor of a bus or have it extended outward or else someone might trip over it or it could get stepped on and broken.
118. The city bus driver needs to store the cane and then find you a seat.	118. False. To be independent, keep the cane and find your own seat.
119. It is okay to let someone store your cane for you after you have found a seat in the classroom, restaurant, library, etc.	119. False. Each individual is responsible for storing their own cane and knowing where it is at all times.
120. Allowing someone take your cane from you at any time is not okay.	120. True. Your cane is your responsibility so you need to be the one to take care of it.
121. The cane needs to be used at every walking opportunity outside the home.	121. True! Whenever you walk outside your home, your cane is your tool for mobility. Keep it with you.
122. In order to walk straighter, one needs to walk quickly.	122. True. This is especially important when crossing the street. It also comes in handy when walking down a long straight hallway, sidewalk or open areas.
123. A long white cane makes a person look independent.	123. True. The cane is the tool used for independent travel.
124. When in the grocery store, the cart can be pulled while walking the isles.	124. True. Pull the cart behind you while using the cane in front of you to ensure the area is clear of obstacles.
125. While traveling in snow, the cane can help detect the edge of the sidewalk.	125. True. By using the Touch & Slide technique, the edge of the sidewalk can be found when traveling in snow.
126. While traveling in rainy, wet weather, traffic can sound louder and closer than it actually is.	126. True. Clouds help bend soundwaves downward, slowing the atmospheric absorption and causing the traffic sound to be louder.
127. A person using crutches can use a long white cane at the same time.	127. True. Although this is difficult, it is doable. The cane must sweep the area before each step forward.
128. Only a folding or telescoping cane is permitted on a plane, train or in a movie theater.	128. False. Although one may prefer a folding or telescoping cane on the plane or train, it is not required.
129. In some cities, when an individual has a long white cane visible, the public bus will stop in front of that person and announce their bus number.	129. True. Sadly, some cities do not do this. If you live in such a city, you need to ask the driver for their bus number before you step on just to ensure you are getting on the correct bus.

TRUE/FALSE QUESTIONS	ANSWERS
130. A long white cane can be used as a tool to find lost items under the bed, couch, or behind the refrigerator.	130. True. This is done by laying the cane on the ground and sliding it around. This works for locating some dropped items, as well.
131. While standing in the elevator, the cane must be held upright.	131. True. Don't have it extended outward or else it could get stuck in the elevator door as it closes.
132. Store a long, rigid cane behind the front seat when in a standard pickup.	132. True. Since the cane can't be stored between the door and the seat, storage of the cane behind the front seat is best.
133. For utmost independence, the cane can be stored in the trunk of the car when traveling by automobile.	133. False. The cane is not easily accessible when it is in the trunk.
134. It is not safe to use the cane with roller skates.	134. False. The cane needs to be used at every walking or, in this case, rolling opportunity. However, some people prefer not to use a cane when holding the rink's edge or a friend's hand.
135. It is safe to use your cane as a sword to play fight with other people.	135. False. The cane is a tool for mobility, not a toy.
136. Individuals who have some vision can achieve better results by wearing sleep-shades during O&M lessons.	136. True. Sleep-shades help you focus on your other senses to help you develop your intrinsic feedback.
137. Running up or jumping down stairs while holding the cane is not safe.	137. True. Running with the cane while going up or down stairs may be harmful to the individual and/or others.
138. Twirling the cane like a baton, when no one is around, is perfectly fine.	138. False. Twirling the cane may be dangerous. It could accidently hit something.
139. When walking with the cane, it is okay to have the chain or handle loop snug around the wrist like a bracelet.	139. False. Having the loop around the wrist may harm the wrist if the cane accidentally trips another person and is yanked out of the individual's hand.
140. If sleep-shades are used during O&M lessons and/or games, one must not peek.	140. True. Peeking does not allow individuals to focus on their senses. Peeking conveys that vision is necessary to complete a task.
141. Storing the cane under the table at restaurants is fine.	141. True. It can get dirty there but sometimes that is the only place to store it. Look for nearby corner to prop it.
142. Using your cane like a hiking stick while going upstairs is fine.	142. False. Using this is not the proper method for going upstairs.
143. It is okay to store the cane next to the classroom door in familiar classrooms.	143. False. The cane needs to be easily accessible to the individual who uses it, especially in the case of an emergency.

TRUE/FALSE QUESTIONS	ANSWERS
144. Storing extra canes in the trunk of the car when traveling by automobile is fine.	144. True. The key word here is extra. It is important not to store the cane currently in use in the trunk.
145. It is okay to swing the cane tip high in the air when arcing it from left to right as wide as the shoulders.	145. False. When the cane tip is high in the air when arcing, it makes it difficult to detect slight changes in the sidewalk.
146. The cane needs to be used at every walking opportunity outside the home.	146. True! Perhaps by now, you comprehend you must use your cane whenever you leave your home.
147. The cane can be used while pulling or pushing a suitcase on rollers.	147. True. This is the best way to travel with a suitcase while using the cane.
148. As you get taller, your cane needs to get longer, too.	148. True. The cane needs to be the length from your toes to your nose.
149. Some people name their canes.	149. True (e.g., Candy Cane, Hurricane, Sugarcane, Novocain, or even Leroy).
150. The cane must be used when walking to and from the cafeteria or dorm.	150. True. The cane needs to be used every time outside the home environment.
151. Whenever possible, use human guide rather than the cane.	151. False. Being dependent on only traveling with a human guide removes independence.
152. The cane does not need to be used at every walking opportunity outside the home.	152. False! For independence, the cane needs to be used at every walking opportunity outside the home.
153. The pencil grip needs to be used when traveling in congested areas.	153. True. The pencil grip needs to be used in congested areas so that the cane does not accidently go under tables or between chair legs. If that happens, the body can run into objects.
154. When sitting at the lunch table, the cane may be stored along the floorboard or propped in a nearby corner.	154. True. You are responsible for your cane. Be responsible on where you store your cane. Along the floorboard or propped in a nearby corner is just fine.
155. While standing and waiting, the cane needs to be upright.	155. True. This is cane etiquette. By holding it upright keeps it and other people safe.
156. The cane can be used to detect a step(s).	156. True. The cane, when used correctly, will detect the step(s).
157. It is okay to walk with the cane tip off the ground.	157. False. If the cane tip is off the ground when walking, it will not detect anything on the ground, including steps or curbs. This may cause harm to the user.
158. It is okay to leave the cane propped in the corner or in the closet at home when going out with friends (parents. because they can be your free human guides.	158. False. If the cane is not in use, it is not serving its purpose. Going human guide without a cane makes you dependent on others. Also, it is never a good idea to take advantage of parents or friends.

TRUE/FALSE QUESTIONS	ANSWERS
159. It is okay to leave the cane propped in the corner or in the closet at home when going out with parents because they can be your free human guides.	159. False. It is never a good idea to take advantage of parents. If the cane is not in use, it is not serving its purpose.
160. The cane needs to be stored near the student's desk, not by the classroom door.	160. True. The cane needs to be easily accessible to the individual who uses it, especially in the case of an emergency.
161. It is okay to arc the cane tip high in the air without touching the ground.	161. False. When the cane tip is arced high in the air, it is not providing terrain information.
162. The proper way to find low tree branches, is to arc the cane over the head.	162. False. The proper way to find low tree branches is to use upper body protective technique.
163. Parents can be human guides.	163. True. Often parents are the child's first human guide.

Extra Space to Add True/False Questions

O&M ENCOUNTERS
Going to Mickey's House
Dr. Merry-Noel Chamberlain, NOMC, TVI

This is an independent mental mapping, problem-solving activity where YOU decide your destiny. As you read *O&M Encounters: Going to Mickey's House*, you will encounter various travel problems. You will be given up to four options as listed in the KEY:

C—Continue Walking Forward; S & I—Stop & Investigate (check cardinal directions, use senses for cues); R—Retrace Steps, or; O—Other options (double check directions, verify current location, obtain assistance).

YOU, the reader, make the decisions on the best way to resolve each encounter. YOUR decisions will guide you through this O&M Encounter opportunity and direct YOUR destiny. Are you ready to go on an O&M Encounter? **IF SO, LET'S GO!!!**

KEY	
C	Continue walking forward
S & I	Stop and Investigate - Check cardinal directions - Use senses for cues (i.e., listen, feel sun & wind)
R	Retrace Steps
O	Other options - Double check directions - Verify current location - Obtain assistance

Start here → It is 8:00 in the morning and you decide (if you are a child, you were given permission) to walk to Mickey's house that is three blocks away. Although you have been to his house before, this will be your first time walking there by yourself. You live in a quiet residential neighborhood and feel confident that you can do this independently. From your home, which faces the south, you know that you must: (1) Walk to the sidewalk in the front of your house; (2) Turn east; (3) Cross two streets; (4) Turn north; and (5) Go to the third house on the right from the corner. Mickey told you his house does not have a sidewalk leading from the street. You remember when you get rides there, the sidewalk to the house is off the driveway by the driver's side of the car. You grab your cane that is next to the front door and exit the house. At the sidewalk in front of the house, you… (Pick one) 　　　　Turn right—Go to #1 　　　　Turn left—Go to #2		
#1	You start walking and your cane hits something that makes a 'thunk' sound. You acknowledge this could be a problem. However, you've heard this sound before and decide that it is a big rubber trashcan on the sidewalk. You…	C—Go to #3 S & I—Go to #5 R—Go to #9 O—Go to #11
#2	You start walking and your cane hits something that makes a 'thunk' sound. You acknowledge this could be a problem. However, you've heard this before and conclude that it is a big rubber trashcan on the sidewalk. You…	C—Go to #4 S & I—Go to #6 R—Go to #10 O—Go to #12
#3	If you keep on walking, you will run into the object again. Go back to #1 and select a different option.		
#4	If you keep on walking, you will run into the object again. Go back to #2 and select a different option.		
#5	You decide you did not need to check cardinal directions and your nose tells you that it is trash day so it is probably a trashcan, like you thought. You decide to investigate/explore nearby so you swing the cane to the right of the trashcan and discover there is a fence. There is not enough room to walk past the trashcan that way. Then, you swing the cane to the left of the trashcan and you find the edge of the grass but there is enough room for you to walk between the grass and the trashcan so you do. Go to #7.		

#6	You decide you do not need to check cardinal directions and your nose tells you that it is trash day so it is probably a trashcan, like you thought. You decide to investigate/explore nearby so you swing the cane to the left of the trashcan and discover there is the brick wall. There is not enough room to walk past the trashcan that way. Then, you swing the cane to the right of the trashcan and you find the edge of the grass but there is enough room for you to walk between the grass and the trashcan so you do. Go to #8.	
#7	You walk around the trashcan and continue walking. Just when you hear a car pass you on your left, suddenly your cane drops down. You…	C—Go to #13 S & I—Go to #15 R—Go to #17 O—Go to #19
#8	You continue walking. You feel the sun on your face and you hear a car pass on your right. You feel the sidewalk slope down on the right so now you feel like you are walking on the side of a small hill. You…	C—Go to #14 S & I—Go to #16 R—Go to #18 O—Go to #20
#9	Are you sure you want to do retrace your steps?	Yes: Go to #21. No: Go to #1 and make a different selection.
#10	You turn around and find yourself at the entrance to the sidewalk that leads back to your house. You know this is your house because you smell your mother's perfume! You conclude she is watching you! You want to reassure her that you know your way so you say out loud. "Mom, I got this!" (just in case your suspicion is correct) and promptly turn around and walk back to the trashcan. Go to #6.	
#11	This is independent problem solving—you can figure this out yourself! You got this! Go back to #1 and select a different option.	
#12	This is independent problem solving—you can figure this out yourself! You got this! Besides, you are just outside your home. You are not lost. You are just a little disoriented. Go back to #2 and select a different option.	
#13	If you take a step off the curb, you might get hit by a car. That could possibly happen if you do not pay attention to the traffic and wait until it was safe to cross the street. If you get hit by a car, you will get hurt and everyone will be upset. Please remember, whenever your cane drips down unexpectantly, you need to STOP! Listen for sound cues to determine if you are at a street. Then, when the time is best, cross the street. Go back to #7 and select a different option.	
#14	You continue walking as straight as you can. You know this is a driveway to your neighbor's house. The slope down on the right leads directly into the street so you do not want to let the slope direct you that way, which is very easy to do. If you walk straight (which can be difficult to do on a slope, sometimes), you will be lined up with the sidewalk on the other side of the drive way. Go to #22.	
#15	You decide you do not need to check cardinal directions. You determine that you are at an intersection because you can hear automobiles passing by on your left. You…	C—Go to #23 S & I—Go to #24 R—Go to #17 O—Go to #19

#16	You decide you do not need to check cardinal directions because you know you are facing the east because you can feel the sun on your face so you investigate/explore nearby. Your cane swings to the right and to the left and all you can find is sidewalk. You listen and a car drives by on your right which confirms that you are still walking in the correct direction. Despite the slope, you try your hardest to walk straight. Go to #22	
#17	You suddenly realize the sound of the car was on your left! That means, you turned the wrong way when you left your house. So, you walk back toward the trashcan and pass it. Go to #2.	
#18	Are you sure you want to retrace your steps?	Yes: Go to #47 No: Go back to #8 and select a different option.
#19	You decide you to ponder other options. First, you think about the directions. You remember that you must exit your home and turn left, go two blocks, then turn left and Mickey's house is on the right. You have walked this with Mickey. So, you think you are on the right track. You decide that you do not need to call anyone to get direction clarification. Besides, you know you can do this so you conclude that you need to verify your current location. You swing your cane around to check out the area as a tactile way to verify your location. You determine that you are at the first intersection and you want to do this independently. When you swing your cane to the left, you feel the grass edge. You also find a grass edge on the right. You stand and listen. Two cars pass on your left and one car passes in front of you. Suddenly, you know what to do. You…	C—Go to #23 S & I—Go to #24 R—Go to #17
#20	You decide that you do not need to double check directions or verify your location because you know you are going the correct direction. Nor, do you think you need to call Mickey to get direction clarification. This is not a directional problem. Frankly, the terrain is a bit off… yes, that's it! You have walked on a driveway with your mobility instructor so you remember that you must simply work on walking straight! Didn't your mobility instructor tell you once, "the faster you walk, the straighter you will walk?" You conclude this is your neighbor's driveway, so you proceed forward. Go to #22.	
#21	You turn around and decide to check the width of the sidewalk. You find grass on your right and the fence on our left. You hear a car drive by on your right and realize that you actually turned the wrong way on the sidewalk and are now walking the correct direction. Go to #2.	
#22	You reach the other side of the small slope and you find grass. You move your cane from the left to the right while lowering the tip to the ground every few inches. Suddenly, you hear the sidewalk sound on your right so, you veer over to the right and position your body to where you think you are in the middle of the sidewalk then you use constant contact with the cane from the left and to the right. The cane finds grass on both sides. You conclude you are back on track because sidewalks usually are the same width. You proceed to walk east on the sidewalk. Go to #25.	

#23	You wait until it is safe to cross the street, then you cross. When you get to the other side of the intersection, your cane finds the curb and you step up—except there is no sidewalk! You suddenly realize that you went the wrong way when you left the house because you have made this mistake before. You could have realized this when you heard the car on your left instead of on your right. You turn around, wait until it is safe to cross the street. You cross the street, walk past the trashcan, and the sidewalk leading up to your house. Go to #2.	
#24	You decide to re-check cardinal directions. The sun comes up on the east and goes down on the west. Since it is morning, you note that you feel the heat of the sun on your back. This means that you must be walking west. You conclude that you must have turned right instead of left when you left your house so you walk back to the trashcan and pass it. Go to #2.	
#25	You pass another trashcan and have come to a second driveway. This time, after you walk the slope of the drive-way, instead of finding grass on the other side, you felt yourself level off and then your cane went under something and your body bumps into something hard. You…	C—Go to #26 S & I—Go to #27 R—Go to #28 O—Go to #29
#26	Seriously? You can't move forward. Your body hit something hard! Go back to #25 and select a different option.	
#27	You decide to investigate/explore nearby. A car passes on your right and you still feel the sun on your face so you know you are going the correct direction. But, wait, did that car sound closer? Slowly, you reach the back of your hand outward toward the object in front of you and you conclude it is the hood of a car. You surmise that you veered too much on the right because that has happened before. Your mobility instructor told you that it is too easy to let your body walk in the direction of the slope and if you are not careful, you can walk right into the street without even knowing it! Go to #35.	
#28	You turn around and walk away from the object. You feel like you are walking in a little valley and you don't remember walking in a little valley. Using constant contact, you conclude the sidewalk goes up slightly on both sides. After a few feet, your cane hits a cement wall on the right side. You raise your cane slightly and discover the cement wall is not very high at all! You hear a car pass on your left. You take a couple more steps and your cane tip slips under something and your body hits something hard! You…	C—Go to #38 S & I—Go to #39 R—Go to #33 O—Go to #39
#29	You decide you do not need to double check the directions because you feel the heat of the sun so you know you are still on the same path. For the same reasons, you do not feel you need to call anyone for direction clarification. You know you are near your home and you know you are not lost. You conclude this is a minor disorientation problem and you can figure this out yourself. Go back to #25 and make a different choice.	
#30	You can figure this out by thinking about the situation. No need to call anyone right now. You know the directions to Mickey's house, you are just a little disoriented right now. Stop and think about what you did. Go to #39.	
#31	Seriously? You can't move forward. Your body hit something hard! Go back to #25 and select a different option.	

#32	Since you are now on the edge of the street, you turn to the right, find the curb. You sweep your cane over the ground to make sure the area is clear of obstacles before stepping onto the grass. Arcing your cane wide, you walk away from the street and seek the sidewalk. When you hear the familiar sound of the cane hitting the sidewalk, you step into the sidewalk and turn right to face the sun and the east. You arc the cane to the right and left, finding grass on both sides. You conclude the girth is the correct distance to be a sidewalk. So, you proceed forward walking as straight as possible. Go to #37.	
#33	Are you sure you want to retrace your steps?	Yes: Go to #48 No: Go to #28
#34	You turn around and walk away from the object and walk back through the little cement valley. You hear a car pass on your right so you know you are going the right direction. After a few more steps, your cane hits a cement wall on your left. You raise your cane slightly and discover the cement wall is not very high at all, just like on the other side! This time, you conclude it is a curb and all of a sudden, you realize you can feel the sun on your face again. You take a few more steps and your cane tip slips under something but you stop yourself before your body hits whatever it is. Go to #35.	
#35	Since you realized you veered too much to the right when you crossed the driveway, you turn to the left and find the curb. Before you step up, you arc your cane across the top of the ground (grass) to be sure there is not a sign post. Since the area is clear, you step up. Arcing your cane wide, you walk away from the street to seek the sidewalk. When you hear the familiar sound of the cane hitting the cement, you step into the sidewalk and turn right to face the sun again. You arc the cane to the right and left, finding grass on both sides you conclude the girth is the correct distance to be a sidewalk. So, you proceed forward. Go to #36.	
#36	As you walk, you arc the cane to the right and left. About every other time, you touch the grass line on the left. When you find openings on the left, you pass by them because you conclude they must be sidewalks leading to houses. You walk around any trashcans you encounter and you don't have any problems crossing driveways. Then suddenly your cane drops down. You…	C—Go to #40 S & I—Go to #41 R—Go to #43 O—Go to #46
#37	You quickly find yourself back at the second driveway. You make a conscious effort to not let the slope guide you to the end of the driveway again. You successfully cross the driveway and find the sidewalk on the other side. Go to #36.	
#38	Seriously? You can't move forward. Your body hit something hard! Go back to #28 and select a different option.	
#39	You decide to re-check cardinal directions. You determine you are facing west but you need to be walking east. You thought about what you just did… you crossed a driveway, you bumped into something, then you turned around and followed a little valley. Now you have bumped into something else. You hear another car pass on your left. Was that car on your left? Yes, it was. You already know you can't move forward but you reach the back of your hand out to explore the object. Finding it, you turn your hand around and discover it feels like an automobile. You remember that you just heard a car on your left when traffic needs to be on your right. You conclude that you veered when you crossed the driveway and ended up at the base of the driveway so you now have two options. You can turn right and walk back to the sidewalk then you can turn right again and cross the driveway for a second time. Or, you can turn around and follow the little valley to the other side of the driveway, then turn left and walk to the sidewalk and then turn right to get back on track. You decide to: Turn right—Go to #32 R—Go to #34	

#40	*Oh no! You take a step and walk directly into the street!* Luckily, there was no car this time and you are okay. However, if you take another step, you might get hit by a car. That could possibly happen if you do not pay attention to the traffic and wait until it was safe to cross the street. If you get hit by a car, you will get hurt and everyone will be upset. Please remember, whenever your cane drops down unexpectantly, you need to *STOP!* Listen for sound cues to determine if you are at a street. Then, when the time is best, cross the street. Go back to #36 and select a different option.	
#41	You decide you do not need to check cardinal directions. You can feel the sun on your face. You determine that you are at an intersection because you hear a vehicle pass in front of you. You…	C—Go to #42 R—Go to #45 O—Go to #46
#42	You wait until it is safe to cross the street, then you cross. When you get to the other side of the intersection, your cane finds the curb. You quickly sweep your cane over the ground above the curb to make sure the area is clear of obstacles. Not finding any, you step off the street. Go to #44.	
#43	Are you sure you want to retrace your steps? You know you need to cross two streets and this is only the first one. Go back to #36 and select a different option.	
#44	After you step up, you sweep your cane over the ground. The metal tip of your cane informs you that the sidewalk is to your right. You veer in that direction and then you swing the cane to the right and left. You conclude that you are indeed back on the sidewalk because your cane helped determine the width of the sidewalk. You are happy that you have reached this block because it is a city park and there is a nice sidewalk that goes entirely around the block. You continue walking east at a nice pace because you are walking-in-step and you know that it is a nice straight sidewalk. As you walk, you hear children playing on the playground to your left and occasionally you hear a car on your right. Then, all of a sudden, your cane encounters something on the ground. You…	C—Go to #50 S & I—Go to #51 R—Go to #57 O—Go to #58
#45	Are you sure you want to retrace your steps? You are on the right track! Go back to #41 and select a different option.	
#46	You think about the directions and remember that you need to cross two streets. This is the first street in your directions. You take your cane and 'look around' by moving it around the ground the verify your current location. You determine that you are indeed at an intersection because you feel the curb in front of you. No need to call for assistance. You decide that you need to cross this street and proceed. Go to #42.	

KEY	
C—Continue walking forward	R—Retrace Steps
S & I—Stop and Investigate Check cardinal directions Use senses for cues (i.e., listen, feel sun & wind)	O—Other options Double check directions Verify current location Obtain Assistance

#47	You turn around and find that trashcan again. You decide that you are heading back to the house and you don't want to do that. So, you turn around again and go back to the sloping sidewalk. Go to #8 and select a different option.	
#48	You turn around and walk away from the object. You walk back through the little cement valley. You hear a car pass on your right so you know you are going the right direction. After a few more steps, your cane hits a cement wall on your left. You raise your cane slightly and discover the cement wall is not very high at all, just like on the other side! This time, you conclude it is a curb and suddenly you realize you can feel the sun on your face again. You take a few more steps and your cane tip slips under something but you stop yourself before your body hits whatever it is. This is the second time you have found this object. Now is time to really think about the situation. You decide to re-check cardinal directions. You determine you are facing east so that is correct. You think about what you just did… you crossed a driveway, you bumped into something, then you turned around and followed a little valley and bumped into something else so turned around and followed the little valley back. Now you are facing that object again. You hear another car pass on your right. Was that car on your right? Yes, it was. You already know you can't move forward but you reach the back of your hand out to explore the object. Finding the object, you turn your hand around and discover it feels like an automobile. You conclude that you veered when you crossed the driveway. Go to #35.	
#49	You stop and investigate with your cane and determine it must be another bike. You check to the left and the right and conclude that you can pass it on the left so you do. BOOM! You find yet another encounter in the sidewalk! You are beginning to get a little upset now. You…	C—Go to #54 S & I—Go to #52 R—Go to #71 O—Go to #61
#50	If you continue, you will walk on top of whatever is in the path of the sidewalk. Go back to #44 and select a different option.	
#51	You stop and investigate the area with your cane using the pencil-grip. Because of being able to hear the children on your left, you conclude that it must be a bike or a child's toy. You check to the left and the right of the item and you determine that there is space for you to go around to the right so you do that and continue on your way until your cane encounters another object. You…	C—Go to #53 S & I—Go to #49 R—Go to #60 O—Go to #59
#52	For the third time, you use the pencil-grip to investigate the sidewalk. You determine there is no path to the right or left of the object. You…	C—Go to #68 S & I—Go to #56 R—Go to #69 O—Go to #70
#53	If you continue, you will walk on top of whatever is in the path of the sidewalk. Go back to #51 and select a different option.	
#54	If you continue, you will walk on top of whatever is in the path of the sidewalk. Go back to #49 and select a different option.	

#55	As you continue forward, the footsteps seem to get louder. They sound like a woman because of the click-click-click of the shoes.
	As the footsteps approaches you, you say, "Hello."
	A lady says, "Hi. I saw that you were having some problems with the bikes on the sidewalk. I came over to see if you needed any help but by the time I got here, I saw that you got it all figured out!"
	You stop walking and reply, "I'm just fine. Thank you. I did wonder what those obstacles were, though. Thanks to telling me."
	The lady continues, "Well, now that I'm here, can I help you with anything?"
	You continue to walk east and answer, "No thanks, I'm okay."
	The lady says, "Okay. Have a great day. I'm going to get those kids to move their bikes off the sidewalk. Bye."
	You say "Bye" back to her and continue walking. Even though you think you are still walking east, you are not quite certain because this park has so many trees and you no longer feel the sun. Just when you were thinking about calling out to that lady, you hear a car on your right. Great! You think to yourself that you are still going the right way. Besides, you never turned. In the distance, you hear a car in front of you. You…
	     C—Go to #63
	     S & I—Go to #64	

#56	Using the pencil-grip, you investigate beyond the sidewalk with your cane and determine that you could still go around the object by walking on the grass to the left of the object. This means you will need to step off the sidewalk. You now are walking on the grass and shore-lining the object on the right. You do this by arcing your cane left and right and each time your cane goes to the right, it encounters the object. After about five arcs of the cane to the right, your cane swings further over to the right so you know you have reached the end of the object. You veer to the right, toward the sidewalk to see if it is clear to step back on. As you get onto the sidewalk, you check to make sure it was a sidewalk by arcing the cane to the right and left. After checking the width of the sidewalk, you continue on your way. You don't hear the children as loud as before. Rather, you hear the birds singing, an occasional car, and some footsteps coming toward you. You…	C—Go to #55 S & I—Go to #65 R—Go to #66 O—Go to #67
#57	If you turn around, you will be walking back to the intersection. Why do that when you know you are heading in the right direction? Go back to #44 and select a different option.	
#58	This is simply an obstacle in the path. No need to call for assistance. Go back to #44 and select a different option.	
#59	This is simply an obstacle in the path. No need to call for assistance. Go back to #51 and select a different option.	
#60	If you turn around, you will be walking back to that obstacle and then to the intersection. Why do that when you know you are heading in the right direction? Go back to #51 and select a different option.	
#61	This is simply an obstacle in the path. No need to call for assistance. Go back to #49 and select a different option.	

#62	If you turn around, you will be walking back through those two obstacles and then to the intersection. Why do that when you know you are heading in the right direction? Go back to #49 and select a different option.	
#63	Since you heard a car in front of you, you figure that you are approaching the next intersection. You slow down and begin looking for a drop-off by using the constant-contact technique with the pencil-grip. When your cane drops down, you…	C—Go to #73 S & I—Go to #74 R—Go to #75 O—Go to #76
#64	Since this car is in the distance, you decide that you need not come to a complete stop. So, you continue forward. After several steps, you hear another car in front of you. This time, the car sounds closer. Go to #63.	
#65	You tell yourself this sidewalk is open to everyone. No need to stop. Go to #55.	
#66	No need to turn around. This sidewalk is open to everyone. Go to #55.	
#67	No need to seek assistance. You just got through all those obstacles. You got this! Go to #55.	
#68	Seriously? You want to try to walk on top of these objects? If you do that, you might trip and fall. Please go back to #52 and select a different option.	
#69	Are you sure you want to turn around and walk all the way around the block instead of problem solving in order to continue walking on this sidewalk?	Yes—Go to #72 No—Go back to #52 and select a different option.
#70	You are frustrated because there are so many obstacles on the sidewalk. You just stand there wondering what you will do. You explore with the cane some more and come to the same conclusion that the sidewalk with blocked with something. You are thinking about calling out to the kids to come over and help you handle this encounter. Ahead of you, you hear the footsteps that seem to get louder. They sound like a woman because of the click-click-click of the shoes. As the footsteps approaches you, you say, "Hello." A lady says, "Hi. I saw that you were having some problems with the bikes on the sidewalk. I came over to see if you needed any help." You reply, "Oh, yes, I could use some help. There seems to be a lot of obstacles on the sidewalk." The lady says, "Well, now that I'm here, can I help you?" and suddenly, you feel a hand on your arm. You say, "Oh, how about I take your arm? Thanks." You take the lady's arm and follow her movements using your cane in a pencil-grip. Then, quickly, you are back on the sidewalk. The lady says, "The rest of the sidewalk is clear. But, is there anything else I can help you with?" You let go of the lady's arm and say, "No, thank you. I'm fine now." The lady says, "Okay. Have a great day. I'm going to get those kids to move their bikes off the sidewalk. Bye." You say "Bye" and "Have a great day, too." and continue walking down the sidewalk. Even though you think you are still walking east, you are not quite certain because this park has so many trees and you no longer feel the sun. Just when you were thinking about calling out to that lady, you hear a car on your right. Great! You think to yourself that you are still on the right path. Besides, you never turned. Then, in the distance, you hear a car in front of you. You… C—Go to #63 S & I—Go to #64	

KEY	
C—Continue walking forward	R—Retrace Steps
S & I—Stop and Investigate **Check cardinal directions** **Use senses for cues (i.e., listen, feel sun &** **wind)**	O—Other options Double check directions Verify current location Obtain Assistance

#71	You are upset. This is true, but you tell yourself that you have gone too far to turn around now… Go back to #49 and select another option.	
#72	You turn around and make your way through the obstacles on the sidewalk. Although you are dreading walking around the entire block, you tell yourself that this is an alternative technique when the intended path is inaccessible. You walk west and shoreline on the right. When you find an opening on the right, you turn right. Then, you walk north. After several feet, you begin to shoreline on the right. When you find an opening, you turn right and then walk east. As you walk east, the sound of the children become louder. Then suddenly, the sidewalk ends and you find yourself walking on something soft and squishy. You…	C—Go to #79 S & I—Go to #80 R—Go to #81 O—Go to #82
#73	Remember, before you continue forward, you need to stop! This is a street and you need to make sure it is safe to cross before you step off the curb. Go to #74	
#74	You realize you have come to the intersection. You listen to determine if there is any traffic. You hear a car on your right and it continues without turning. You hear another car on your left and it stops. You think maybe it would be okay to cross but then the car moves on. Then, you remember this intersection has one of those crossing buttons. You turn left and using your cane, you arc your cane above the grass to look for the pole with the crossing button. Ting. You found the pole with the button. You walk to it, find the button and push it. Quickly, you return to the curb and listen for the time to cross. Great. You think to yourself. Now there is no traffic. Hearing none, you decide it is okay to cross the street. Go to #77.	
#75	You are almost to Mickey's house. You just need to cross this street, turn left and Mickey's house is the third one on the right. You got this! Go to #74.	
#76	You know how to cross a residential street. You can do this without any assistant. Go to #74.	
#77	You lower your cane and, listening again, you hear nothing, so you proceed across the street. As you walk, you feel the camber, which is the little hill in the road to help drain rain water off. You go up slightly and then you feel yourself go down a little. Then, you feel yourself go up a little ramp with bumps. When you get to the top of the little ramp, you determine you went up a truncated dome, which most people call a wheelchair ramp. You are pleased with yourself for a straight crossing. You… Continue straight—Go to #84	Turn right—Go to #90 Turn left—Go to #86

#78	Now, you hear the traffic on your left! You walk several feet and then begin to shoreline on the right. When you find an opening on the right, you turn right and conclude you are walking east. You walk several feet and then begin to shoreline on the right again. When you find an opening on the right, you turn right and surmise that you are walking south. You walk several feet before you begin to shoreline on the left. You find an opening on the left so you turn left. Suddenly, you hear a car right in front of you. Go to #63.	
#79	You continue walking and then your cane hits something that makes a tink sound. You hear children playing all around you. You reach your hand forward and feel a metal pole. Exploring some more, you find the slide. Oops! You conclude you are in the playground. You…	Stop and play a while—Go to #83 R—Go to #81
#80	You stop and listen. The children are playing all around you. You determine that you have reached the playground. You…	C—Go to #79 R—Go to #81
#81	You turn around and follow the path back to the main sidewalk and turn right. Go to #78.	
#82	You feel very confused. You thought you could walk around the block but how did you end up in the playground? You decide that maybe you need help but you do not want to ask a child for help. So, you explore some more and decide you do not want to walk forward because that would take you off the sidewalk and doing that is like walking in no-man-land. You turn around and follow the path back to the main sidewalk and turn right. Go to #78.	
#83	After playing for a while, you get hot and then you remember you were supposed to be going to Mickey's house. You find the path back to the main sidewalk and turn right. Go to #78	
#84	Shore-lining on your right, you continue forward and walk for a long time before you come to an opening. As you walk across the opening, you notice there is a slope descending down on the right. At that same time, you hear a car on your right. You…	C—Go to #87 S & I—Go to #88 R—Go to #89
#85	It is not always a good idea to turn around in an open area because that can cause a person to really get disoriented. Go back to #87 and make a different choice.	
#86	You remember that Mickey's home is the third house on your right. So, as you walk, your cane follows the edge of the sidewalk on the right side. You count three large openings on the right side. You conclude they are driveways. At the third opening, you…	C—Go to #96 S & I—Go to #97 R—Go to #98 O—Go to #99
#87	You continue to cross the opening and decide it is a driveway. But, this feels like the driveways on your block and then it dawns on you that there was traffic on your right. You begin to think something is wrong. You…	C—Go to #92 S & I—Go to #93 R—Go to #85
#88	After some thought, you realize you heard traffic on your right and it was supposed to be on your left because you are looking for a house on your right. You decide you need to turn around. Go to #89.	
#89	You decide that you need to turn around because the traffic is on your right where the houses are supposed to be. You conclude that you walked straight instead of turning north after crossing the street. You turn around and walk back to the intersection where you…	Turn left—Go to #90 Turn Right—Go to #86

#90	Immediately you feel yourself descend. You determine that you are standing on a truncated dome (i.e., wheelchair ramp). You feel the sun on your left cheek so that means you are facing the south. You determine that you are facing the opposite direction and you definitely don't want to cross the street. You… Turn left—Go to #94 Turn 90 degrees—Go to #91 Turn right—Go to #95
#91	You turn around and skip the sidewalk on your left and right. You continue walking north. Go to #86.
#92	You continue to the next driveway. While doing so, you hear more traffic on your right. Then suddenly it dawns on you that if you hear traffic on your right; there are no houses on your right! You feel the sun on your face and conclude that you are walking east when you need to be walking north. Go to #89.
#93	You walk to the other side of the driveway because you think it is never a good idea to stop in the middle of a driveway. You do some problem-solving by taking your cane and checking the area to make sure you are on the next sidewalk. You listen for several seconds and determine that you are facing the east. You remember that you are supposed to be going north to Mickey's house. You realize you must have missed a turn, but where? You know for sure where you were when you crossed the street. Hmm, you think that after you cross the street, you were supposed to turn north. Apparently, you did not turn north. So, you decide you need to retrace your steps and go back to the intersection. You turn around and walk back to the intersection where you… Turn left—Go to #90 Turn Right—Go to #86
#94	Now, you feel the sun on your face. You…	Turn left—Go to #91 Turn right—Go back to #90
#95	You no longer feel the sun on your left cheek. You hear some traffic on your left side so you decide that you are going in the correct direction because that means houses will be on your right. But then you realize that you are still in the wheelchair ramp. You turn around until you feel the sun on your right cheek. Now you know you are walking north. Go to #86.
#96	You continue past the driveway and come up to the sidewalk on the other side. You turn right and shoreline the edge of the driveway on your left. When you find an opening, you turn left and know you're almost there. You follow the sidewalk leading up to the front door. Go to #100
#97	You take a second to remember which side of the driveway has the sidewalk leading to the house. Then, you remember that when you arrive by car, you always get out of the car and go around to the driver's side of the car to find the sidewalk leading up to the house. So, you decide you need to continue to the other side of the driveway. Go to #96.
#98	You are pretty sure that you counted correctly and this is definitely the third driveway. However, you just want to double check. So, you turn around and use your cane to shoreline the left side of the sidewalk as you walk back to the corner. You count two driveways before you find another sidewalk. Great, you did count correctly. At the corner, you turn around and shoreline the right side to get right back to this exact spot. Go back to #86 and select another option.

#99	You are pretty sure that you are near Mickey's house but not exactly sure. On the one hand, you think you would like to call Mickey to let him know you are out front and that maybe he will come out and give you a sound clue as to where to go. On the other hand, you really want to get to Mickey's house totally independent. Go to #98.
#100	You are now at the door, so you ring the doorbell. Soon you hear someone coming to the door and Mickey answers the door! Congratulations! You made it to Mickey's house!!! You feel so good that you did this independently! You want to jump up and down and get a high-five from Mickey but you want to act cool so you don't say anything. Perhaps another day you will tell him about this O&M encounter.

THE END

Dr. Merry-Noel Chamberlain with two students, Oliver and Noah, at the zoo on a mobility lesson.

NOTES

_____

_____

_____

_____

_____

_____

_____

PART III

CHAPTER 15

THE TRUE STORY OF OWIN M.

By Dr. Merry-Noel Chamberlain, NOMC, TVI
Illustrated by: Ashley Roth

Owin M. is a character who happens to be blind and wishes to educate the reader in the skills necessary to travel independently using the long white cane.

The ABCs of Structured Discovery Cane Travel for Children, pages 167–198.

TO

Martin, Royene and Ashleah
for standing by me.

Heidi Unkrich
for countless editing hours.

The National Federation of the Blind
and The National Blindness Professional Certification Board
for opening the doors of opportunity for blind individuals everywhere.

and

The National Organization of Parents of Blind Children* (NOPBC)
for providing education and support to all.

ACKNOWLEDGEMENTS

Roxanne Bullard, NOMC (Chapter 8)

And

All my students, who have been "my" teachers

INTRODUCTION

Owin M. is a character that happens to be blind and wishes to educate the reader in the skills necessary in order to travel independently using the long white cane. It is intended for individuals of all ages with visual impairments who want to learn more about Orientation and Mobility (O&M). My desire is that this book will capture the reader's interest in learning techniques that will enhance their O&M skills. The True Story of Owin M. is not only to educate the cane user but also to provide information to parents, guardians, classroom teachers, and anyone else interested in learning more about O&M so they can offer support and guidance to those with visual impairments.

CHAPTER 1
THE TRUE STORY OF OWIN M.

You may have heard of <u>Orientation and Mobility</u>. A lot of people call that O&M for short. My name sounds like O&M but it's spelled capital O-w-i-n, space, capital M, period. Orientation and Mobility are big words that basically mean knowing where you are and knowing how to get from one place to another. I want to tell you all about how I move around my neighborhood and get to school using my long white cane. Would you like to know how I do it? That's great because I want to tell you.

Like most of you, when I was little I held my mom or dad's hand. It makes parents feel good when you hold their hand. But now that I'm bigger, I go places by myself and when I do that, I use my long white cane. My cane is my very own tool. A tool is something people use to do a job. My dad uses a hammer for putting nails in wood. My mom uses a spoon for scooping out icing from a bowl. A hammer and a spoon are tools. My long white cane is my tool for getting from one place to another.

Sometimes my friends, like you, wonder about how and when I use my cane, so I thought I'd tell you all about how I use my cane in just one day. Well, most every morning I use my cane to walk to school. But along the way, I usually stop by Ronald's house. He has been my best friend since we were in preschool. That's a long, long time! How about coming with me today and I'll show you how I use my long white cane?

The first thing I do before I leave my house is grab my cane from the corner next to the front door. When I hold my cane in front of me, it stands almost as tall as my nose. My cane needs to be long so that it gives me plenty of time to stop if I need to. If I had a short cane, I might not stop in time, and I might bump into something or someone. Plus, the longer cane allows me to walk faster, and that's way cool.

From my front door, I walk down the sidewalk that leads to the street in front of my house and when my cane touches the front gate, I stop. I open the gate, turn left, and walk down the sidewalk holding my cane in front of me. When I walk, I hold the cane outward in front of my tummy, near my bellybutton, and point the end of the cane outward in the direction I am walking. I hold it like this to find things ahead of me so I don't trip on them. I move the tip of the cane back and forth, left and right, just as wide as my shoulders so it will clear the way for my feet to go. Sometimes kids leave bikes and things on the sidewalk or adults leave the trash out to be picked up, but that is okay because I just find stuff with my cane, and I easily walk around whatever it is.

When my cane tip moves to the right side of my body, my left foot is forward, and when my cane tip moves to the left side of my body, my right foot is forward. I call this kick-the-cane game, but it is really called <u>walking-in-step</u>. It was a little hard for me to learn at first, but now that I have the hang of it, it feels sort of like dancing.

When I use my cane to follow something, like the edge of the sidewalk, it is called <u>shore-lining</u>. It is similar to walking along the beach and following the edge of the ocean waves. I did this last summer with my mom and dad. We had a great time as we walked along the shore with the water rushing up to greet us. I could feel the water splashing against my feet and then quietly returning to the ocean. I remember my toes sinking deep into the sand, and I could hear the ocean better out of one ear than the other.

As I walk to Ronald's house, I feel the edge of the grass along the sidewalk with my cane just as when I walk along the shore. Unlike the ocean, the grass is quiet so most every time when my cane tip goes to the left, it touches the grass and the sound is a little different. That lets me know I'm still on the sidewalk. Shore-lining helps me as I count four driveways and three sidewalks to get to Ronald's house. I need to arc my cane to the left to touch the grass to find the sidewalks and the driveways. When I move my cane to the left and the grass is gone, then it is either a driveway or a sidewalk. It takes longer to cross a driveway than a sidewalk; therefore, I can tell the difference because the grass is missing a few more steps for a driveway than a sidewalk. Also, the driveways sometimes have a little slope towards the street which makes me feel as though I'm walking sideways on a small hill.

When I find the fourth sidewalk, I turn left and follow that sidewalk right up to the first step leading me to the porch. My cane lets me know when I reach the steps because it stops. (If my cane were shorter, I might trip on the stairs!) Then I hold the cane up and down, lift it just a little and push it forward a tiny bit. When I step up, my cane tip moves forward and like magic, it finds the next step. Bam! I do this again and poof, there is another step. When I get to the last step, my cane swings forward and that tells me there are no more steps. That is good to know because before I used a cane, I never knew when I was at the top step, and sometimes I ended up taking an imaginary step into nowhere land. It's kind of embarrassing actually. Ronald told me that I need to count the stairs but if I did that, I would need to remember so many numbers! I sure don't want to have to memorize numbers! I already have to memorize my spelling words each week!

Ronald is usually late, so I wait on the porch swing. I sure like the way the breeze dances across my face as I swing and listen to the crows squawking. It reminds me of when I was little and I used to believe that the crows were counting the cars for me. If the crow said, "Caw, Caw, Caw," that meant there were three cars parked nearby. I know that's not true now. I laugh out loud to myself and hope that no one heard me.

When Ronald shows up, we run to school so we will not be late. We run so fast that sometimes my foot slips off the sidewalk, so I use my cane to help me stay on the sidewalk. When I run, I try not to shore-line because that would slow me down. I tap my cane from side to side; I can hear the same sound on my right and left that my cane makes. But when I veer a little, my cane lets me know because the tap isn't loud on the grass. I just step quickly back onto the sidewalk and keep on running, trying to stay in the middle of the sidewalk—not touching the edge.

Pretty soon we stop running because we are coming to a street we need to cross. Crossing streets took a little practice until I learned how to do it safely, but now I'm a pro. I try to listen ahead of where I am walking. I know when I am approaching the intersection because I hear the traffic. When my cane lowers, I know I have reached the curb, so I stop walking and I wait. I hold my cane straight up and down and listen to the traffic. I keep the cane up and down until I know when it is safe to cross the street. Also, by keeping the cane up and down, I'm letting the drivers know that I am just waiting, and I am not ready to cross the street. When I hear the traffic move in front of my face, I know it is NOT a good time to cross the street. But when I hear the traffic on the right side of my head, I know it is safe to cross the street in front of me. I keep the sound of the traffic on my right side when I walk to school and on my left side when I walk home from school. It is like shore-lining the sound of the traffic.

When we get to the school, I walk up several stairs to the front door of the building. Sometimes I hear people move out of my way as I approach them. They really don't need to do that because my cane will find them, and I can easily walk around them. Plus, I can hear some of them talking or laughing which is a signal for me to move around them.

Inside the school building, Ronald goes down the right hallway. I take several steps down the left hallway, and then I shore-line the wall on the right to look for my classroom door. The tip of my cane sounds a bit hollow when it hits a closed door, and it sounds solid when it hits the wall. Ting, ting. There's the water fountain. I know my classroom is two doors from here. The first door is closed, and then at the next door,

my cane swings farther to the right as if pointing the way for me to go. That means the door is open, so I walk right in.

I walk directly to my desk by pulling my cane tip close to me so that it doesn't get caught under desks or chairs. This is called the <u>pencil grip</u>. I hold my cane like it is a giant pencil, and I am writing in the sand at the beach with a stick. At my desk, I lay my cane on the floor next to me and sit down. I keep it beside me so that I always know where it is, and I can get it quickly whenever I need it. You know how much teachers like to have fire drills? Well, when that happens, I just grab my cane and go outside—just like my classmates.

My cane is my tool all day. I use it in the lunch line by placing the tip of my cane next to the heel of the person in front of me. I do have the tip raised just a tad, and I place a tiny pit of pressure towards the shoe of the person in front of me. When that person steps forward, my cane swings slightly so I know I can step forward, too. Most of my classmates are used to my cane touching their shoe. But at first, I needed to explain to them why my cane was touching them. They didn't mind at all! Sometimes I don't need to put my cane beside their shoe because I can hear them talking and hear their voices move away from me.

One of the cafeteria staff used to help me with my tray at lunch. But now I can carry my own tray and use my cane at the same time—all by myself! I just hold my cup with my left pointy finger and thumb. I use my other fingers of my left hand to carry the tray and press the tray against my body. My right hand is free to use my cane to find a seat. I try to sit with Ronald because he is so funny. Usually I follow my classmates to the table, and Ronald calls out to me so I know where he is by following the sound of his voice.

At recess, I put my cane on the ground near the monkey bars and climb on up. The other guys and I hang up there until the girls come, and then we play tag with them for a while. Then we go to the slide where there is a bridge, and we pretend we are pirates in the deep blue sea.

In P.E. class, I use my cane for almost all of the activities. I like it when we get to jump on the trampoline because it is so fun! Of course, I don't use my cane on the trampoline! I leave it nearby, but I always know where it is so I can get it quickly when I need it.

After school, I walk home by myself because Ronald has to go to his dad's house. I don't mind walking by myself. It gives me a chance to think about my school day. When I get home, I put my cane back in the corner next to the front door because I don't need it in my house. At home I know where things are so I feel comfortable going around without it. But whenever I leave my house, I grab my cane.

Later when we go out for dinner, I snuggle my cane between the front seat and the door in the car. When I get taller, I will get a longer cane. My cane needs to always be taller than the floor to my chin. When it is longer, my cane will reach all the way to my mom's feet in the front of the car. I can't wait!

A restaurant can be crowded so sometimes my mom will ask me if I want to go <u>human guide</u>. That is when I hold on to her elbow as she follows the hostess to our table. When she moves to the right, I move to the right, too. When she moves to the left, I move to the left, too. When she goes up or down stairs, I do the same. It's like follow the leader, and she's the leader! It's okay to use the human guide method when there is a big crowd, when the place we're going has a lot of twists and turns, or if we are in a hurry to get someplace like an emergency. If I were going human guide with someone and that someone took my arm to lead me around, then I would not be in control—they would. It's a lot better for me be independent by holding on to my human guide's arm because then I can let go quickly if I ever do not feel comfortable or safe. Of course, holding my mom's hand is not the same as going human guide. I hold her hand sometimes because I know she loves that. When I hold her hand or go human guide, I still use my cane to make sure I don't bump into doorways or miss steps. It is not her responsibility to watch over me as I walk. I'm old enough to do that myself.

When we get to our table, I lay my cane under my chair making sure not to let it stick out in the aisle. Sometimes in restaurants, I prop my cane against the wall or corner behind me or lay along the wall or on the floor beside me like at school. There are many places to store a cane just so long as it is out of the way so no one can trip over it.

My long white cane is my tool but it does not only help me travel from one place to another. It also symbolizes to other people (like the waitress) that I can't see very well. Whenever I meet someone new, I don't have to tell them that I can't see, my cane tells them that for me.

Well, now you have it, my story—the true story—of Owin M. The long white cane is my tool for life! Is your cane your tool, too?

CHAPTER 2
OWIN M. GOES TO CAMP

Hi! It's me Owin M. and guess what? Today I'm going to camp for the weekend! I'm so excited, but I'm a little nervous, too. Have you ever been to camp? Would you like to come to camp with me? That's great!

I packed my suitcase last night, so I'm all set to go. Oh, I can't forget my tool. My tool? Yes, my tool is my long white cane. I use my cane to help me get around, and I'm going to need it at camp! When I was younger, I sometimes forgot to take my cane with me when I left the house, but I now know that the cane is part of me. The cane is my eyes to the world—the extension of my arm to touch my surroundings. My cane allows me to be independent. I bet you are wondering what the word independent means. Well, it means being able to do something without help from others.

Some people think I need to take a folding or telescoping cane rather than my long, white, rigid cane to camp because it's easier to put away when I don't need it. But I use my long, white, rigid cane all the time except when I go tandem bike riding or horseback riding. All the connections in the folding cane can make it harder to feel the uneven bumps in the paths or cracks in the sidewalk. To be able to find those cracks is important so I don't trip and fall. A telescoping cane is a cane that collapses like an antenna. Gosh, when I had a telescoping cane it kept shrinking when it hit a crack so I had to stop several times to fix it along the way. For me to get to where I was going took forever because I had to stop so many times to fix my cane! I prefer a long, rigid cane as my tool because it does not collapse. I know I will be doing a lot of hiking and rocks will be along the trail for my cane to find. To always have a dependable cane with you at all times is very important.

I just heard Mom calling. Let's go, or we'll be late! I'll pull my suitcase to the van. Pulling a suitcase behind you is pretty easy. I can pull the suitcase with one hand and still use my cane in the other. I'll sit behind the driver today. My cane can easily slide between the door and the driver's seat. My dad is going to take us to where we'll meet the bus.

Oh, great! The bus is coming. Do you hear it approaching? The first step onto the bus may be a little high, so I use my cane to check how high I need to step up. I can move my cane over to the side of the first step until it stops at the edge, and then I can find the handrail, grab it, and pull myself up. I then hold my cane up and down in front of me to help me find the next step. Sometimes the steps turn to the left at an angle, so I feel the steps carefully with my cane.

On the bus I need to find an empty seat. Want to see how I do that? Okay! As I walk down the aisle of seats, I hold my cane in a <u>pencil grip</u> and sweep it back and forth to make sure nothing is on the floor of the bus. If I hear voices or people shifting as I pass by each seat, I know those seats are not empty. When I think there might be an empty seat, I'll ask if the seat is free. If I no one replies, I slide my cane between the seats to see if it touches anyone's knees. If my cane does not stop, then I have a pretty good idea that the seat is empty. But just to make sure, I check the seat with the back of my hand to confirm nothing or nobody is there. Once I've determined the seat is empty, I can sit down. Look! Here is a seat for both of us! I'll sit by the window and slide my cane between the seat and the window where it'll be safe until I need it again. I have apples in my bag. Do you want one?

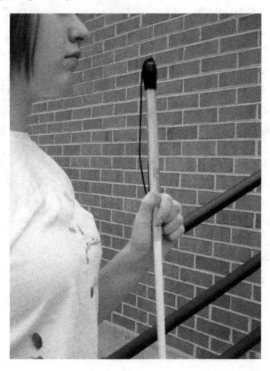

Wow! Don't you love this camp? It looks like we'll be in the same cabin! Do you like the top bunk or the bottom? It doesn't matter to me. I'll just prop my cane next to the bed. I could lay it on the floor, but it could get kicked under the bed by accident, so I won't do that. I heard that we need to unpack quickly because we are supposed to meet at the camp circle as soon as possible. The camp counselor told me we walked by the camp circle on the way here. This is the first time I've gone to this camp, so I don't know anyone but you. I may need to have someone to show me around. But I heard that it's the first time for most everyone, so we all need to be shown around. Right?

I'm ready to go to the camp circle, are you? There sure are a lot of campers here, so I'll hold my cane in the pencil grip around the camp circle to be respectful of others. The long white cane is a symbol of independence and just by using it I am proud because I am independent. I am able to walk to the camp circle by myself but let's walk there together.

I heard that we're going on a hike tomorrow morning and swimming at the pool in the afternoon. There is also a lake here that we will take paddleboats on. I can't wait!

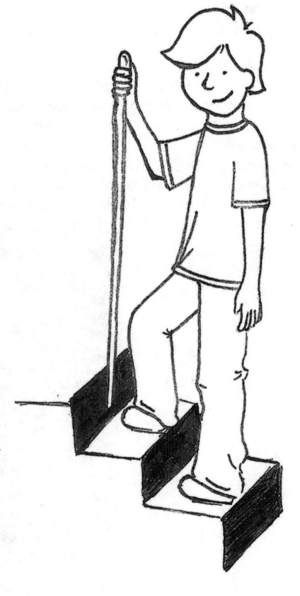

Some campers wonder about my long white cane. They think I can't go on the hike because I can't see. I just tell them that some people might think that it is hard to go on a hike without sight. But my cane helps me go wherever I want to go because I know how to use it. When I go on a hike, I stay on the main path. If I can't move my cane freely, it may be stuck in tall grass, weeds, branches, or twigs. That means that I have veered off the path a little bit, so I will need to correct my body by moving back towards the path. It's easy-peasy-lemon-squeezy.

When I am on the hiking trail and I feel the path is clear, I will extend my cane outward and walk faster, but when the ground is uneven, I use the pencil grip and take smaller steps in order to pay more attention. It is important to be safe on a hike. I'm taking my Braille compass with me. It is tactual so I can feel the cardinal directions. When we are in the woods, it may be hard to feel the direction of the sun.

At the pool tomorrow, I'll take my cane with me, too. Sometimes I go human guide to the edge of the pool and leave my cane with my towel. But that depends on how many people are there. If not a lot of people are at the pool, I will take my cane with me to the edge of the pool and lay it down by the stairs so I can get it easily when I get out of the pool. What? Take the cane in the pool? No, I don't do that!

Super, we made it to the camp circle. Let's find a couple of seats together. Ok?

CHAPTER 3
TRUE/FALSE QUIZ FOR OWIN M.

1. A cane is a tool for people who are blind or visually impaired to use to do a job.

    TRUE   FALSE

2. A cane needs to be about as tall as the floor to one's nose.

    TRUE   FALSE

3. When the cane tip is moved from the right to the left as wide as one's shoulder, it is called arcing the cane.

    TRUE   FALSE

4. Kick-the-cane game and walk-in-step does not mean the same thing

    TRUE   FALSE

5. When Owin M. uses his cane to follow something, like the edge of the sidewalk, it is called "walking along the shore."

    TRUE   FALSE

6. When Owin M. was a little boy, he thought that if the crows made the sound, "Caw, caw, caw," that meant there were three cars parked nearby.

    TRUE   FALSE

7. In Orientation and Mobility, the pencil grip is used so that the cane does not get caught under desks or chairs.

    TRUE   FALSE

8. Owin M. can lay his cane on the floor beside him so that he can get it quickly whenever he needs it.

    TRUE   FALSE

9. A cane cannot be stored against the wall or propped in the corner.

    TRUE   FALSE

10. The long white cane symbolizes that the user can't see very well or not at all.

    TRUE   FALSE

11. The cane is an extension of one's arm to touch surroundings.

    TRUE FALSE

12. The cane allows an individual who is blind or has low vision to be independent.

    TRUE FALSE

13. All the connections in a folding cane can make it easier to feel the uneven bumps in the paths or cracks in the sidewalk.

    TRUE FALSE

14. It is important to have a dependable cane at all times.

    TRUE FALSE

Answers Provided by Owin M.

1. True. My cane is my very own tool. A tool is something that people use to do a job. (Chapter 1)

2. True. When I hold my cane in front of me, it almost stands as tall as my nose. My cane needs to be long so that it gives me plenty of time to stop if I need to. If my cane were short, I might not stop in time, and I might bump into something or someone. (Chapter 1)

3. True. When I move the cane tip as wide as my shoulders I am making an arc with my cane. (Chapter 1)

4. False. When my cane tip moves to the right side of my body, my left foot is forward, and when my cane moves to the left side of my body, my right foot is forward. I call this kick-the-cane game but it is really called, walking-in-step. It was a little hard for me to learn at first, but now that I have the hang of it, it feels sort of like dancing. (Chapter 1)

5. False. When I use my cane to follow something, like the edge of the sidewalk, it is called shore-lining. It is similar to walking along the beach and following the edge of the ocean waves. (Chapter 1)

6. True. Yes, when I was a little boy, I really thought the crows counted the cars. If the crows made the sounds, "Caw, caw, caw," that meant there were three cars parked nearby. I know that's not true now. (Chapter 1)

7. True. I walk right to my desk by pulling my cane up close to me so that it doesn't get caught under desks or chairs. This is called the pencil grip. I hold my cane like it is a giant pencil, and it is as though I am writing in the sand at the beach with a stick. (Chapter 1)

8. True. At my desk, I lay my cane on the floor next to me and sit down. I keep it beside me so that I always know where it is, and I can get it quickly whenever I need it. (Chapter 1)

9. False. I can lay my cane under my chair making sure not to let it stick out in the aisle. Sometimes in restaurants, I lay my cane against the wall behind me or beside me, or I prop it in the corner. (Chapter 1)

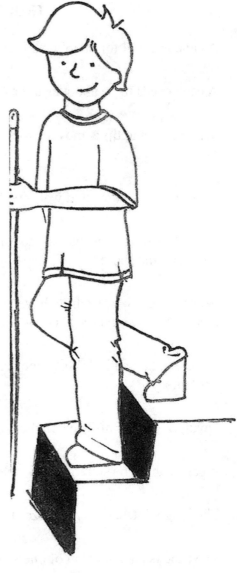

10. True. My long white cane is my tool, but it does not only help me travel from one place to another. It also symbolizes to other people (like the waitress) that I can't see. (Chapter 1) Whenever I meet someone I don't know, I don't have to tell them that I can't see, my cane tells them that for me.

11. True. The cane is my eyes to the world, the extension of my arm to touch my surroundings. It allows me to be independent. (Chapter 2)

12. True. I bet you are wondering what the word independent means. Well, it means being able to do something without help from others. (Chapter 2)

13. False. All the connections in the folding cane can make it harder to feel the uneven bumps in the paths or cracks in the sidewalk. (Chapter 2)

14. True. (Chapter 2)

CHAPTER 4
OWIN M. AT GRANDMA'S HOUSE

I'm so happy my grandma said you could come with me today. We're going to have a lot of fun at her house. My dad is going to drop us off on his way to work this morning. He's in the car now, so we'd better head for the garage. I need to grab my cane first. Do you have yours? Great! We need to take it with us everywhere we go even if we are going someplace that we've been before and feel comfortable. But you've never been to my grandma's house before.

Oops! Did you hear that? That's my dad honking the horn. We'd better hurry.

Where do I store the cane in the car? I slide it between the seat and the door. It will be safe there and will be out of the way of people's feet. Sure, both canes can be stored in the same side of the car, but you can put yours on your side, and I can put mine on my side. "Dad, here comes my cane."

Gosh, that was a quick ride. We're here already. Grandma will be happy to see us. I bet she'll have cookies fresh from the oven waiting for us. Grab your cane. Let's go!

That's nice that you thanked my dad for the ride. I try to remember to do that, but sometimes I forget.

There is a sidewalk on the side of the driveway that leads to the front door. I bet you can find it with your cane. It's near the front of the car on the left side. Great! You found it! The sidewalk has a little curve in it but we can just shore-line the edge and it'll lead us right up to the front steps. I hear the screen door opening right now! Mmm, I smell cookies!

I know my grandma's house just like I know my own house, so I don't use a cane here. But you might want to since this is your first time here. Let me show you to the kitchen; it's straight ahead. You can prop your cane in the corner by the kitchen table while we have our cookies. After we eat, let's go in the backyard to play in the tree house.

When I go in the backyard, I take my cane with me because Grandpa is always working on one project or another and leaves stuff on the ground. The backyard has a pond with a path around it. The tree house is on the other side. So, let's go. Wait! I need my cane. No, we don't need the canes *in* the tree house, but we do need them to get *to* the tree house.

I'm glad we have our canes to find our way through this stone path that Grandpa made around the pond. We can use the canes to distinguish between the stepping stones and those river rocks. Let's just leave our canes on the ground near the wooden ladder to the tree house. They will be fine there.

Grandma says after we are done playing here, she has a *descriptive video* that she checked out from the library if we want to watch it. Oh, what is a descriptive video? Well, a descriptive video has a narrator who tells us what is happening in the story when no one is talking. Later my cousins are coming over. You'll like them. When there are so many people here, I will keep my cane with me. Some of my cousins are little and tend to leave toys all over the place. I would hate to trip over them or my little cousins for that matter. It's safer for me to have my cane with me than to leave it in the corner when there are lots of people or little children around. Our canes can't help us if they aren't being used. Right?

POP QUIZ

1. When I go to the pool, I can either go human guide from my towel to the pool or use my cane to walk independently to the pool and leave my cane by the edge of the pool.

    TRUE   FALSE

2. A descriptive video is having a narrator who tells us what is happening in the story when no one is talking..

    TRUE   FALSE

3. It is safer for me to leave my cane in the corner when there are lots of people or little children around. .

    TRUE   FALSE

4. Our canes can't help us if they aren't being used..

    TRUE   FALSE

Answers by Owin M:

1. True. Sometimes I go human guide to the edge of the pool and leave my cane with my towel. But that depends on how many people are there. If not a lot of people are at the pool, I will take my cane with me to the edge of the pool and lay it down by the stairs so I can get it easily when I get out of the pool. (Chapter 2)

2. True. A descriptive video has a narrator who tells us what is happening in the story when no one is talking. (Chapter 4)

3. False. It is more important than ever to use your cane when there are a lot of people around and small children. (Chapter 4)

4. True. If the cane is propped in the corner, it isn't being used. Just like if the car is parked in the driveway, it is not being used. (Chapter 4)

CHAPTER 5
OWIN M. AT THE MALL

Our Friend, Sara, is sure going to be happy to see us at her birthday party. At first, I thought I couldn't go because my dad had to work and I wouldn't be able to get a ride there, but then my mom suggested I take the city bus and my dad said it was okay. Mom says it is always fun to have lots of people at a birthday party—that means more presents for the birthday person.

When we get to the mall, the bus will drop us off at the main entrance. Are you ready? Let's go.

Okay, let's find the front door to the mall. I hear some people walking over to my left. I've been to the mall before, so I remember that the main entrance is to the left of the bus stop. If I didn't remember that, I would simply ask the bus driver if he could direct me to the main entrance. So, let's go left. There—did you hear that? The automatic door opened. Come on. The sound came from over here.

Yes, this is the correct entrance. I hear the music from the merry-go-round on my right. We have to walk through the Food Court, through the mall to the department store that we also need to walk through to get outside so we can walk to the pizza place where the party is going to be held. I know that sounds like a lot, but we can do it because we have our long white canes. Remember, the cane is our tool!

It's pretty easy to walk through the Food Court because the textures on the floor change around the tables and up close to each of the food vendors. Vendors? Oh, that is all the different types of food choices offered at the Food Court. I <u>glide</u> my cane across the floor here instead of tapping the cane. The main walkway through the Food Court is smooth. The texture of the floor is a bit rough near the food venders and around the tables. If we keep our cane tips on the floor without tapping it, we can feel the difference between the smooth and rough textures which is very helpful because sometimes it is so loud here that I can't hear the sound of the taps of my cane. I use this technique quite a bit in food courts. But not all food courts are set up like this. The one near your home may be different.

When we pass the Food Court, we need to turn right and go down a huge hallway. We can't shore-line here because there are lots of little and big doorways. If we did shore-line here, we'd be going in and out and in and out—that's a waste of time and can also make a person <u>disoriented.</u> Let's walk quickly, and that'll help us to walk straight through this hallway.

Oh! Smell that? We are passing a hair salon place. Someone must be getting a perm! I've smelled that before when my mom got a perm! UCK!

Sometimes I can hear an echo change to my right from listening to the sound of the tap of my cane. That echo sound might mean there is a little cove area. My mom says that the cove area leads to special doors that the store owners use to get into their stores. Customers must use the store's main entrance.

Now I smell leather. This store sells leather jackets, purses, and belts. I suppose just about anything that can be made out of leather may be sold here. I love the smell of leather, don't you? Ha ha. That reminds me of something. One time, my mom bought a leather jacket for my dad for Christmas. She had to pack it in a double plastic bag so that he couldn't smell the leather before the big day. Then it ended up to be a lady's jacket instead of a jacket for a man. We all laughed about that!

We are now in a real open area. I can tell because the sound of my cane tip does not echo so much. A metal cane tip allows me to hear an echo when I tap it. Do you hear the fountain to our right? It is down that hallway. We need to go straight here and find the hallway ahead of us.

A sitting area is in the middle of this courtyard with a gazebo and a lot of plants and little trees. We'll need to go around that so we will need to veer a little and try not to lose track of our final destination. Come on. Let's go. I don't want to be late for the party.

I smell the flowers around the gazebo now. Don't you? Okay. Let's keep the flowers on the left for a bit. Now, let's veer to the right and start looking for that hallway. Listen to your cane taps which will guide us and show us the way.

Good, I think we found it. I'll know for sure as soon as we pass by the. . .mmm. Yes, we found it. The bulk candy shop! Nope, we can't stop now. Let's keep going. We need to go through this department store to the exit on the other side.

See? It was easy getting through that store. We just stayed on the main path by gliding the cane. We could feel the texture change and shore-line that edge. It was a breeze finding the main path on the left. Then we found the escalators with our ears, went down one level, and now we are outside. It seems strange that we had to find the escalators to go down a level. That's because the back of the mall is lower than the front of the mall. Some malls, just like houses, are built on hillsides.

You did great with the escalator, by the way. We listened for the sound of the escalators and headed towards them. By using our canes, we could feel the different texture on the floor in front of the escalators. We also used the cane by moving the tip back and forth to find the edge of the walkway that led us to the handrail. By feeling the moving handrail, we were able to determine if the escalator was going up or down. When we found the one going down, we used our cane tip to move forward while we had our hand on the moving handrail. When the cane began to move forward on its own, we had found the top step and we then stepped forward onto the moving step. We moved the cane tip to the step ahead but below us and went for a little ride. When the cane began to move upward on its own, we knew we were at the bottom and simply stepped off the escalator. It is important to step off the escalator quickly and move forward a few steps to give room to the person behind to step off, too.

Now that we are outside, we need to shore-line the building. We'll keep the building on our right and the curb on our left so we stay on the sidewalk. At the end of the building, we have to cross the driveway to the pizza place. We're almost there! I'm getting excited. Are you?

Great! You found the <u>drop off</u>. The drop off is where we step off the sidewalk to cross the driveway.

Shhh, listen for traffic. Do you hear any? I don't. Let's cross the driveway.

I'm so happy you were able to go to the party. The pizza place entrance will be here soon. This building is brick and the front doors are metal. Ting! There it is. I bet Sara will be happy to see us! I'm hungry! How about you?

Pop Quiz

1. The echo of the metal cane tip may let you know if the area is open or enclosed..

                      TRUE   FALSE

2. In O&M a "drop-Off" is where you get out of an automobile..

                      TRUE   FALSE

3. Walking quickly can help you walk straighter..

                      TRUE   FALSE

4. The long white cane is a symbol of independence..

                      TRUE   FALSE

Answers by Owin M.
1. True. If you pay close attention to the sound the metal cane tip is providing, you can detect sound changes provided by the echo of the cane tip as it taps the floor. (Chapter 5)
2. False. In O&M a 'drop-off' is a step down off a sidewalk, stair, wall, curb, etc. (Chapter 5)
3. True. When you walk slowly, it is easier to walk crooked. Try it out on a long straight sidewalk or hallway. (Chapter 5)
4. True.

CHAPTER 6
OWIN M. TAKES THE PLANE

I'm a little bit nervous because I've never been on a plane before. Have you? As usual, I am bringing along my *Braille notetaking device* to journal about new experiences. I was a little worried about my long white cane on the plane. My friend told me planes can be rather small. He said luggage is stored in the belly of the plane and carry-on luggage must be able to fit under the seat or above the head. Above the head? What could there ever be above the head? Anyway, I know now. There is a bin above the head that has a door on it that can store all your stuff in it while the plane is in the air. But wait—I'm getting a head of myself. Get it? A HEAD

My mom and I arrived at the airport a long time before our first plane was to take off. We have to take two planes to get to my aunt's house. Mom says that is called a transfer. The first thing we have to do is check in. When we arrived at the ticket counter, the man behind the counter asked for our names. I heard some beeping sounds, and then he gave my mom something. He asked us if we needed any assistance to the gate which is where you leave the building to get on the plane. The gate is not like the one in front of my house. My mom asked him to point us in the right direction. He told us we needed to turn to our left and go to the security check-in line that was in the center of the building. I took her hand, we turned to the left and walked. My cane echoed in the huge room, and then the sound changed slightly when we went into a little hallway. The echo wasn't as loud. After a few steps the sound changed again because we were in another huge room. I noticed a change in the floor which had some ridges in it making the sound of the tip of my cane different. We heard some beeping sounds to our right and turned towards that sound. We found the end of the line by asking people who were standing there.

I'm not afraid to ask people questions when it is appropriate such as asking people in line where the end of the line is. I learned in school that it is not nice to cut in line even if someone offers to let you do so because it wouldn't be fair to the people who are waiting farther back in line behind. Sometimes people have offered to let me cut in line ahead of them because they may think they are doing something nice for a person with a disability, but I want to be as independent as everyone else.

We found the end of the line and waited our turn through security. My mom has traveled before, so she knew what to do in the security line. We had to remove our shoes and put them in a tote. My mom had her computer, and I had my Braille notetaking device, which needed to go in the tote, too. The security person looked at our boarding pass, the piece of paper the person at the check-in counter gave us. Actually, everything we carried had to be put in totes. We had four totes that were lined up on a long table almost like the lunchroom tables at school. Then the security person wanted to take my cane and put it through a machine. Mom explained to me that the machine is like an x-ray. It looks inside the cane to make sure there is nothing harmful inside it that would hurt the plane or passengers. I handed my cane to one security person while another security person took my hand, and guided me forward a few steps. I was told we were walking through a doorway. Then my cane was given back to me. It was as simple as that. My mom went through the doorway right behind me. She said that sometimes the security guard lets a person walk through the doorway with their cane but every airport has its own way of doing things.

I used my cane to continue to follow the long table and was able to locate the totes with our stuff in them. Mom and I collected our things and asked the security guard where gate 4B was located. He told us to walk to the end of the hallway, and it would be on our right.

Mom and I walked down the hallway. I think it must have been the longest hallway I have ever been down in my whole life! It was also the largest hallway I have ever known because the echo of my cane was so loud! I could hear lots of people going this way and that way. It was easy to hear them because many of them were pulling suitcases on wheels. Some suitcases made clicking sounds as they rolled over the tiles on the floor. Other suitcases were so quiet that I was only able to find them with my cane. Some ladies wore high heel shoes that went click, click, click when they walked. I could hear how fast they were walking because the clicks of their shoes. You can hear them for a long time, and that gave me information about how long the hallway was.

I held my mom's hand because the airport is a huge place with lots of people from many different parts of the world going everywhere, and we didn't want to get separated. Sometimes we veered in the hallway. I could tell because my cane would find the edge of a carpeted area. Sometimes the hallway sounded more open, but we kept on walking straight ahead. We walked quickly, too. My mobility instructor told me that I could walk straighter if I walked faster, so I've been practicing on the sidewalk on my way to and from school. The practice paid off because before I knew it, we were at the end of the hallway. We stopped and listened and heard what sounded like passengers talking to a flight attendant. We walked towards that area until we heard the flight attendant more clearly as she checked something on the computer. We waited in line, and soon she asked us if she could assist us. Mom checked if we were at gate 4B. We were told we needed to go across the hallway to be in the right spot. We turned around and the attendant asked us if we needed any assistance, but Mom said we were fine. Gosh, there are so many helpful people here. Mom said that it is always good idea to double-check on some information because not everyone is correct in the directions they give even though they try to be. We were told the gate we needed was on the right side but it was actually on the left side of the hallway.

We continued on our way and searched for the help desk to make sure we were at the correct gate. Mom asked where the gate opening was so we could find a seat near the door to wait for the time to get on the plane. It was easy to find an empty seat because we heard some people talking in the area. We walked over, and I moved my cane along the front of the seat to feel for knees. Making sure the seat is empty before sitting down is important because some people use empty seats to store their belongings. We found two seats together.

As we sat there, I heard the flight attendants speaking over the intercom. Several times, I heard them saying, "For passengers sitting in the 4B area, heading for…please be prepared to board…" This message reassured me that we were in the correct place and wouldn't miss our plane.

One time, a flight attendant came up to us and asked us if we would need assistance in getting on the plane, but Mom said we were just fine. Mom explained to me that people with small children or people needing assistance could get on the plane ahead of the other passengers, but we were fine and didn't need assistance because she's traveled many, many times.

Soon our flight number was announced, and we could get on the plane. We gathered our things and walked towards the gate where we were directed to enter the plane. It was way cool to walk down a small hallway that had a railing to hold onto. The hallway had a curve in it like an elbow. When we stepped into the plane, a flight attendant asked us if we needed assistance. Mom showed the attendant our ticket and confirmed that our seats were seats 7A and 7B. Mom then asked if it were 7 rows down and if seats A and B were on the right or left. The flight attendant told us that the seats were going to be on our right. As we walked down the path between the seats, we counted seven seats. When we got to the seventh row, we stopped and turned to the right. The walkway reminded me of my friend's bedroom. His room was so messy that I always have to walk in a small path to get to his computer when I visit him.

My mom told me I could put my back pack under the seat in front of me or in a storage area above my head. I decided to store it under the seat in front of me so I could get to it easier once the plane was in the air. She showed me how to store my cane between my window seat and the window of the plane. It slid right in and was long enough to reach the seat in front of me and a little to the seat behind me. The people in front of me and behind me were very friendly and helped my cane slide in very easily.

My mom showed me the little buttons above my head, so I could control the personal air blower. She told me there was a special little light for each person and a button to push for assistance from the flight attendant, if needed. As Mom was showing me the buttons, a flight attendant stopped by and said his name was James and that the emergency exit was five rows behind us. James also asked us if we were going to need any assistance when we landed. My mom said that she thought we would be fine. James said that he was going to call ahead to have someone there for us just in case. Mom thanked him. Later she told me to put on my seatbelt, and the plane took off. I felt the plane move slowly at first. Then it got faster and faster, and I felt my head press against the seat. The nose of the plane moved upward towards the sky, and I felt like I was lying in a recliner at home. The nose of the plane is the front of the plane. After a while, the nose of the plane moved downward a little, and I felt like I was sitting level. Mom showed me how to open up a little table in front of me. I got my Braille notetaking device out and started my journal.

It's later now, and I'm at my aunt's house, but I wanted to tell you about the rest of my plane trip. After I wrote in my journal, James stopped by with peanuts and cookies. Then he stopped by with soda and water which was a nice snack in the middle of our trip. Then when I was just starting to get bored, I could feel the nose of the plane move down slightly. Soon after that, I heard the captain say over the speaker that we would be landing soon. I started to get excited about seeing my aunt again. We had to stay in our seats until the plane came to a complete stop. After a little bit, I heard a beeping sound. Mom said that meant they had turned off the seatbelt light, so now we could undo our seatbelt and gather our things to exit the plane.

This time when we exited the plane, we were directly outside! I knew because I immediately felt the wind and smelled the outdoor air. We then stepped down a very narrow stairway. When we arrived at the bottom of the stairs, a man met us and said he was there to assist us. I held on to Mom's hand, and we followed the man to the building. It was very loud; I couldn't hear the tip of my cane. Mom told me later that it was so loud because the engine of the plane was still running.

We followed the crowd through a maze to the building. It was kind of fun—like I was a mouse working towards a treasured piece of cheddar cheese. We got to the door of the airport, followed the crowd up some stairs, and then we were in the airport. The man asked if we needed assistance finding our next gate. Mom accepted his help. He talked into a walky-talky, and the voice on the other end told him which gate we needed to go to for our next plane. The man took my mom's arm to help guide her to the next gate, but Mom politely told him that she could follow him. Fortunately, I had all my stuff in a backpack so I could use my cane with one hand and hold Mom's hand with the other. Mom asked the man several questions along the way to the gate. I was happy that this man was there to help us because the hallway in this airport was carpeted making it hard to hear my cane so I couldn't determine the main path very well. The walk to our next gate was super long, and once we were there, I was relieved. Mom went up to the courtesy counter and double-checked that we were at the right gate. She then asked the nice lady about the nearby restaurants. She told us that a fast food restaurant was just farther down the hallway. We ventured off to find it which was easy because soon we just followed our noses.

When we arrived back to the gate, we found a seat and waited our turn to get on our last plane. We had to take two planes to get to my aunt's house. Sometimes trips are like that. While we were waiting, I heard a motor like a small golf cart drive towards the courtesy counter. It stopped, and I heard a man tell the attendant that Mrs. Cloud had arrived and would need assistance. I turned to my mom and asked her why we didn't ride in the cart, too. She said sometimes some people need more assistance than others.

Pop Quiz

1. Gliding the cane across the floor will not help you find different textures..

     TRUE   FALSE

Answers from Owin M.:

1. FALSE: The texture of the floor is a bit rough near the food venders and around the tables. If we keep our cane tips on the floor and move it back and forth without tapping it, we can feel the difference between the smooth and rough textures which can be very helpful when in loud places. (Chapter 5)

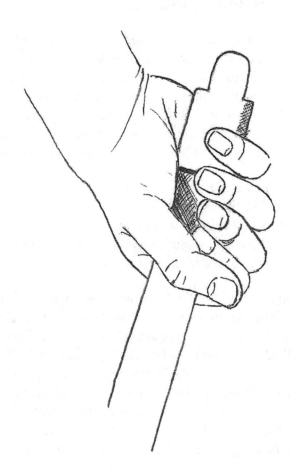

CHAPTER 7
OWIN M. AT THE DOCTOR'S APPOINTMENT

Dear friend,

I'm so proud that you are now using the long white cane all the time. I know that it was difficult at first to remember to take your cane with you whenever you left the house, but now it has become part of your life. The long white cane is my eyes and ears—my eyes because it finds things on the ground and protects me from falling, and my ears because the metal cane tip allows me to hear echoes so I know when I'm approaching buildings or parked cars. Don't you feel proud when you are able to walk independently where you want to go and when you want to go? Of course, you always need permission before you go wherever you want to go!

Well, I'm happy you called me the other day about your doctor's appointment because you were nervous about taking your cane. It's good to be able to have someone to go to for questions about blindness. Sometimes when I have questions, I call my friends at the *National Federation of the Blind.* If they don't know the answer, they know someone who does! Frankly, I don't think there is a blindness question to which they don't know the answer! Anyway, I'm sorry I couldn't talk to you the other day because I was on my way out the door. I thought I'd write you a letter about the time I went to the doctor for a sports physical and what I did with my cane.

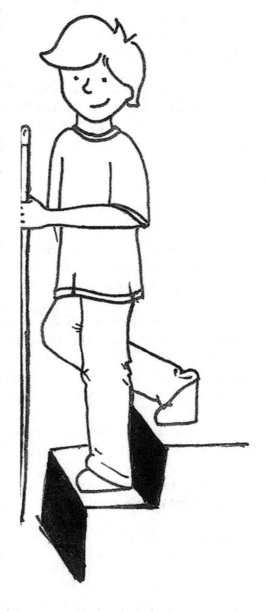

Hmmmm, let's see. I think it was about a year ago I went for my physical. I needed one so I could play *Goalball*. Have you ever heard of Goalball? Well, it's a game that was designed way back in 1946 for individuals who were blind. Now it is a regular event at the Paralympics! Teams throw or roll balls that have bells inside them to score a goal on the other side of the court. What's so cool about it is that all the players have to wear blindfolds or sleep shades; therefore, everyone must focus on their hearing. Of course, the spectators, the people watching, have to stay very, very quiet so the players can hear the balls. The players have to use their whole body to stop the ball from scoring a goal. There are only three players for each team on the court at a time, so a player may have to actually lie down to stop a ball from rolling into the goal. Oh gosh, I'm getting off topic. You'll just have to come watch me play sometime. Okay, I hear you asking me, "How can I watch you when I can't even see that well?" You just watch me in a different way than someone who can see. You can watch me with your ears. Besides, at the game, if you're quiet, you can listen to the bells in the ball yourself and get a picture in your mind of what is happening.

I better get back to the doctor's office. Most doctors' offices are the same. You will enter a room that is filled with many chairs for people to sit on while they wait to see the doctor. First, you need to find the check-in counter which is usually pretty easy to find. Just listen for a ringing phone or people talking. Tell the person behind the counter your name, and then use your cane to find a seat. By holding your cane up and down, you can slide it across the front of the seat. If your cane touches something, you have most likely found someone's knees. Usually the person will say something like, "Hello," before you actually touch them. Which reminds me, you can also listen—be a detective and listen for voices, magazine pages turning, children chatting with their parents, or couples having a conversation. Or it could be that everyone has stopped talking and is watching you because they are interested in seeing how you get along being a blind person. Just go ahead about your business of finding a seat, and they will eventually get back to whatever they were doing, too.

Slide your cane over to the front of the next seat. If it smoothly runs across the front of the seat, then you know the seat is empty, but also check the seat with the back of your hand to make sure nothing is left on the seat, such as books, magazines, someone's purse, or coat. Then you sit and wait for your name to be called.

And wait.

And wait.

Listen while you wait. From the sounds, you can get a good idea of where the seats are located in the room. Also listen as patients are called to see the doctor. Listen as patients follow the nurse through a door to where the examination rooms are located. When your name is called, you'll know exactly where to go.

Follow the person who called your name. Make note on which directions you turn as you walk to the examination room. Once you are in the examination room, the nurse may need to take your weight and your temperature, and ask you why you need to see the doctor. When you do that, you can rest your cane against the wall, the corner, or lay it on the floor against the wall. After that, you may need to sit on a little bed and wait for the doctor to show up.

When you are finished with the doctor, retrace your steps to the waiting room. Stop at the front counter, and then you are done. There you have it, the basic Orientation and Mobility methods for a doctor's visit.

When you feel up to it, come to a Goalball game, okay? If you have any more questions, you can email me at: OwinM@yahoo.com. Oh, and remember, whenever you leave your home, take your cane with you!

Sincerely,

Owin M.

CHAPTER 8
OWIN M. AND THE DISCOVERY METHOD

Today I am on my way to the Student Center to meet some of my friends. A week-long event is happening. I have been to the Student Center a few times with my buddies, but I went using the human guide technique. I have never traveled there on my own, so this is going to be an adventure for me.

From my house, I walk east right into the morning sun, and then I need to turn north. I've been on that sidewalk before because I have a friend who lives that way. But today I have to walk farther north than I've ever done by myself. Want to come with me? Great! It'll be fun to have you along.

Okay, here is the sidewalk going north; I feel the slight incline. When I walk on this sidewalk, I feel like we are climbing a small hill. Here I need to shore-line the left side of the sidewalk. (Remember shore-lining is when I use my cane to locate something or follow something. In this case, I'm using my cane to locate the sidewalk leading to the entrance of the Student Center.) My cane finds the edge of the sidewalk so I continue forward, checking for the sidewalk leading for the entrance from time to time. Do you feel yourself going upward?

Wait a second. My cane just extended farther left than it had been doing, so we need to turn left. Oh no, I immediately felt a slight decline so we need to stop. Let me check out this sidewalk. I need to extend my cane to the right and left, wider than my shoulders. Oh, I understand, this sidewalk is too narrow to be the entrance to the Student Center. Let's turn around, continue north on the sidewalk, and occasionally shore-line on the left to find the entrance.

The sidewalk just leveled off. I don't feel like we are going upward any more. Do you? Oops, spoke too soon. The sidewalk is going upward again. Oh, look, here is another opening on our left, so let's check it out. It seems wide enough when I check with the cane on both sides. What's this? It feels like a rubber mat. I bet we found the door to the Student Center because often there is a welcome mat in front of doors. Wait. Do you hear something? I hear a hum of a motor running that sounds like it is right in front of us. Tap. My cane just felt something. Let's check it out. I'll reach forward and hope to find the door. Oh, it is a soda machine! I don't remember there being a soda machine! Maybe I didn't go north on the sidewalk far enough. Let's go back to the sidewalk and continue north.

I'll continue shore-lining on the left side, and I hope the next time there is an opening, it'll be the Student Center. Here's another opening, and a welcome mat and great, a door! My cane made a different sound as it hit the door this time, and I don't hear a motor running. Everything looks good! I found the door handle. Oh no! It's locked! Let me see what time it is. I can check my <u>Braille watch</u>. Hmmm. It's not too early. The Student Center has already been open for quite some time. Let's return to the sidewalk and continue north again. We are bound to find it!

I found the shore-line on the left but something has stopped my cane from touching the grass. I'll take a few more steps forward and see if it is still there. Yep, my cane still stops. I wonder what is on the right side of the sidewalk. Oops, my cane did the same thing on the other side. Hmm, I'll raise my cane an inch or two and see what I find. It's a small retaining wall with a little tinny sound—like metal hitting metal right above it. I'll check it out with the back of my hand. Oh, it's a handrail. I don't remember ever coming to a small retaining wall or handrails before! Hmm. Maybe I missed the sidewalk to the

Student Center. So, let's turn south and shore-line on the right side of the sidewalk. Now I feel like we are walking down the small hill. Do you feel that, too?

I find the opening to the locked door, so let's walk pass it. I find the opening to the soda machine, so let's walk pass it as well. Ok, the sidewalk has leveled off again. Stop. Here is another opening on the right. Let's check it out. I don't feel myself descend. Great! My cane finds a welcome mat, so let's walk forward. I hear a familiar tinny door sound as my cane taps it. Super! The door is unlocked! I hear music, too. Let's go in!

"Hi! I'm happy you made it here. Come on in!"

My trip to the Student Center took 37 minutes. Tomorrow I'll be heading there again. I know it won't take me as long.

The Next Day

Today I'm heading to the Student Center. I'm happy you had so much fun yesterday and want to join again. Let's head out. Remember, we go east and then head north.

Here is the sidewalk going north with the slight incline. I'll walk on the left side so I can shore-line on the left. Look, here is an opening on the left. Let me check it out. Oh, it's the sidewalk with the slight decline, so we don't want this one. Let's continue.

The sidewalk just leveled off. I remember this from yesterday. Let's continue onward. Here is another opening on our left, so let's check it out. Here is the rubber mat, but I hear a motor running. Oh yes, it's the soda machine. We need to turn back. We missed the door to the Student Center.

Now, I'll shore-line on the right, and we'll find the door. The sidewalk leveled off again. Oh, here is an opening. I found the rubber mat. Did you hear that? It was the familiar tinny door sound my cane made as it hit the door yesterday. Super! We found it! Let's go in.

Today my trip to the Student Center took me 21 minutes.

The Third Day

I'm happy you're here. Come on. Let's go to the Student Center. Do you remember that we go east and then head north on the sidewalk with the slight incline? I'll shore-line on the left and look for the opening. Let's skip the first opening because it is the one with the slight decline and not the one we need.

Feel that? The sidewalk just leveled off. I remember this from yesterday. Hmm, yesterday we walked past this and found the soda machines so let's not do that today. Great! I found the sidewalk on our left. Come on, here's the welcome mat and there's the familiar tinny door sound because my cane tapped the door. Wonderful! We found the Student Center! Let's go in.

This time the trip to the Student Center only took me ten minutes! I used problem-solving skills, generalizing, discovery, and prior experiences in order to successfully complete this journey to the Student Center. By finding the Student Center, I enhanced my knowledge of all of these skills. From this experience, I'm not only less likely to miss the sidewalk leading to the Student Center again, but I also discovered the soda machine for future use. The knowledge that I obtained is only accessible because I was allowed to make mistakes, discover, generalize, and problem solve. If I didn't have this opportunity, my experience would not have had the same impact, and if someone would have stopped me from discovering, I would have missed this valuable opportunity that contributed to my development of independence.

Pop Quiz

1. When I hear the traffic move in front of my face, I know it is NOT a good time to cross the street..

   TRUE   FALSE

2. Goalball began in 1946..

   TRUE   FALSE

Answers from Owin M.

1. TRUE: When crossing a street, keep the sound of the moving traffic on the side of your ears—not in front of you! (Chapter 1)
2. TRUE: it's a game that started in 1946 for individuals who were blind. Now it is a regular event at the Paralympics! Teams throw or roll balls that have bells inside them to score a goal on the other side of the court. What's so cool about it is that all the players have to wear blindfolds or sleep shades; therefore, everyone must focus on their hearing. (Chapter 7)

CHAPTER 9
OWIN M.'S INSTRUCTIONS ON
HOW TO MAKE AN O&M SNOWMAN

I've heard, "When life gives you lemons, make lemonade." But what about when you're given snow? I say, "When life gives you snow, build a snowman!" That's exactly what I did in Orientation and Mobility (O&M) class. You might ask how can building a snowman be incorporated in an O&M lesson? Orientation and Mobility class is more than learning how to use the long white cane. Learning how to interpret environmental cues is also important.

One major component of incorporating O&M with building a snowman is what to do with the long white cane; after all, the cane isn't exactly needed when psychically bending over and pushing a snowball around a field. But the cane can't simply be dropped in the snow or else it can easily be lost until spring! When not needed, the cane can be placed along a scooped sidewalk edge or propped against a tree, fence post or building.

When entering a snowy field, pay close attention to the information provided by the environment such as the sun, wind, and traffic cues. If it is in the middle of the day, the sun will most likely be directly overhead and/or slightly south. As the day progresses, the sun is more in the westerly or southwesterly direction. The sun can be felt on your body if you pay attention to the location of heat on your body. If it is a cloudy day, then pay attention to the traffic sounds. Perhaps there is a major street to the east. Keep the sound of that traffic noted and one will always know where east is located. If there is a breeze, that may help, too. Pay attention to the direction of the breeze before walking away from the cane. The sound of a distant train can also provide information. Knowing where that train track is can be quite handy.

Of course, one can also use a Braille compass when traveling in a snowy field. If the cane was stored along the scooped sidewalk north of the field, then wherever one travels in the field, the individual can always use the compass to find north to locate the sidewalk and then follow the sidewalk's edge to retrieve the cane. Knowing the location of the stored cane is important in order to retrieve it upon completion of the snowman.

Now having the cane safely stored and having knowledge of how to be orientated to the snowy field, we come to the fun stuff. First pack a snowball as tight as you can. Add more snow as you roll it forward (or away from your body.) With each roll of the snowball, gently pack the new snow against the ball. Sometimes it is important to gently push down on the snowball as it is rolled forward to help pack the new snow to the snowball. As the snowball gets bigger and heavier, it will naturally get packed by its own weight as it is rolled. Sometimes it will even pick up all the snow on the ground leaving a line of bare grass in its wake.

Be sure to plan ahead to determine where you want the snowman and roll your snowball in that direction. The first snowball is the base. Make a second and third snowball the same way you made the first except the second snowball needs to be slightly smaller than the first, and the third slightly smaller than the second.

Gently rub off some of the snow from the top of the first snowball to make it somewhat flat. Lift the middle snowball onto the first snowball. Gather extra snow and pack it (like glue) between the two snowballs. Repeat this procedure to add the smallest snowball to the top. Wrap an old scarf between the middle and top snowball. Add a hat if desired.

For my snowman, I used broken cane handles as arms and a broken cane tip as a nose. My snowman wore a pair of sleep-shades, and another cane was propped against his body—after all, this snowman was in Orientation and Mobility class!

CHAPTER 10
OWIN M. ON THE TRAIN

Now that I'm old enough, my mom and dad are allowing me to take a train ride all by myself to Baltimore, Maryland, to visit my cousin for two weeks. I'm so excited. I'm taking my electronic Braille notetaking device with me so I can keep a journal about the trip. It's fun to keep a journal because whenever I want to remember something, I can go back and read all about it.

Today Mom and Dad took me to the train station. They let me go up to the counter to get my ticket all by myself. It was really easy because they bought the ticket online, and I just needed to pick it up at the ticket counter. I had to show the person behind the counter my state I.D. card. The state I.D. card is like a driver's license, but it does not permit me to drive. I felt really grown up. I picked up my ticket, and we waited for the train to come. The person behind the counter told us where we needed to go to get on the train when it arrived. He also asked if I needed any help getting to the train, but I told him that I was fine. All I needed to know was which letter to stand by. This train station had large letters along the track and people with various types of tickets such as first class or coach needed to stand by particular letters. Dad travels by train a lot so knew exactly where to go. Besides, he told me that if I tried to get on the train at the wrong spot, the steward would correct me.

Soon we left the train station and walked down a sidewalk, crossed the parking lot driveway, and got onto another sidewalk that leads us to the train platform. We turned left and a group of people were standing there. Dad said this was letter N, so we walked some more. There was another group and at the next group, we stopped and waited. "This is the letter L," Dad said. Too bad the signs are not in Braille or else I could have done it myself. If I were traveling alone, I would ask someone standing by the signs.

When the train arrived, my dad talked to the steward and mom hugged me goodbye. Then I got on the train where the steward selected a seat for me. When I get older, I can select the seat myself. As for now, I stayed in my seat the whole time. Well, except for when I needed to go to the bathroom, which wasn't far away at all. The steward stopped by and asked for my ticket, and I showed him. It sounded like he put a piece of paper above my head, and then I heard him ask the person across the aisle for her ticket.

I got out my Braille notetaking device and wrote in my journal. I then read a book that I had downloaded onto it.

Over the speaker, I heard someone announce some stops along the way. I knew my stop was the one after Washington, D.C., because Mom, Dad, and I have taken the train to Washington, D.C., before. It wasn't a long ride. Just when I was at a great part in the story I was reading, we were leaving Washington, D.C. I decided I'd better pack my Braille note-taking device away and listen for my stop. I could feel butterflies in my tummy because I was excited to see my cousin.

Soon the steward told me my stop was coming up and asked if I was ready. I told him I was and before I knew it, the train stopped. The steward was at the exit helping everyone because it was a huge step off the train. He told me to be careful of the gap between the train and the platform. Gosh, I would hate to lose my cane down there! Thank goodness, I always pack a folding cane in my suitcase just in case I break my rigid cane.

My cousin greeted me while my uncle talked to the steward. How exciting to be spending two weeks playing games, go swimming, camping, hiking, bowling, fishing, boating and, of course, my cane will be with me!

Pop Quiz

1. You need a long white cane in order to make a snowman..

    TRUE   FALSE

2. When entering a snowy field, it is important to pay attention to the environment such as sun, wind and traffic..

    TRUE   FALSE

3. It is not a good idea to double check the information people give you because everyone is always correct in the directions they provide..

    TRUE   FALSE

Answers by Owin M.:

1. FALSE: You need your cane to get to the snow to make the snowman but not to bend down and roll the snowball. (Chapter 9)
2. TRUE: Since you don't have your cane with you, it is very important to pay attention to the environment such as the warmth from the sun and the sound of the traffic when entering a snowy field to make a snowman. (Chapter 9)
3. FALSE: When a person provides information, it is a good idea to double check that you have arrived at the desired destination or have understood the information provided. People providing information may not always provide the correct information because they may be confused, things may have changed since they were there last, or they simply don't know the correct information. (Chapter 6)

CHAPTER 11
QUESTIONS AND ANSWERS WITH OWIN M.

Why do you carry a long white cane?

I carry a cane because I want to be able to stand up proud. I want to be able to hold my head up and face it in the direction in which I am traveling. Before I used a cane, I would walk with my head down in order to watch for curbs, steps, and uneven sidewalks. But now, I can hold my head up and let my cane do the work my poor vision tried to do. The long white cane is a symbol of independence and using it makes me feel proud because I am independent. I bet you are wondering what the word independent means. Well, it means being able to do something without help from others. I am able to walk to my classroom by myself. That is being independent. I don't need to hold someone's arm and be led someplace. I can do it myself! You can be independent, too, if you use your long white cane.

What is the difference between a rigid cane and a cane that is able to become smaller?

The long white cane is a rigid cane. Rigid means it does not fold or bend. Sometimes folding canes are helpful though, like when I go tandem bike or horseback riding. A folding cane is also helpful when going to the movies or a play because those seats can be kind of small and close together. I even bring an extra folding cane in my suitcase on trips just in case my long, rigid cane happens to break. I simply fold the cane and pack it away.

However, if I'm walking with a folding cane, all the connections in the folding cane can make it harder to feel the uneven cracks in the sidewalk, and it is important for me to find the cracks so I don't trip and fall. I prefer a rigid cane because it offers more tactual feedback.

A telescoping cane means that it closes up like an antenna instead of folding up like a folding cane. Telescoping canes are just as helpful as folding canes because they can become smaller for storage, but telescoping canes can sometimes collapse (close) when the tip hits something like a curb or wall.

Overall, it is important to have a cane for Orientation and Mobility. The choice as to whether it's a long, rigid cane, a folding cane, or a telescoping cane is yours—but do choose one!

Will the long, rigid cane ever break?

As with anything, the cane can break. If you are rough with your cane and bang the tip down on the ground, it can break near the bottom. If it gets caught in the car door, it can break, too. Most canes can last a long time if you use it correctly. But as you grow, you will need to get a longer cane. (For a free cane, go to http://www.nfb.org/nfb/Free_Cane_Program.asp)

What about using a long white cane on the school bus?

First of all, I always get the bus at the same spot so the bus will stop to pick me up there. I can usually hear it as it approaches. The first step may be a little high, so I use my long white cane to check how high I need to step up. Usually I sit in the same seat on the bus, but the first time I ever get on the bus, I need to find an empty seat. Want to know how I do that? Well, as I walk down the aisle of seats, I hold my cane in a pencil grip and sweep it back and forth to make sure nothing is on the floor of the bus. I also listen for voices or people shifting in their seats as I pass by to let me know if those seats are empty or not. When I think there might be an empty seat, I'll ask if the seat is free. If no one replies, I sweep my cane in front of the seat to see if it touches any legs. If not, I check the seat with the back of my hand to make sure nothing is there. If I don't find anything, I sit down.

I know when the bus gets near the school because I hear everyone starting to collect their things. After the bus stops, I hear everyone standing up and getting off the bus.

What about the city bus?

I stand right by the bus stop so the bus driver is able to see me and my cane. After the bus stops, the driver will sometimes announce the bus number. If the driver does not announce the number of the bus, I will walk up to the door of the bus and ask the driver what the bus number is. If it is not the bus I want, I'll say, "No, thank you," and step away from the door. If it is the bus I want, I'll thank him and get on the bus.

Sometimes, before I start to get on the bus, I hear a hissing sound and some beeping sounds. That means the bus driver is lowering the front of the bus so it is easier for people to get on or off.

I use my long white cane to find the first step of the bus. By the driver's seat, there is a machine where I put the money in to pay the fare. I tell the driver where I want to be dropped off the bus, and he will announce that stop so I'll know it's time to get off the bus. Sometimes the driver will announce other stops along the way.

I hold the cane in a pencil grip to locate a seat on the bus just like I do on the school bus (see previous question). I usually find a seat near the front of the bus so I can hear the driver announce the streets and bus stops.

How do you walk in crowded areas with your long white cane?

I'm glad that you want to know how to walk safely with your long white cane in a crowd. It's good to be polite to others as you maneuver about. Remember that the cane is a tool to find obstacles in the way. I use the pencil grip and keep the tip of the cane closer to my body when I'm in a crowded area. With the pencil grip, I arch my cane as wide as my shoulders and walk-in-step to get to the place I need to go. Many times, when people see me walking towards them with my long white cane, they sometimes move to the side. I don't mean to tap them with my cane, but sometimes my cane will touch them. That's okay, my mom tells me, because the cane is meant to be used to find things and that even includes finding people!

What is walk-in-step?

Walk-in-step or walking-in-step is when you hold your cane extended outward from your belly button, arcing the tip of the cane to the left and right as wide as your shoulders. When the cane tip is on the right side of your body, your left foot extended forward. Then your cane moves to the left side of your body, your right foot extends forward. Sometimes, I call it kick-the-cane game because it is almost like kicking the cane from side to side.

How high do you arc the tip of your cane off the ground?

I just lift the cane tip slightly above the ground only about a half an inch as I move it from the left and the right as wide as my shoulders. If I lift the cane tip much higher than that, I will not be able to feel small curbs, drop-offs or other changes in the terrain.

How do you use your cane in loud locations?

It is sometimes hard to hear the metal tip of my cane when I'm in the school lunchroom or when I'm at a basketball game in the school auditorium, so it is important to be able to know what information the feel of the cane is providing. For example, in a loud area, I may drag or glide my cane over the floor a little more so I can feel the texture of the floor. Sometimes there is a walking mat to follow. The mat may sit a little higher than the floor and you can follow the edge of the mat to find your way to the door, perhaps. Some stores have a smooth texture on the floor for their main walkway and a rough texture in their vegetable section to help with water and deter slipping. The cane can easily pick up on this change whereas the naked eye may not.

It is extra important to be sure to use the cane correctly when in loud areas. Sometimes if you are traveling with a friend, you can maintain a conversation with him or her and follow the sound of their voice. Tell your friend ahead of time that this is a technique to use in order not to lose them in the crowd.

If you are working on crossing a street and someone is mowing the lawn and you can't hear, you may want to walk down the street to the next corner to cross and then come back and continue on your way.

Do you ever take your cane with you to the movies?

Of course, I take my cane with me to the movies, but this is a time when I may want to bring my telescoping or folding cane. In the movies, the seats are sometimes on steps where the row of seats in front of me is on a step lower. If I put my long white cane on the floor, my cane may fall behind the row of seats in front of me making it difficult to get the cane out. Sometimes movie theatre floors can be dirty with spilled popcorn or drinks, so I am a little hesitant to put my long white cane on the floor. If I have my telescoping cane, I can simply fold it up, put it in my bag, sit back, and enjoy the movie!

How to you respond to relatives or friends who don't think you need to take your cane with you?

Well, I do have some relatives who used to think they were actually helping me by telling me that I don't need to bring a cane with me because they would be there to help me. I know they are just trying to be helpful, but really that does not allow me to be independent, does it? What if I need to go to the bathroom? I don't really want my friend or relative to have to come with me into the bathroom and wait for me to be done. Or what if they need to go to the bathroom? I may not want to go with them either! But they may feel like they are not taking good care of me if they leave me alone. Then what if they do leave me alone and something happens like a fire alarm goes off? I won't have my cane with me to help me get out.

When a friend or relative tells me I don't need my cane, I politely thank them and tell them that I would feel more comfortable bringing my cane with me because the cane allows me to be independent. If they still are insistent that I go without my long white cane, I tell them what I just told you about the bathroom scenario. Usually they are understanding and never ask me to leave it at home.

Is it okay to let others hold your cane for you?

If someone else were holding my cane for me, then it would not be working for me, right? There might be a situation where someone may hold it for me for a minute or two while I am buttoning up my coat and trying to carry a stack of books at the same time, but usually I will prop it against the wall or lay it on the floor while I get myself organized, and then grab it and be on my way. However, there is an exception such as when I am at an amusement park. (See next question.)

What do you do with your cane at the amusement park when you want to ride the Ferris wheel?

Well, if my family or a trusted friend is with me and not going to ride the Ferris wheel, then I will use my cane until I get in my seat on the ride. I will ask somebody I trust to hold my cane for me until the ride is over. That person will meet me at the ride exit. But if everyone I'm with is going to ride the same ride, then I ask the ride attendant to hold or store it for me. I think they've done that many times before because they always seem more than willing to help. The ride attendant is usually waiting for me as soon as the ride is over to give my cane back to me.

How to you store your cane during a school performance?

If I'm in the audience, then I lay it on the floor in front of me. If I'm in the chorus and am standing on the risers, I will take my cane with me to get to my spot, then I will lay it on the floor in front of me because usually I'm in the front row anyway since I'm short. However, if I am ever not in the front row, I can easily prop the cane next to my shoulder and hold it there with my arm. Sometimes if I'm on the second or third step up, an assistant will store my cane for me off stage when I get to my spot and give it back to me when I am ready to exit the stage. I have tried using a telescoping cane but it can be awkward to fold up or extend it out when there are so many people around. I don't always have a deep enough pocket to store it, too. If I'm going to sit in a chair on stage, then I will lay it beside my chair. If I'm in a play, I will use it as I would anywhere else.

What about using a long white cane at a school dance?

I take my cane with me everywhere—even to school dances. When I'm on the dance floor, I will usually dance near the edge of the dance floor and lay my cane on the floor at the edge of the dance floor or along the bottom of the stage. Sometimes I dance with it propped up on my shoulder. Another option is to go human guide to the dance floor and leave my cane at my seat.

Do you take your cane with you to church?

Yes, my cane goes with me everywhere.

What about when you go someplace new? Do you take your cane with you?

Traveling to someplace new is the most important time to take your cane with you! The cane will help you locate items in your path and help you get to where you need to go.

Where do you store your cane in a car or van?

I slide my cane between the seat and the door of the car. I can do the same in the van, too. But I never store my cane in the trunk of the car.

Where do you store your cane when you are sitting on the floor?

I lay it behind me, beside me or in front of me as I sit on the floor.

What do you do in a fire drill?

I do the same thing you do. I walk out quickly and quietly with my classmates. Usually my cane is close by so I just grab it and go. But if it isn't with me, I will go human guide.

Would you take your cane with you to the circus?

You already know the answer to this, don't you? Yes!

Are there any times you don't take your cane with you?

I can't think of any time I don't have my cane with me when I'm outside my house or yard. Wait, there was one time. I was at school, and I was in the library. I put my cane near the door entrance and then there was a fire drill. We all had to leave the school quickly, but we had to go out a different door. There was no time for me to get my cane, so I went human guide to the outside safe spot. Although I was happy to have the human guide in the event of an emergency, I was not happy that I didn't have my cane with me.

After the drill, I had to depend on the human guide to get back to the library to get my cane before I could go to my next class. I ended up being late for that class. If I did have my cane with me, I would not have been late. Keeping the cane within reach allows me to be as independent as possible.

One time my cousin left her cane by the door in her classroom, and she tripped over a box the teacher left on the floor by her desk. I'm sure the teacher didn't mean to leave the box there. I've learned to keep my cane with me at all times or at least to keep in within reach.

How do you know where the towels are in the public restroom?

Touching the wall to look for the towel dispenser can make your clean hands dirty, so I look for the towel dispenser when I first enter an unfamiliar bathroom. I can then easily find the towel dispenser after I wash my hands, or I can get a clean towel and hold it under my arm while I wash my hands. Usually my cane can't locate the towel dispenser because the dispenser may be built into the wall. My cane can help me find the sink and the trash can. Sometimes I put the paper towel partly in my pocket before I use the toilet so that way I have it handy right when I need it. I learned this from a blind guy I know.

Where do you store your cane in a cab?

In some cabs, the cane can't slide between the door and the seat, so it has to lie on the floor across the back of the front seat or propped up on my shoulder with the tip on the floor.

Since the cane is so long, is it okay to store the cane in the trunk of the car?

No! It is never okay to store the cane in the trunk of the car. An independent person who is blind always keeps his or her cane where he or she can easily get to it. If the cane is in the trunk, then it can't be reached easily.

What is the proper way to hold the cane in a crowd?

I use the pencil grip when I'm in the crowd. When the cane is held up and down, it is not extended outwards where it can accidently go between people's feet causing them to trip and fall.

Are you ever afraid to take your cane to meet new people?

No, the cane is a large part of me. It is who I am. My cane is my tool and allows me to be independent. I am not ashamed of my cane.

Have you ever used your cane for other things besides walking?

Yes, I have used it to find things on the floor, under the couch, under my bed. One time I dropped a game piece, so I just laid my cane on the floor and slid it to the right and left. I listened very carefully and heard when my cane touched it. Then I just followed my hand down the cane and was able to find the game piece.

Would a person who is deafblind use a cane, too?

Yes. People who are deafblind use a cane just like a person who is blind. They use the cane the same way as all other blind people do but they may not hear the auditory feedback that the cane offers.

OWIN M. CHAIR: TO ENCOURAGE CANE USE
Created by Dr. Merry-Noel Chamberlain, NOMC, TVI

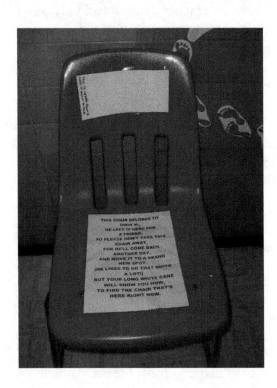

1.   Get a chair and place the following poem (in print and Braille) on the chair:

> This chair belongs to Owin M.
> He left it here for a friend.
> So please don't take this chair away,
> For he'll come back another day,
> and move it to a brand-new spot.
> (He likes to do that quite a lot!)
> But your long white cane can show you how,
> to find the chair that's here right now.

2.   From time to time, move the chair to various places. Everyone enjoys discovering the chair in various locations.

PART IV

CHAPTER 16

FLOWERS' BLOOMING

By: Dr. Merry-Noel Chamberlain, NOMC, TVI

CAST: (In Order of Appearance)

Sarah Siebold: student
Mrs. Siebold: Sarah's mother
Students: extra high school students—nonspeaking parts
Miss Colman: school secretary
Mr. Unkrich: social studies teacher
Glenn: student
Royene Flowers: Sarah's new friend
Elsie Bea: Sarah's new friend
Mrs. Oma: home economics teacher
Cashier:
Ashleah (pronounced Ash-lee-ah): Sarah's new friend
Mr. Kirsch: music teacher
Usher:
Bobby: Ashleah's brother
Marty: Bobby's friend
Mr. Gatewood: announcer

The time: Present.

The location: A small junior high school in Anywhere, USA.

The ABCs of Structured Discovery Cane Travel for Children, pages 201–222.
Copyright © 2021 by Information Age Publishing

ACT ONE: SCENE ONE

In front of closed curtains. Sarah and Mrs. Siebold enter the stage from the right. They are walking slowly across the stage, side by side, toward Miss Colman who is sitting behind a desk on the left side of the stage. A telephone and some papers are on the desk. Miss Colman is moving the papers around and talking quietly on the phone.

Sarah has a school backpack and is walking independently from Mrs. Siebold. With Sarah's right hand, she is holding a long white cane extending outward from her stomach. She is tapping the bottom of the cane from the left to the right as wide as her shoulders.

Several students are in small groups throughout the auditorium and a couple of groups are on the stairs leading up to the stage. Some are whispering as they stare at Sarah and her mother. Other groups stop talking altogether and simply stare at them. Ashleah, Royene, Elsie Bea and Glenn are included. Mrs. Siebold notices the students but ignores them.

Sarah:	What if the kids don't like me?
Mrs. Siebold:	I'm sure they'll like you.
Sarah:	But what if they've never seen a blind girl before? I mean, this is a smaller school in a smaller town and all.
Mrs. Siebold:	That doesn't have anything to do with whether or not they'll like you, Honey. Just be yourself, and you'll do just fine.
Sarah:	Yeah, but I'm sure they will ask a lot of questions and everything.
Mrs. Siebold:	Sarah, we've gone over this before. You know what to say. (Pause) Listen, if you don't feel comfortable talking to the class, I suppose I can stay for a while if you want.
Sarah:	(Smiles and nudges her mother in a teasing way.) Now, Mom, *that* would embarrass me!
Mrs. Siebold:	(Chuckling) I suppose it would. But are you sure you don't want me to hang around?
Sarah:	(Trying to sound reassured.) No, I'll be fine.
Miss Colman:	(Looks up and says something into the phone. Hangs up the phone and approaches them, smiling.) Hello. You must be Sarah. I'm Miss Colman. I met your mom yesterday, so I've been looking forward to meeting you. (Turning to Mrs. Siebold.) So, are you getting all settled into your new job?
Mrs. Siebold:	Oh, as good as to be expected. The city library is so large; I'm just trying to find my way around the building at this point. (Shaking her head.)
Miss Colman:	I am so pleased they are getting a new computer checkout system there. It's been needed for quite some time.
Mrs. Siebold:	The new system will cut down a lot on check-out time, and it will also keep a better record system. (Turning to Sarah.) Sarah, if everything is okay, I really must be getting along. I'll see you later, okay? (Patting her on the shoulder.)
Sarah:	(Smiling.) Sure, Mom.
Mrs. Siebold:	Have good day. (Leaves)
	(School bell rings)
Miss Colman:	(Jumps and returns to her desk.) Oh, that's the early bell. That means you have ten minutes to get to class and into your seat. (Picking up a sheet of paper from her desk.) Your teacher's name is Mr. Unkrich, and he is expecting you. (Returns to

Sarah:	Sarah's side.) He's a real nice teacher, and all the kids just love him. (Big smile.) He's in room 205. (Reaches for Sarah's arm and starts to guide her to turn around.) (Gently moves away slightly.) You don't need to take my elbow, just tell me where I need to go.
Miss Colman:	(Surprised.) Okay...hmm...We need to turn to the left and go to the end of the hall to the stairs.

(Miss Colman and Sarah exit.)

Off stage sound:	(The audience hears the taps of the cane as it shorelines a wall.) Tap, tap, tap, clunk, tap, tap, tap, clunk, tap, tap, tap.

(The curtain opens to a classroom. Miss Colman's desk is now turned to face the students' desks which are in angled rows facing Miss Colman's desk. The phone has been removed from the desk and now there are several piles of books and papers. In the far back left side of the stage is a large whiteboard angled towards students' desks. Mr. Unkrich is talking to Glenn who is standing in the back center of the stage. Some students are sitting at their desks. Others are standing in groups of two or three. No one is sitting at the two desks, which are up front and in the middle of the stage. Elsie Bea and Royene are together near Elsie Bea's desk, which is to the right of the stage. Miss Colman and Sarah enter the classroom on the far right of the stage but stop a few steps in.)

Miss Colman:	We can go on in. Mr. Unkrich is talking to a student right now. I'm sure he'll be with us shortly.

(Sarah takes a few steps into the room and stops when her cane touches a desk.)

Mr. Unkrich:	(Excuses himself from Glenn and approaches Sarah.) This must be Sarah. Thank you, Miss Colman, for bringing her up to me.
Miss Colman:	Oh, I didn't bring her to you, I just walked with her. (Pause.) Well, I'm sure you two can handle things from here. (Almost questioning.) Talk to you later?

(Mr. Unkrich nods to Miss Colman. Miss Colman smiles back at him and leaves.)

Mr. Unkrich:	Sarah, your mom said you could talk to the class about yourself and blindness, but if you don't feel okay about doing that, then that's fine.
Sarah:	No Problem, Mr. Unkrich.
Mr. Unkrich:	Great! Let's see. To start off with, your desk is right over here. (Walking toward the desk.) —to your left and about four steps.

(Sarah follows his directions. As she passes students, she says, "Hi" and "Excuse me." Students quickly move out of her way replying, "That's okay," and "No prob.")

Mr. Unkrich:	(Stops at an empty desk.) This is it.

(Royene leaves Elsie Bea and walks to her desk, which is right next to Sarah's desk.)

Sarah:	Okay. So, is the front of the classroom in this direction? (Pointing to the north.)

Mr. Unkrich:	Why, yes, it is. (Sounding surprised.)
Sarah:	Where is your desk from here?
Mr. Unkrich:	It's right over there… (Pointing just as she had done, but then noticing the confused look on Sarah's face)…in the northwest corner of the room and facing the class. It's to your left and straight ahead.
	(School bell rings. Suddenly chairs are skidding along the floor and bumping into desk legs as the students rush to the seats. Sarah runs her hand over her desk and chair. She puts her cane on the floor beside the desk and sits down, opens her school bag, and gets out a slate, stylus and a couple of sheets of Braille paper.)
Royene:	(Watching Sarah.) What's that?
Sarah:	(Turning her head towards the sound of the voice.) Are you talking to me?
Royene:	Yeah. What's that silver thing you just put on your desk? A ruler?
Sarah:	Oh, that's my slate. I use it to write Braille. Want to see it?
Royene:	Sure.
Sarah:	(Handing over the slate and stylus.) What's your name?
Royene:	Royene. (Looking down at the slate and stylus.) So how do you work this thing?
Sarah:	I put a piece of paper between the metal sheets and use the stylus to punch in the letters, (Attempting to pronounce Royene's name correctly.) Roweene.
Royene:	(Looks up at Sarah.) No, it's pronounced Roy-eene. (Looking back down at the slate, opening, and closing it.) This is really cool. Here, (Holds the slate and stylus towards Sarah.) you'll have to show me how to do it sometime.
Sarah:	(Reaching her hand out to retrieve the slate and stylus.) You bet, Royene. My name is Sarah.
Royene:	Yeah, I know. (Putting the slate and stylus in Sarah's hand.) Mr. Unkrich told us yesterday that you'd be coming. He said you just moved here from Louisiana. We already studied Louisiana. Home of Mardi Gras, you know?
Sarah:	(Chuckles, makes an ugly face and wiggles in her seat.) Yeah, and fire ants and poison ivy.
	(Sarah and Royene Giggle.)
Royene:	UGH!
Mr. Unkrich:	Okay, class, let's get started. We've got plenty to do this hour. First of all, I would like to welcome Sarah Siebold to our class. She has moved here from Louisiana and has graciously agreed to educate us all about being visually impaired. (Turning to Sarah) Please, Sarah, tell us about yourself.
Sarah:	(Thinking for a moment.) Last week I moved here from a large city in Louisiana. My mom works for the National Library Systems Center and got transferred here. I enjoy reading and bike riding. English is my favorite subject. I don't have any pets but want to have a cat someday. (Pause) What else would you like to know?
Mr. Unkrich:	Plenty of students around here enjoy bike riding. I had a friend in college who was blind, and we used to go tandem bike riding all the time. Do you use a tandem bike?
Sarah:	Yes, my mom and I have a tandem. (Chuckling) But she won't let me sit on the front seat.
Mr. Unkrich:	(Chuckling) I would have to agree with her. I never let my friend in front either. What about reading?
Sarah:	I read Braille or listen to books on cassette.

Mr. Unkrich:	(Looking around the classroom.) So, does anyone else have any questions for Sarah?
	(The students silently look around the room at each other.)
Mr. Unkrich:	Okay, then. It seems to me that, for the first time ever, my class has lost their tongues. (Looking at Sarah.) Sarah, let's say the class is reading a chapter in their social studies book.
Students	(only a couple): UGH!
Mr. Unkrich:	How would you do that? I mean, is that book on cassette?
Sarah:	A lot of the books are in Braille or audiocassette. Some are even on the Internet now. I will be using Braille or maybe download some stuff off the Internet. I was told that the textbook for this class is also on cassette.
Mr. Unkrich:	Do you take notes in Braille then?
Sarah:	I have a slate and stylus to write Braille with. But mostly I use a Braille notetaking device. (Retrieving the Braille notetaking device from her bag.) It's a little computer. (Holding it up so everyone can see it.)
Elsie Bea:	I bet that costs a lot.
Sarah:	Quite a bit.
Mr. Unkrich:	And that is why no one will ever touch it except Sarah. Sarah, are there any helpful hints you could pass our way since we are all new to having a visually impaired student in our class?
Sarah:	If people could say their name at the beginning when they speak to me, I could get to know their voice. That would be a big help.
Mr. Unkrich:	All right. This is Mr. Unkrich speaking.
Sarah:	(Laughing) I don't think you need to say who you are, Mr. Unkrich. I bet there aren't too many adult men's voices in this room.
Students:	(Chuckle)
Mr. Unkrich:	(Laughing.) Okay. Any other suggestions?
Elsie Bea:	(raising her hand.) I have a question.
Mr. Unkrich:	Okay, (pointing to Elsie Bea) Elsie Bea?
Elsie Bea:	Well, my grandma can't see very well, so she has a special watch to tell time. Do you have one, too?
Sarah:	(Turns her body towards Elsie Bea) I have a Braille watch. I open the top like this. (Opens the face of the watch and placing her right index finger on it.) Then I can feel the hands to tell the time.
Mr. Unkrich:	Okay, any other questions?
	(Elsie Bea. raises her hand again.)
Mr. Unkrich:	Yes, Elsie Bea?
Elsie Bea:	My grandma has a watch that talks. Does the one you have talk, too?
Sarah:	No. This kind does not talk. I have had that kind before but they don't do so well in school. Some teachers don't like talking watches because they can make noises during class. (Chuckling) Especially around lunchtime.
Students:	(Chuckle)

Elsie Bea:	My grandma gets really upset if I try to help her too much. But I really like to help her.
Sarah:	Yeah, I don't mind if people want to help me sometimes. I'd just appreciate if they asked me first rather than just taking my arm and dragging me around or something.
Mr. Unkrich:	(Looking around the room.) Any other questions? Comments?
Royene:	I'm Royene. I've met Elsie Bea's grandma, and it really is amazing how she gets around and cooks and all. Do you cook, too, Sarah?
Sarah:	I try to do some simple stuff, but I make a pretty big mess.
Royene:	So does my mom. (Laughing)

(Everyone laughs, too.)

Mr. Unkrich:	Okay, okay, let's get down to business. Oh, just one important announcement before we get started. Anyone who is interested in participating in the All-School Talent Show must sign up as soon as possible! Remember the show will be two weeks from Friday. Now please get out your journals.

(Sarah turns on her Braille notetaking device. The students groan loudly as they get their notebooks out of their book bags.)

Mr. Unkrich:	Okay, everyone, you have ten minutes to complete this sentence and expand upon this topic. Everyone is talented in their own way. I am talented in....basketball, poetry, singing, making people laugh…. (He reads out loud as he writes the following sentence on the chalkboard as the curtain closes, "Everyone is talented in their own way. I am talented in….)

Curtain

ACT ONE: SCENE TWO

Curtain Open. Several tables are set up around the stage. On each table is a recipe card and four students are seated at the table. Sarah, Royene, Elsie Bea, and Glenn are sitting together at a table in the center of the stage. On a table to the left are ingredients for peanut butter cookies. Cooking supplies are at another table to the right. Mrs. Oma is standing just to the right of the stage putting measuring cups on top of cookie sheets.

Royene:	I'm so happy you are in Home Ec. with us. This is such a fun class.
Sarah:	So, what all do you do in Home Ec.?
Royene:	We cook mostly. I suppose it's because there are so many kids who stay home alone nowadays. (shrugging her shoulders.) At least, that's what my mom says anyway.
Elsie Bea:	(Making a funny face.) But then we get to eat what we cook. Oh, I'm Elsie Bea
Sarah:	L (hesitate) -C-B?
Elsie Bea:	Elsie, E-l-s-i-e and then the B-e-a...
Royene:	Hey, do you know what your schedule is?
Sarah:	Yes, I do. (She gets out a sheet of Braille paper and reads off it by running her fingers over the Braille.) After Home Ec., I have lunch and then computer class followed by English.

Royene:	Darn. We don't have any other classes together today. What about tomorrow? Do you know what your alternate schedule is?
Sarah:	Just a second. I'll take a look. Tomorrow I've got chorus and...
Mrs. Oma:	(Interrupts but is very cheery and walking around the tables.) Okay, class. It's time to get started.

(Sarah puts her class schedule away.)

Mrs. Oma:	We're going to make some of the very best peanut butter cookies ever known to mankind. (Putting her hands together as in prayer.) So, you ask me, how do I know this? Well, I know this because my grandma and I used to make these exact same cookies when I was your age. That's how I know. (Stops walking and stands near Sarah.) Everyone, please make sure you are in your regular groups.
Elsie Bea:	(Leans towards Sarah.) Hey, Sarah, you can join our group. We've always been one short.
Mrs. Oma:	(Turns to Sarah and Elsie Bea) That is exactly what I was thinking myself. (Turns back to the class.) Okay, class, on each table is the list of ingredients you'll need. Please collect those items and let's get started. You all know what you need to do, so let's do it. (Turns back to Sarah.) I'm Mrs. Oma. Let me know if I can do anything to help you, Sarah.
Sarah:	Sure, Mrs. Oma.

(Mrs. Oma leaves to attend to some other students.)

Royene:	Let's see... (Looking at the recipe card.) We need some butter, brown sugar, white sugar, vanilla, peanut butter, eggs, and flour to start off with.
Sarah:	(Feeling around the table.) Where is everything?
Elsie Bea:	We have to collect them from the supply tables over by the front of the classroom. But we can get everything, Sarah, don't worry.
Sarah:	(Protesting.) No, no. I can help. How much peanut butter do we need?
Royene:	Hmm... (Looking at the card) ...one cup.
Sarah:	Okay, I'll get the peanut butter and how many eggs do we need?
Royene:	(Gives a surprised look towards Elsie Bea and then glances down at the recipe card.) We need two eggs.

(Sarah walks up to the front table and gently glides her hand over the table looking for the peanut butter. Finding a jar, she opens it up and smells the contents. Realizing its peanut butter, she places the jar under her left arm. She continues to glide her hand over the table again. She finds a bowl with two eggs in it. Holding the bowl with the eggs with her left hand, she uses her right hand to maneuver her cane and returns to her seat. Meanwhile, Elsie Bea, Royene, and Glenn collect the other items on the list, including measuring cups, knife, and spoon. Other students move out of Sara's way and silently watch her. Mrs. Oma gives the students scowling looks and motions them to get back to work.)

Sarah:	(Sitting at the table.) Does anyone know where the measuring cups are? They were not on the front table.
Elsie Bea:	They're right here. Which one do you need? They are all on a ring.

Sarah:	All we need is one cup. That is the biggest one on the ring. Oh, I also need a knife to scoop out the peanut butter.
Elsie Bea:	(Looks down at the measuring cups.) Wow! You're right! It is the biggest one. (Handing over the measuring cup and a knife to Sarah.) Here.
Sarah:	(Reaching out for the items.) Thanks. But knowing that was no big deal. My mom and I cook quite a bit.

(Elsie Bea, Royene, and Glenn watch Sarah as she fills the measuring cup with peanut butter, and then levels the cup with the knife.)

Sarah:	(Handing the cup to group.) Here is one cup of peanut butter.
Glenn:	(Takes the cup.) So, Sarah, how did you learn all that stuff?
Sarah:	Learn what?
Glenn:	How to walk over there, get that stuff, come back, and things like that?
Sarah:	I went to summer programs for teens to learn some skills. I was with other kids who were blind or had little vision, and we all learned together. It was really fun, too. We went swimming, camping, rafting, shopping, and all sorts of things. We even went diamond digging... (chuckling)...didn't find any, but we had lots of fun.
Glenn:	I would have rather spent the summer fishing.
Sarah:	Oh, we did that, too. The summer went by so fast, I was sad to see it end. We all had some sort of job, too. I was able to make some extra money for some CDs and stuff.
Elsie Bea:	Were there cute guys there?
Sarah:	Yes. There was a guy named Roland that all the girls were after.
Elsie Bea:	On second thought, I suppose it really didn't matter if they were cute or not.
Sarah:	What do you mean?
Elsie Bea:	Well, I mean...um...if you can't see what they look like then it didn't matter if they were ugly or not.
Sarah:	Oh, I don't know of any girl who wouldn't mind having a cute boyfriend, whether she was able to see him or not.
Royene:	Hey, you guys. Looks don't matter. It's what's in the heart that matters.
Mrs. Oma:	(Walking up to the table.) Okay, okay. This table is doing way too much talking and not enough mixing. Let's get back to work.

Curtain

ACT TWO: SCENE ONE

The curtains are opened on the right side. We see lunch tables with a few students sitting around them. The curtains are closed on the left side of the stage. In front of the closed curtain is a cafeteria line. Several students enter the stage in a line. There are a couple of students ahead of Royene who is standing just in front of Sarah. Elsie Bea and Ashleah are standing together, and a couple of students behind them are whispering to each other. Glenn is there, as well. Sarah has her cane touching the side of Royene's shoe and the line moves slowly. As they walk through the cafeteria line, they face the audience. Thus, the food line is between the students and the audience. At the end of the food line is the cashier.

Royene:	So, do you usually buy a lunch, Sarah? (Taking a step forward.)

Sarah:	Yeah, mostly. Except when I don't care for what's for lunch, then I'll bring something. (Stepping forward when her cane moves.)
Royene:	(Chuckling.) Same here. (Serious.) Um…how do you know when to move up?
Sarah:	Well, there are two ways. First of all, I hear your voice move away. Second, I have the end of my cane touching your shoe. So, when you move, I move, too.
Royene:	Oh, I wondered why you were touching me with your stick. I didn't want to say anything about it.
Sarah:	I was going to ask you about it but it slipped my mind. By the way, I prefer to call it a cane.
Royene:	What?
Sarah:	This. (holding up her cane) I prefer to call it a cane, not a stick. But to some people, it doesn't matter what you call it.
Royene:	Oh, ok. What do you want for lunch? Hot dogs or cheese pizza?
Sarah:	Cheese pizza for me. What about you?
Royene:	Same here. Do you want white or chocolate milk?
Sarah:	I think I'll have the white milk. Chocolate milk gives me zits.
Royene:	(Grabs two white milks and puts one in Sarah's hand.) I know what you mean.
Sarah:	(Holding up a small carton of milk.) Where did you get this?
Royene:	Oh, down here. They're in crates, and you just get the one you want. The white milk is usually on the left, and the chocolate is on the right.
Sarah:	Okay. (Moving her hand to the area, Royene was talking about.) Right here?
Royene:	Yeah. Um…well, then there are trays with pizza on it next.
Sarah:	(With the back of her hand, she touches a tray.) Here?
Royene:	Yes, Sarah. (Turning to the cashier.) Three dollars even, right?
Cashier:	As always, Royene. (Chuckling.) You say that every day!

(Royene steps asides and waits for Sarah.)

Cashier:	(Turning to Sarah and notices her long white cane.) Oh now, hang on, sweetie. I can get someone to carry your tray for you.
Sarah:	(Reaches into her pocket and pulls out a folded bill.) No, that's okay. I can get it. Thanks. (Unfolding the bill and handing it over to the cashier.) Here's a five.
Cashier:	(Looking at the bill.) Why, yes, it is. And here is your change, two dollars.

(Sarah takes the bills and folds them in half. She puts the bills in her pocket.)

Cashier:	Are you sure you don't need any help? I can get someone here really quick.
Royene:	Sure, she's sure. Come on, Sarah. I usually sit over here.

(The left side of the curtain opens. The lunch line is rolled off stage. Behind the curtain is the rest of the lunchroom. Royene moves to an empty table almost to the center of the stage. Sarah carries her tray propped up against her left hip. She sweeps her cane in front of her as she follows Royene to the table. When her cane taps against a chair, she gently lays her tray down on the table. Sarah lays her cane on the floor beside her and sits down. She takes her fork and moves it around her tray. Elsie Bea and Ashleah join the table.)

Elsie Bea:	Hi, Sarah. It's Elsie Bea
Ashleah:	And I'm Ashleah.

Sarah:	Hi, Elsie Bea Hi, Ashleah. Are you in Mr. Unkrich's class, Ashleah?
Ashleah:	(Plopping down in her seat.) Nope. I'm in Miss Mean Moore's class. You're lucky you're in Mr. Unkrich's class. He's pretty cool. You know he's dating Miss Colman, don't you?
Sarah:	Are you serious?
Elsie Bea:	(Sitting down.) Now don't go giving out all the school's secrets, Ash-Lee-Ah. (Over pronouncing her name.)
Ashleah:	Hey, I'm not saying anything that hasn't been said before.
Elsie Bea:	Hurry up and eat, you guys. I want to check out that new boy in Moore's class. Tell me more about him, Ashleah.
Ashleah:	(Teasing.) Oh, you mean Mar-ty. What more can I tell you that I haven't told you already? (Stuffing some food in her mouth.)
Elsie Bea:	Whatever you know. Tell me.
Ashleah:	I've told you everything already.
Elsie Bea:	Well, then let's just hurry up and get to the courts.
Royene:	Oh, Elsie Bea, you just want to see if Marty is there.
Elsie Bea:	(Giggling.) So what if I do?

(Everyone eats in silence for 5 seconds.)

Sarah:	Tell me what people wear around here.
Royene:	Jeans mostly. Hey, you look okay, Sarah. Don't worry.
Sarah:	Oh, I was just wondering. What are you wearing today, Royene?
Royene:	I'm wearing a flowered skirt with a red top.
Sarah:	(Teasing.) I thought you said jeans.
Royene:	(Laughing.) Yeah, well, mostly I wear jeans.
Sarah:	So, what are you wearing, Elsie Bea?
Elsie Bea:	Both Ashleah and I have jeans on.
Ashleah:	(Changing the subject.) Cool! After lunch I have computer class.
Sarah:	Really? So do I.
Ashleah:	(Doubtful.) How can you work a computer?
Sarah:	I have a Teacher of the Visually Impaired and she set up a program called JAWS on the computer.
Ashleah:	JAWS, like the movie?
Sarah:	(Chuckles) No. JAWS is a type of computer program that has a voice that tells me what's on the computer screen.
Ashleah:	Oh, I can't wait to see (pause) that.
Sarah:	Look, it's okay to say words like see and look to me. I just look and see in a different way than you do. Okay?
Royene:	What do you mean?
Sarah:	Well, say for example, you got a new dress. You could describe it to me. You could tell me the color of it. Maybe you could let me feel the material, especially if it has a special texture to it.
Ashleah:	But what about TV? Do you go to the movies?
Sarah:	Yeah, I watch TV and go to the movies. Just like anyone else. Usually, I have someone who reads for me. That is, a person who tells me what's going on when no one is talking. Kind of like what you did when we went through the cafeteria line, Royene. But in a movie, a reader does not need to tell me every little detail like how

short a girl's skirt is or that the guy is having a bad hair day unless it's important to the plot. They have Descriptive Videos now, too. It's like having a reader built into the movie.

Royene: Wow! That's neat. Do you have a lot of those videos?

Sarah: I have a few. I usually check them out at the library.

Elsie Bea: This is all quite interesting, you guys, but can we hurry up and get to the courts while we still have some lunch time left?

Royene: Yeah, yeah.

Ashleah: Oh. Do we have to? (Protesting in a teasing way as she gets up.)

Sarah: Yeah. Let's go. I'm done. I just got to see what this "Marty" guy is all about. (Giggling.)

Curtain

ACT TWO: SCENE TWO

(Elsie Bea, Royene, and Sarah are standing in front of closed curtains on the left side of the stage.)

Elsie Bea: So how are you getting home? Oh, this is Elsie Bea, by the way.

Royene: (Looking around.) Is someone going to come and pick you up?

Sarah: No, I know the way home.

Royene: Did that teacher of the visually impaired help you with that, too?

Sarah: No. She works with me on Braille and independent living skills—those kinds of things. I have an Orientation and Mobility Instructor who teaches me cane travel; how to walk with my cane. A few days ago, he worked with me on the route to and from school.

Royene: Cane travel? Never heard of it.

Sarah: It's when you walk around from one place to another with the long white cane. We just call it O&M for short. I like it when we work on routes to new places like to the mall or convenience store.

Elsie Bea: That's cool. Where do you live?

Sarah: Just south a few blocks and west a block, over on Dorothy Avenue.

Royene: That's not far from me. I just live a couple of blocks from there. I'll walk with you.

Sarah: Great.

Elsie Bea: Well, I live in the other direction. I'll see you guys later. Bye. (Waving as she heads off stage to the left.)

Royene and **Sarah:** Bye, Elsie Bea

(Both girls start walking to the right of the stage.)

Royene: How do you know where to go?

Sarah: Well, what I'm doing now is called shore-lining. I'm following the edge of the sidewalk with my cane. I'm touching the grass each time my cane goes to the right. When it goes to the left, I'm touching the sidewalk. See?

Royene: Yes, but how do you know when you come to the corner?

Sarah: My cane tells me that, too. It'll feel the curb and sometimes the sidewalk goes down a bit.

Royene: But what about crossing the street? Isn't that scary?

Sarah:	I'll show you that when we come to it, ok?
Royene:	Look, I'm sorry if I'm asking too many questions. It's just that I've never met a blind person before.
Sarah:	Don't worry about it. I'm used to it. Besides, I'm happy you're interested. After a while you'll know these things, and we'll talk more about other stuff. I've met lots of blind people at the National Convention for the National Federation of the Blind. My mom and I go every year.
Royene:	National Federation of the Blind?
Sarah:	NFB for short. Thousands of blind people from all over the world gather for a weeklong convention every year. It's always around July 4th, Independence Day. Independence for people who are blind, too. I have so much fun with the teen programs and catching up with all my old friends. It's almost like attending a huge family reunion. All kinds of people come: blind lawyers, teachers, and computer experts. Hey, the corner is here. See how the sidewalk is lowering a bit? It's because this is a wheel-chair ramp.

(Both girls stop walking.)

Royene:	Wow, you're right!
Sarah:	Okay. Now close your eyes and listen. Do you hear any traffic?
Royene:	(With closed eyes, points to the right.) Yeah, I think there's a car to my right.
Sarah:	Okay, let's wait for it to pass. (Pause) Okay, it's clear for us to cross now. (Walks forward.)
Royene:	(Pauses, opens her eyes, looks to the left and right, then runs after Sarah.) Hey, wait for me! Gosh, you're so talented. I couldn't do that in a million years.

Sarah and Royene cross the street.

Sara turns to Royene:	Royene, this is not being talented. These are skills I had to learn. Talent is something people seem to be born with. Skills are things people learn.
Royene:	I never thought of it that way. Gosh, I didn't mean to hurt your feelings.
Sarah:	You didn't. It's just that a lot of people get this all confused. Sometimes people think I'm amazing because I can do this or that. It's just that I've had training and because of that training, I am able to do this and that. I wish I was talented to do something special, but I'm not talented at all. I can't even tune a piano, which is something most people think blind people are supposed to know how to do. But I have absolutely no ear for music.
Royene:	(rather quietly) I do. I love to sing.
Sarah:	Great! I'd love to hear you sing sometime.
Royene:	I've thought a thousand times about entering in the All-School Talent Show but have always chickened out.
Sarah:	Why?
Royene:	Why what?
Sarah:	Why do you chicken out?
Royene:	I don't know.
Sarah:	I bet you do.

Off Stage Sound: (Similar to a crow.) Caw! Caw! Caw!

Sarah:	Hmm. There must be three cars parked along here.
Royene:	(Looking both ways.) Why do you say that? I don't see any cars.

| Sarah: | (Laughing) I was just teasing. I had a friend back home who used to say those crows would spend the whole day hanging around and counting cars. (Imitating the crow.) Caw! Caw! Caw! |
| Royene: | (Making a face and nodding.) You had a weird friend. |

(Both girls continue walking off stage.)

ACT THREE: SCENE ONE

Sarah is walking in front of closed curtains. From behind, Royene runs up to her.

Royene:	Hey, wait up. It's Royene.
Sarah:	(Stops.) How's it going?
Royene:	Oh, not bad. Are you ready for another day of Mr. Unkrich's class?

(The girls continue walking slowly.)

Sarah:	Yeah, he seems cool.
Royene:	Oh, he is. But sometimes he can be a drag if you get on his bad side, though. Hmm......umm..... Sarah, I was wondering about a few things last night.
Sarah:	You can ask me anything. I'll answer it, but if it's too personal...
Royene:	No, no. It's nothing personal, I don't think. Well, maybe it is, sort of.
Sarah:	Then just ask me. I can always refuse to answer.
Royene:	Well, I was wondering how you became blind and what exactly can you see. (Pause.) Well, I guess that is a little personal, after all.
Sarah:	That's okay. People ask me that all the time. I was born with cataracts on my eyes. I don't see much now. But several of my friends who are blind can see some light or shadows. Some can't see anything at all.
Royene:	Gosh, Sarah. I'm really sorry.
Sarah:	(Stops and turns to Royene.) Don't feel sorry for me.
Royene:	(Shaking her head.) I'm sorry. I just can't help it.
Sarah:	Don't be sorry for me because I don't feel sorry for myself. Okay?
Ashleah:	(Approaching Sarah and Royene) Hey, did you hear about the All-School Talent Show?
Sarah:	Not really.
Ashleah:	Well, it's going to be really special this year because it's our school's 75th anniversary. The All-School Talent Show has been going on each year since the beginning. There is no first or second prize or anything like that. It's just an opportunity for anyone who wants to, to get up on stage and show off their talent. It's a lot of fun. It's supposed to be a week from next Friday. Elsie Bea was thinking about doing some clogging number. That's some kind of dance where you pound your feet into the floor. It sounds really neat! I think I'm going to read some of my latest poetry. That's what I do. I write poetry.
Sarah:	That sounds like fun. I heard some cloggers a while back but I've never tried it. (Shaking her head.) I'm sorry, but I can't recognize your voice yet.
Ashleah:	Oh, sorry. It's me, Ashleah.
Sarah:	Will you be in the Talent Show, Royene?
Royene:	No way!
Sarah:	But I thought you liked to sing.

Royene:	Yeah, I like to sing, but not in front of all those people.
Ashleah:	But you sing in the school choir, Royene. What's the difference?
Royene:	Well, in choir I'm not the only one standing up there, you know.
Ashleah:	Yeah, yeah. I know. (Turning to Sarah.) Sarah, we've been trying to get her to do this every year, but she says the same thing year after year after year.
Elsie Bea:	(Approaching the group.) Hi, it's Elsie Bea, here. So, what's year after year after year?
Ashleah:	Oh, getting Royene to sing in the talent show. It's a lost cause. (Turning to Elsie Bea) Hey, Elsie Bea, I hear that the new guy, Marty, already has a girlfriend from his old school. Bobby told me last night. (Turning to Sarah.) Bobby is my brother, Sarah.
Royene:	Too bad, so sad. But we better get going. The first bell is going to ring any second now.

(The school bell rings. Curtains open to a music class. There is a piano in the corner. Chairs are in rows forming a half circle. Mr. Kirsch is standing behind the piano, moving some music papers around. Students enter the stage and go to their seats.)

Mr. Kirsch:	(Approaches Sarah.) I'm Mr. Kirsch, your music teacher, and you must be...?
Sarah:	Sarah Siebold.
Mr. Kirsch:	Oh, yes. That's right. Do you like to sing, Miss Siebold?
Sarah:	Not really because I'm not too good at it.
Mr. Kirsch:	Well, we'll just have to change that, now won't we? It just so happens that I have an empty seat here next to Miss Flowers. It's between the altos and the sopranos. We'll start you off there so I can get an idea of what tone you sing. Oh, I don't have any Braille music yet. I was told that it would take a couple of weeks. Just do what you can for now. Okay?
Sarah:	Sure. (Doubtful.) I'll try.
Mr. Kirsch:	Now if you would like to take my arm, I will guide you to your seat. The classroom is a bit in disarray right now because of the All-School Talent Show.
Sarah:	Okay. Sounds like you have experience guiding people.

(Sarah takes Mr. Kirsch's arm, using proper human guide technique they walk to her seat.)

Mr. Kirsch:	Why, yes, I have. My best friend in college had vision problems. Most of the time he was just fine but when things got moved around a bit such as my classroom right now, I would help him
Royene:	(Just before Sarah reaches the seat.) Super, you get to sit next to me.
Mr. Kirsch:	Good, you two already know each other.
Royene:	You bet.
Mr. Kirsch:	Great. (Returns to the piano.)
Sarah:	(Sitting down.) Are you Miss Flowers?
Royene:	Yeah, Mr. Kirsch likes to call us Mr. and Miss. He says it's his way of showing us respect.
Sarah:	I think it's kind of neat. And I really like your last name—Flowers. What a pretty last name. So why do you sit between the altos and sopranos?
Royene:	It's because I can sing both. Mr. Kirsch has me sing where he needs me the most. So he says. Actually, I enjoy going back and forth. It's more interesting that way.
Mr. Kirsch:	(Plays the scale on the piano.)

Royene:	That's our cue to practice the scales. (Singing.) La, la, la, la, la.
Sarah:	(Joins in singing.) La, la, la, la, la.

(Usher walks across the stage with a sign: FIFTY MINUTES LATER)

Mr. Kirsch:	That was great! Remember the All-School Talent Show next Friday. Let me know if you want any extra practice. Have a great day.

(The students gather their things and exit the stage. Sarah and Royene stand in the middle of the stage.)

Royene:	Hey, do you have any plans for Saturday night? A few friends are coming over for a while. It'd be great if you could come, too.
Sarah:	No plans yet. I think it'll be okay with my mom. What time?
Royene:	About eight. My mom said we could order some pizza, so long as everyone brings soda or snacks. Maybe you could bring one of those talking movies, too.
Sarah:	Okay, and I'll bring some chips and dip. Hey, Royene, have you thought any more about singing in the talent show?
Royene:	(Shaking her head.) No. I just can't do that sort of thing. I just hate to stand in front of a whole bunch of people. I just know my voice would crack and make all sorts of funny noises. I'd sound like a dork or something. I just can't do it.
Sarah:	Just think about it. I happen to think you can do it. I've been listening to you sing, and you're great!
Royene:	Oh! That was different. That's in chorus. I'm not standing there all by myself with everyone's eyes glued to me alone.
Sarah:	Royene, I'm used to people looking at me all the time, and it doesn't bother me.
Royene:	That's because you can't see them all staring at you.
Sarah:	You're right. I can't, but I know they are. (Showing excitement, as if a light just turned on.) That's it! That's your problem. You're all hung up on the thought of people looking at you. You've got to get past that and not let it get you all uptight. (Nodding her head.) It's a matter of the mind. What we need to do is start off small.
Royene:	What do you mean *we*?
Sarah:	*We* need to get you in front of a small group and work our way to a larger group. (Pause.) I got it! Meet me at the city library on Saturday morning at 10:00 sharp.
Royene:	What for?
Sarah:	Just trust me, okay?
Royene:	(Doubtful.) Okay, but if I don't think I'm going to like it, then I'm going to back out.
Sarah:	You'll like it. Besides, I won't let you back out.

Curtain

ACT THREE: SCENE TWO

Sarah is standing in front of closed curtains.

Royene:	(Approaches Sarah.) Okay, here I am.
Sarah:	(Holding two Print-Braille books under her arm.) Great, you made it. I was beginning to wonder if…

Royene:	I'm here, but I'm not sure I want to be.
Sarah:	You see, I used to read to the children at the city library in Louisiana, so when I moved here, I wanted to keep it up. I've been doing this here on Saturdays now for two weeks. I'll read a story, and then you can. Okay?
Royene:	(Doubtful) Umm...O.K.
Sarah:	I am going to read, *Happy Birthday, Grampie*, by Susan Pearson. It is a twin-vision book. It has Braille that I can read and pictures that the little ones can look at.
Royene:	Yes. But I can't read Braille.
Sarah:	You don't have to. Twin-vision books have print, too. Here, you can read, *See the Ocean* by Estele Condra (Hands the book to Royene.) These are both great books that have blind characters. Just follow my lead. You're going to have so much fun!

(Sarah and Royene leave the stage.)

(Usher walks across the stage with a sign: FORTY-FIVE MINUTES LATER. Usher turns the sign over and walks back across the stage and exits. The sign reads: ...AND AFTER SINGING *MARY HAD A LITTLE LAMB* THREE TIMES.)

(Sarah and Royene enter the stage.)

Royene:	Wow! Sarah, that was great! I loved it.
Sarah:	Good. I thought you would. But the question is, (Putting her index and thumbs together and placing them above the bridge of her nose. Then spreading her middle, ring, and pinky fingers outward. Looking through her thumb and index fingers) How did it feel having all those little itty-bitty eyes on you, hanging on your every word?
Royene:	(Laughing and protesting.) Hey, that's not fair. You know that is not the same thing as singing in front of a bunch of people.
Sarah:	Not really the same thing, but... (cocking her head to one side.) Look, why don't you just try it? Stand up on that stage and sing as if you were singing to the kids today. I know down deep inside, you want to do it.
Royene:	I'll think about it. Okay?
Sarah:	Well, at least that's a start. Hey, want to meet my mom? Her office is near here.
Royene:	Sure.

(Royene follows Sarah off stage.)

Curtain

ACT FOUR: SCENE ONE

(In front of closed curtains. The audience hears the sound of a doorbell. Sarah and Royene enter the stage from the left. Sarah is carrying potato chips and Mountain Dew.)

Royene:	Super, you found the place. Did your mom bring you?
Sarah:	Yes, she dropped me off on her way to the movies.
Royene:	Cool. We've just ordered the pizza. I see you brought the chips.

(Curtain opens to Royene's house. The couch is on the center of the stage where Ashleah and Elsie Bea are sitting and drinking Mountain Dew. Behind the couch is a large picture window. To the right and left of the couch are two large recliners. There is a coffee table in front of the couch with a stack of CDs, a large empty bowl, paper cups in a stack, and a couple of large bottles of Mountain Dew.

Sarah:	Who all is here?
Royene:	Elsie Bea and Ashleah. Bobby and Marty might stop by later. Come on in. Want some soda?
Sarah:	Sure. What kind is there?
Elsie Bea:	(Laughing.) There's Mountain Dew and Mountain Dew.
Sarah:	(Laughing.) Wow, so much to choose from. I guess, I'll have... Mountain Dew.
Ashleah:	We both brought the Dew; it's our favorite. When is the pizza going to get here anyway?
Royene:	About forty-five minutes. Here I'll take the chips. (Puts them on the coffee table.) Sarah, there are some cups filled with ice on the coffee table so you can pour some Dew.
Sarah:	(Finds the coffee table with her cane and gently moves her hand around the coffee table and locates the paper cups. She fills her own glass with soda.) Forty-five minutes is a long time.
Ashleah:	I'll be fainted on the floor by then. I didn't have any lunch today because I was hanging out with Bobby and Marty.
Elsie Bea:	(Pipes up.) How's Marty's girlfriend?
Ashleah:	Oh, they broke up. Said she couldn't take him living so far away.
Elsie Bea:	Oh, what a shame. (Smiling.)
Royene:	Let's put on some music. What does everyone want to hear?
Sarah:	Anything is okay with me.
Ashleah:	No country! (Opening the bag of potato chips and empties the bag into the large bowl.)
Elsie Bea:	Whatever is fine with me.
Sarah:	Actually, I was wondering if you all wouldn't mind going over a couple of chorus songs with me. Mr. Kirsch told me that it'll take longer than he thought to get the music in Braille, and I'm kind of hung up in a couple of areas.
Elsie Bea:	Sure. (Turning to Ashleah.) Ashleah, I think your class is working on the same songs, aren't they?
Ashleah:	I think so. (Stuffing a handful of chips in her mouth.)
Elsie Bea:	Then let's do it. What song do you want to sing?
Sarah:	*His Eye is on the Sparrow*.
Ashleah:	Oh, sure, we're working on that song, too.

(Sarah, Elsie Bea, Ashleah, and Royene start singing. As the song progresses, everyone drops out one by one leaving Royene to sing solo. Bobby and Marty enter the stage as Royene is singing. They stand quietly and listen.)

Ashleah:	(After the song is over.) Wow, Royene, you have a beautiful voice.
Elsie Bea:	You're going to be the next super star!
Sarah:	See, Royene, if you can sing in front of your closest friends, who, by the way, can be your best critics, then you can sing in front of anyone!

Royene:	(Embarrassed.) Oh, you guys are just saying that because you're my friends and you don't want to hurt my feelings by telling me the real truth. I STINK!
Bobby:	You don't stink. You were great. (Walking over to the bowl of chips and grabbing a hand full.)
Ashleah:	Okay, then it's settled. You're going to sing in the All-School Talent Show, and that's final! (Backhanding Bobby's arm teasingly.) Now what did you two bring to eat? I'm starving!
Bobby:	You're always hungry!
Ashleah:	Am not!
Bobby:	(Teasing.) Are too. Now stop it! Have you all met Marty? He just moved here.
Ashleah:	(Laughing.) Yeah, I know him.
Bobby:	I wasn't talking to you, silly.
Elsie Bea:	Hello Marty. I'm Elsie Bea.
Royene:	Hey Marty. I'm happy you could make it. I'm Royene, and this is Sarah; she just moved here, too.
Marty:	Hi.
Bobby:	Hi, Sarah. I'm Ashleah's big, bad brother.

(Bobby waves his hands over Sarah's face as if to see if she is really blind. Ashleah slaps her brother's arm and gives him a dirty look and shakes her head.)

Sarah:	Hi, Bobby and Marty.
Bobby:	So, um… Sarah. Are you, like, blind, or something?
Sarah:	(Teasing, using the same tone as Bobby.) Yes. Um... are you... like sighted or something?
Bobby:	(Taken back by her candor, steps back.) Umm, yeah... So, Sarah. Do you want to play the piano, or shall we put on the stereo?
Sarah:	Actually, we were just talking about putting on some tunes You wouldn't want me to play any piano if you want to save the keys. I'm lousy!
Bobby:	But I thought all blind people were good at the piano. I think I read that someplace.
Sarah:	Well, it's not true.

(Bobby whispers something to Marty. Marty shakes his head.)

Bobby:	(Goes over and picks up Sarah's cane.) What is this? (Closes his eyes, and walks around the room hitting the cane against the furniture and people.)
Elsie Bea:	(Chasing after Bobby.) Come on, Bobby, that's not nice.
Ashleah:	Stop it, Bobby!

(Marty takes the cane from Bobby and returns it to where it was.)

Royene:	That wasn't nice.
Sarah:	(Teasing.) Bobby, if you want me to give you a proper cane travel lesson, I've got some free time tomorrow. But until then, let's save the furniture around here, okay?
Bobby:	(Looks a bit ashamed.) Darn, I'm sorry.
Ashleah:	Well, you ought to be! (Slapping him on the back.) Shame on you, picking on a blind girl like that!
Sarah:	(Teasing.) Yeah, what would your mom say?
Ashleah:	(Looking out the picture window.) Gosh, when is that pizza going to get here?

Elsie Bea:	(Walks up to Marty.) Marty, how do you like it here, so far?
Marty:	Oh, it's ok.

(Elsie Bea and Marty start talking quietly together.)

Ashleah:	I'm going outside to see if the pizza guy got lost!
Royene:	I'll go with you.

(Ashleah and Royene leave the stage.)

Bobby:	(Walks over to Sarah.) Look, Sarah, I'm really sorry for what I did. Sometimes I can be a total jerk.
Sarah:	That's okay, Bobby. You're not the first person who has ever done jerky things like that before and you won't be the last, I'm sure.
Bobby:	Can I get you another soda or something?
Sarah:	Nope, I'm fine. Thank you.
Bobby:	Well then, I'll put on some tunes. (Looks through some CDs on the coffee table.) Can you dance? I mean, um... Do you want to?
Sarah:	I like to dance but not right now.
Bobby:	(Sitting down on the couch.) I've never met a blind girl before.
Sarah:	(Big smile.) Well, there's always a first time for everything. So my mom tells me.
Bobby:	You're kind of funny. You know that?
Sarah:	Some people have told me that.

(Silence)

Bobby:	(Awkward.) Would you like to feel my face?
Sarah:	Why?
Bobby:	So, you can see that I'm smiling.
Sarah:	I can hear it in your voice.
Bobby:	Cool.

(Silence)

(Royene and Ashleah burst in. Ashleah is holding the pizza.)

Ashleah:	FINALLY! The pizza is here!
Royene:	(Turning to Sarah.) I think I'll ask Mr. Kirsch if he'll help me practice after school next week.
Sarah:	Does that mean you're going to sing in the talent show?
Royene:	Doy!

Curtain

ACT FOUR: SCENE TWO

At the	All-School Talent Show, behind the stage. Ashleah, Royene, and Sarah are peeking out of the curtains at the center of the stage.
Ashleah:	Have you guys heard the news?

Royene:	What?
Ashleah:	Elsie Bea and Marty are going out.
Sarah:	(Shocked.) You're kidding.
Ashleah:	No joke, you guys. I'm serious. Bobby told me that Marty was planning on asking her out today. Peeking through curtain.) Look, they're sitting together... right over there, the third row.
Royene:	(Peeks through the curtain.) They sure are. Gosh, she never said anything to me. I wonder when he asked her.
Ashleah:	Bobby said Marty was going to ask her right after they got out of computer class today.
Royene:	Oh, then that explains why she didn't tell me. I haven't seen her since then.
Ashleah:	(Peeking through the curtains again.) Oh, there is Mr. Unkrich and Miss Colman sitting together.
Sarah, **Elsie Bea**, and **Ashleah:**	Ooooohhh!
Royene:	(Gently pushes Ashleah aside so she could look through the curtains.) Where? Oh, hey! I see your mom, Sarah. She's sitting on the other side of Miss Colman.
Sarah:	My mom said she was looking forward to checking out the talent around here. I just thought I'd come back here and wish you good luck.
Royene:	(Turning away from the curtain.) Oh, thanks, Sarah. I'm going to need it.
Sarah:	(Shaking her head.) Not really. Pretend like you're singing to the children. Just go out there and bloom, Miss Flowers!
Royene:	(Giggling and nodding her head.) Sure, sure...
Ashleah:	(Hugging Royene.) You'll do just great!
Royene:	(Turning to Ashleah.) Good luck to you too, Ashleah. I can't wait to hear your poem. You've been so secretive about it.
Ashleah:	Okay, okay. Darn, now you've made me nervous, too!
Sarah:	(Chuckling.) Well then, I'd better go. (Calling over her shoulder.) See you after the show! (Leaves the stage and joins her mother in the audience.)

(Ashleah and Royene exit. Mr. Gatewood enters the stage with a microphone.)

Mr. Gatewood:	(Sounding like a circus entertainer.) Ladies and Gentlemen! Welcome to our Seventy-fifth All-School Talent Show. Remember, everyone here is a winner tonight. Please, let's welcome, our first guest, Mr. Glenn Calvin. He is going to play the National Anthem on his trumpet.

(Usher walks across the stage with a sign: APPLAUSE. Mr. Gatewood exits. Glenn enters the stage from the center of the curtains. The spotlight is upon him. He blinks his eyes in order to adjust to the light. The usher pushes the United States flag on to the right side of the stage, steps back and places his hand upon his heart. Glenn turns his body slightly towards the flag, places his trumpet to his lips and plays the National Anthem. Afterwards, he bows. The usher removes the flag and Mr. Gatewood enters the stage.)

Mr. Gatewood:	Thank you, Mr. Glenn Calvin for an excellent performance. Now, ladies and gentlemen, let's please give a warm welcome to Miss Ashleah Kline. She would like to present some of her most creative poetry to you.

(Usher walks across the stage with a sign: APPLAUSE. Mr. Gatewood exits. Curtain open. Ashleah enters the stage and stands in front of a microphone.)

Ashleah: (Clearing her throat loudly.) My poem is called, Have You Ever Seen a Fly Pee? (Pausing and clearing her throat again.) (Pointing to the audience.) Have you ever seen a fly pee? (Putting her hands on her hips and nodding her head.) It did, it did, right in front of me. (Pretending to sit with her hands crossed on her lap.) I was sitting there upon a chair. (Standing with her hand by her mouth as if to whisper.) I confess. I did stare. (Putting her hands back on her hip.) And then it happened, clear as day. (Pointing to the audience moving her index finger up and down as if lecturing a small child.)You must believe what I say. (Slowly saying.) For under the fly, a puddle did appear. (resuming her rate of speech) I wouldn't have seen it, if I weren't (Pause.) so near!

(Ashleah bows and exits the stage.)

Curtain

(Usher walks across the stage with a sign: APPLAUSE. Mr. Gatewood enters)

Mr. Gatewood: Very well done, Miss Kline. Okay, ladies and gentleman, our next performer is Miss Royene Flowers. She will be singing "His Eye is on the Sparrow."

(Usher walks across the stage with a sign: APPLAUSE. Mr. Gatewood exits.)

Curtains open. Royene is standing next to a piano. Mr. Kirsch is at the keys. Royene is wearing a beautiful long light blue dress sprinkled with small white daffodils. She appears a little nervous but her voice is loud and strong as she sings beautifully into the microphone.

(Royene bows and her face is gleaming as the curtain close. Usher walks across the stage with a sign: AFTER THE SHOW.)

(Sarah and Mrs. Siebold walk in front of a closed curtain.)

Mrs. Siebold: That friend of yours, Royene, was very good tonight. Don't you think?
Sarah: Yes, she was great! (Laughing.) So was Ashleah's poem!
Mrs. Siebold: Yes. That poem was really funny. I have never seen a fly pee!
Royene: (Running up to Sarah and her mother.) Hey, Sarah, wait up.

(Sarah and her mother stop.)

Sarah: You were super! (Hugging Royene.) I was going to wait for you back stage but I heard that you had left already.

Royene: Sorry. But I had to go find my parents. Sarah, you know, I couldn't have done it without you. (Giving Sarah a big hug then turning to Mrs. Siebold and giving her a hug, too) Thank you so much for moving here.

Mrs. Siebold: (Smiling.) Oh, you're quite welcome.

Ashleah:	(Approaches them.) Hey, you guys, want to come over to my place for a celebration? (Giggling.) I've got plenty of Mountain Dew!
Sarah:	Sounds great! (Turning to her mother.) Mom?
Mrs. Siebold:	(Smiling.) You go ahead and have a great time.
Sarah:	Thanks, Mom. I won't be out too late. (Turning to Ashleah.) Boy, that was a silly poem. I loved it.

(Sarah, Royene and Ashleah start walking back towards the way they entered. Bobby, Marty, and Elsie Bea join them, and they all exit together. Elsie Bea and Marty are holding hands.)

Mrs. Siebold:	(Smiling and watching them all leave, turns in the opposite direction, takes a couple of steps and stops. Looks back to where the group exited the stage and nods to herself.) I told you they would like you. (Exits the stage with a big smile.)

THE END

NOTES

_____

_____

_____

_____

_____

_____

_____

_____

_____

_____

_____

_____

_____

DEFINITION OF TERMS

Cane Arc: The cane mechanics of moving the cane tip to the right and left of the body, as wide as the user's shoulders, to ensure the area is clear of obstacles as well as wide enough for the body to proceed.

Cane Basics: The physical components of holding the cane as well as some of the mechanics of using the long white cane for mobility purposes.

Cane Etiquette: The proper way to store the cane when not in use.

Cane Mechanics: The physical component of moving the cane during mobility: (1) Extended Technique; (2) Cane Arc; (3) Walking-in-Step; (4) Two-Point Touch; (5) Touch & Slide; (6) Constant Contact; and (7) Shore-lining.

Cane Travel (i.e., Mobility): The skill and ability to maneuver from one location to another using the long white cane.

Cognitive Learning Theory: This is an instructional design that utilizes an environment to acquire knowledge and improve comprehension to build and expand upon (Tennyson & Rasch, 1988).

Constant Contact: The cane mechanics which helps to locate small, hard to detect, landmarks that are best found using tactile, and sometimes auditory, methods.

Consumer: Typically, it is a person who utilizes a service (Dictionary.com, 2018). However, in this text, a *consumer* it is a person who is blind or visually impaired—post O&M instruction.

Custodial Paradigm: When things are done for the student (such as guiding them) rather than expecting things from the student (such as traveling independently).

Curriculum: An aggregate list of learning objectives (i.e., skills and knowledge) used to guide instruction (Education Reform, 2015) and these objectives "always reflect the values of those who created it" (Wiles, 2009, p. 14).

Discovery Learning: "A teaching strategy in which the material to be learned is uncovered by the learner in the course of solving a problem or completing a task" (Fazzi & Barlow, 2017, p. 254).

Drop-Routes: An O&M training method typically used to increase self-confidence and mobility competency and for students' final instructional training exam in mobility training. This consists of the following: (1) Create confusion (i.e., taking the student on a meaningless automobile ride with numerous twists and turns so they are unable to use mental mapping to determin their whereabouts); (2) Dropping off the student at a location unknown to the student where they are given the objective to (3) use all their mobility training abilities to (4) return to home-base or given a predetermined location to which they need to walk (Welsh, 2005).

Echolocation: The metal tip of the cane which offers *active* and *consistent* sounds for the user which Johnson (2012) states produces specific signals that reflect off objects.

Extended Technique: The cane mechanics which helps to travel quickly and confidently in open spaces.

Fixed Routes: Routes that have a relationship from one landmark to another regardless of the students' perspective (Long & Giudice, 2010).

Hand Grip: Techniques of holding the cane for mobility purposes: (1) Pencil Grip and (2) Open Palm Grip.

Human Guide: A simple procedure in which the guide walks about a step ahead of the consumer/student who holds the leader's arm above the bent elbow (Ensing, 2016).

Independence Paradigm: When students learn to travel without a guide, the opportunities to travel independently are endless whereby they are not limited to only traveling at certain times or only traveling to certain locations.

Independent Cane Travel: A myriad of opportunities to achieve maximum independence, often through self-dependent mobility, provided by their O&M instructors (Ballemans et al., 2011; Leonard, 1968; Malik et al., 2018; Williams, 1967).

Individual Education Plan (IEP): An educational team which includes parent(s), school staff members (i.e., principal or vice principal, classroom teacher, special education teacher, and paraprofessional), Orientation and Mobility (O&M) Instructor, and Teacher of the Visually Impaired (TVI).

Intrinsic Feedback: Information obtained through internal processing or senses such as: (1) auditory sounds available either through the metal tip of the cane or elsewhere; (2) olfactory; (3) tactile information provided maneuvering or via the cane; (4) internal perception (kinesthetic cues); (5) prior knowledge; and/or (6) memory of spatial information (Long & Giudice, 2010).

Intrinsic Motivation: One of the key components of SDCT curriculum because it establishes goals which are meaningful or significant only to that student (Sarid, 2012).

Kinesthetic: Active engagement through a multi-sensory learning environment whereby internal learning occurs and this involves "movement, testing, trial and error and a non-traditional learning environment to retain information and excel" (Macmillan, 2018, par. 3).

Landmarks: Landmarks items that are Points of Interest (POI) which are stationary, meaning they may be used as reference points that are unlikely to be moved such as water fountains, support column, texture change on the floor (carpet to tile) (Chamberlain, 2017).

Legal blindness: Individuals who have a visual acuity of 20/200 or worse in their better eye, with correction, or those who have a combined (meaning both eyes) visual field of 20 degrees or less (CDC, 2017; Social Security Administration, 2018) and this includes individuals whose visual acuity may be 20/20 within that limited field of view.

Locale Memory: Long-term memory with an unlimited capacity (Payne, 2002).

Locus of Control: "A psychological concept that refers to how strongly people believe they have control over the situations and experiences that affect their lives" (Glossary of Education Reform, 2013, par. 1).

Long white cane: The mobility tool used by consumers to gain surface information from the environment and to identify the user as being visually impaired or blind (Pogrund & Griffin-Shirley, 2018).

Mental Mapping Skills: The ability to create a diagram of the area within the mind (Chamberlain, 2005).

Mild Visual Impairment: This is a visual acuity between 20/30 and 20/60.

Mobility (i.e., Cane Travel): "The capacity or facility to movement" (Jacobson, 1993, p. 3) or actual locomotion to move from one position or location to another (Koestler, 2004) using the long white cane.

Moderate Visual Impairment: This is a visual acuity between 20/70 and 20/180.

National Blindness Professional Certification Board (NBPCB): Established in 1997 when Louisiana Tech University (LA. Tech) teamed with the Louisiana Center for the Blind (LCB) to develop a holistic O&M Master's level training program. It was made possible via a Federal Experimental and Innovative grant from the Rehabilitation Services Administration, U.S. Department of Education (Aditya, 2004). This certifying body that offers the National Orientation and Mobility Certifications.

National Orientation and Mobility Certification (NOMC): This is the certification held by mobility instructors who use the Structured Discovery Cane Travel curriculum.

Normal Vision: A person is considered to have normal vision if they have a visual acuity of "20/20." This means people who have 20/20 visual acuity can all see the same thing when standing 20 feet away from that visual target.

Occluded Training: This instruction provides students the abilities and skills they can depend on, regardless of how much vision they have now or how little vision they may have in the future.

Open Palm Grip: A cane grip that helps to avoid the cane from thrusting into the user's gut when the cane encounters objects when walking.

Orientation and Mobility (O&M) (i.e., cane travel, foot travel): The profession of teaching concept development, techniques and skills to consumers to help them travel efficiently, gracefully and safely in a myriad of locations and situations which include soliciting assistance (if needed), using community resources (i.e., public transportation), and making decisions (Jacobson, 1993; Pogrund & Griffin-Shirley, 2018).

Orientation and Mobility (O&M) Curriculum: This focuses on the foundational skills necessary to develop future independence and sovereignty for individuals who are blind or visually impaired.

Orientation: *Orientation* has two interrelated metaphorical senses, the first being "a positioning and awareness of the location where one stands relative to the world" and the second "a horizon of meaning that points the direction towards the desired destination" (Sarid, 2012, p. 245). It is the perception of space and relationships to neighboring objects (Koestler, 2004).

Paradigm Paralysis: "The inability or refusal to see beyond current ways of thinking" or "beyond the present situation" in which an organization focuses on what is "supposed to work instead of what really works" (Smith & Rigby, 2015, p. XIV, 71, 73).

Pencil Grip: A cane grip that helps to avoid the cane from going under obstacles such as tables and chairs when walking.

Play Facilitators: Individuals who "inspires play, creates space and time for many kinds of playful activities, and adapts his or her role to match where children are as they take on new challenges. Skillful facilitators are able to spot opportunities to integrate learning goals in playful settings without disrupting children's engaged and playful endeavors (Jensen et al., 2019, p. 5).

Profession of O&M: The teaching O&M (concepts, techniques and skills) to individuals who are visually impaired so they are able to *independently* travel safely in a myriad of locations, efficiently and gracefully (Aditya, 2004; Cutter, 2007; Jacobson, 1993) by way of using a long white cane with a metal tip as the mobility tool.

Pre-canes: Alternative Mobility Devices (AMDs) often made out of PBC pipe and are heavy and cumbersome. Such devices do "not encourage the exploration of surfaces and the development of self-directed active discovery" (Castellano, 2017, par. 4).

Problem-Solving: A "metaphor for most higher-order thinking tasks and for most assessment tasks that tap higher-order thinking" (Brookhart, 2014, p. 12). This includes simple decisions to complex followed by selection and implementation of strategies.

Problem-Solving Skills: The process of utilizing techniques to alleviate travel woes.

Scribbling With The Cane: An age and stage appropriate technique of which young children explore with using the cane as a tool because young children have not developed the dexterity to hold the cane correctly (Chamberlain & Mackenstadt, 2018). They add, this is similar to scribbling before developing the ability to print.

Self-Confidence: How much a person feels certain or capable of their decisions, actions, and/or behaviors (Bearden et al., 2001).

Sequential Learning (SL): A curriculum which build skills to use in future lessons to advance the understanding of concepts and skills (Moss & Brookhart, 2012). Sequential Learning follows the Taxon memory system which needs continuous rehearsals and extrinsic motivation to reach perfection (Payne, 2002).

Shoreline: An edge of something (i.e., building, curb, sidewalk, carpet), or tactile surface (i.e., sidewalk crack), which can be followed using the cane or auditory (i.e. echolocation, traffic) methods.

Shore-Lining: The cane mechanics of actively following a shoreline by using the long white cane. (See shoreline)

Sighted Guide: See Human Guide.

Socratic Method: Open-ended probing questions to assist students to "learn through the use of critical thinking, reasoning, and logic" and help focus on the task at hand (Fabio, 2019, par. 3).

Splinter Skills (i.e., gaps of knowledge): When only fragments of an ability or talent are comprehended (Fazzi & Petersmeyer, 2001; Perla & O'Donnell, 2004).

Structured Discovery Cane Travel (SDCT): An O&M curriculum which utilizes transformational knowledge, hands-on experiences, problem-solving opportunities within natural environments, and personal reflection through teachable moments to develop physical and mental mapping skills which can be utilized post instruction, outside the O&M lesson. This specifically involves the experience of cognitive problem-solving under the direction of a mobility instructor who has National Orientation and Mobility Certification.

Structured Discovery: The experience of cognitive problem-solving under the direction of an educator (Dodds, 1984). Dodds describes Structured Discovery whereby he did not receive sighted information second hand; rather he was permitted to experiment through making mistakes and actively exploring his environment to determine possible solutions without external assistance while occluded.

Student: A person who is blind or visually impaired learning Orientation & Mobility; the foundational skill necessary to develop future independence and sovereignty.

Taxon Memory: Sort-term memory with approximately five tasks (Payne, 2002).

Teachable Moment: These are real-life new and/or unexpected educational encounters that engage and stimulate long-lasting concepts and/or memory of specific learning experiences (Hansen, 1998).

Teacher of Blind Students: See below.

Teacher of Students with Visual Impairments (i.e., Teacher of Blind Students or Teacher of the Visually Impaired): A person who has a degree specializing in teaching students who are blind or visually impaired.

Teacher of the Visually Impaired: See above.

Teaching Cane: An educational strategy. A cane that adults use to demonstrate a variety of skills such as tapping the cane to listen to various sounds. Parents use teaching canes whereby the child will hold the shaft of the adult cane to feel the movements (Thorpe, 2007). "This modeling technique allows the parent to play a vital role in helping the child to develop early movement and exploration" states Thorpe (2007, par. 10).

Touch & Slide: The cane mechanics which helps to provide tactile information regarding the terrain and locate landmarks that are best found using tactile methods.

Transformational Knowledge: which is the ability to learn and master techniques within a plethora of settings during training through hands-on experiences and then transfer those skills post training in other settings

Two-Point Touch: Creates auditory, and possible tactile, feedback in various locations.

Vision: A directional foreground modality (Kratz et al., 1987).

Walk-in-Step: The method used that provides *continuous* information that the area in which is about to be traveled is clear of objects).

REFERENCES

Aditya, R. N. (2004). *A comparison of two Orientation and Mobility certifications.* http://studylib.net/doc/6790954/a-comparison-of-two-orientation-and-mobility-certifications.

Alan Beggs, W. D. (1992). Coping with traveling in the visually impaired: A comparison of elite and poor travelers. *Psychology & Health,* 7(1), 15–16.

Ambutech. (2020). *Slimline aluminum identification cane—No grip (san) adult.* https://ambutech.com/collections/aluminum-identification-canes/products/slimline-aluminum-identification-cane

American Foundation for the Blind. (AFB). (2018a). *Being a sighted guide.* http://www.afb.org/info/friends-and-family/etiquette/being-a-sighted-guide/235

American Foundation for the Blind. (AFB). (2018b). *Walking with a sighted guide.* http://www.afb.org/section.aspx?SectionID=66&TopicID=304&DocumentID=3263&rewrite=0

American Optometric Association. (2018). *Low vision.* https://www.aoa.org/patients-and-public/caring-for-your-vision/low-vision

Annual Disability Statistics Compendium. (2017). *Institute on disability. University of New Hampshire.* https://disabilitycompendium.org/

A Veterans Administration Medical Film. (1952). *The long cane: Indoor foot travel. Part 1. Department of medicine and surgery.* https://www.youtube.com/watch?v=D-hDizzZZak

A Veterans Administration Medical Film. (1952b). *The long cane: Outdoor foot travel. Part 2. Department of medicine and surgery.* https://www.youtube.com/watch?v=NnxlX7fstYI

Baldwin, D. (2016). *Bugs, blindness, and the pursuit of happiness: How navigation gave rise to consciousness.* Author.

Ball, E. M., & Nicolle, C. A. (2015). Changing what it means to be 'normal': A grounded theory study of the mobility choices of people who are blind or have low vision. *Journal of Visual Impairment & Blindness, 109*(4), 291–301.

Ballemans, J., Kempen, G. I., & Zijlstra, G. R. (2011). Orientation and Mobility training for partially-sighted older adults using an identification cane: A systematic review. *Clinical rehabilitation, 25*(10), 880–891. DOI:10.1177/0269215511404931

Bandura, A. (1982). Self-efficacy mechanism in human agency. *American Psychologist, 37*(2), 122–147. https://pdfs.semanticscholar.org/8bee/ c556fe7a650120544a99e9e063eb8fcd987b.pdf

Barraga, N. C., & Erin, J. N. (1992). *Visual handicaps and learning.* Pro Ed.

Bearden, W. O., Hardesty, D. M., & Rose, R. L. (2001). Consumer self-confidence: Refinements in conceptualization and measurement. *Journal of Consumer Research, 28*(1), 121–134.

Bell, E. (2015). Transforming the training of professionals in education and rehabilitation for the blind. *Braille monitor.* https://nfb.org/images/nfb/publications /bm/bm15/bm1510/bm151009.htm

Bell, E. (2018). Email correspondence.

Bell, E. C., & Mino, N. M. (2011). A demographic study of national Orientation and Mobility certified instructors. *Journal of Blindness Innovation and Research, 1*(2). https://nfb.org/images/nfb/publications/jbir/jbir11/jbir010201.html

Bénabou, R., & Tirole, J. (2002). Self-confidence and personal motivation. *The Quarterly Journal of Economics, 117*(3), 871–915. https://doi.org/10.1162/003355302760193913

Best, C. (2015). *My three best friends and me, Zulay.* N Farrar Straus, Giroux Books for Young Readers.

Bickford, T. (1993). *Care and feeding of the long white cane.* National Federation of the Blind.

Blaha, L. (1967). Basic techniques essential to Orientation and Mobility. In *Proceedings conference for mobility trainers and technicians.* Handout. http://www.duxburysystems.org/downloads/library/history/1967_mobility_mit.pdf

Blasch, B., Wiener, W., & Welsh, R. (1997). *Foundations of Orientation and Mobility: Second edition.* American Foundation for the Blind.

British Broadcasting Company (BBC) News. (2017). *Completely blind packpacker travelling around the world.* http://www.bbc.com/news/av/disability-42198169/completely-blind-backpacker-travelling-around-the-world

Brookhart, S. M. (2014). *How to design questions and tasks to assess student thinking.* Association for Supervision and Curriculum Development (ASCD).

Bryant, E. (2009). My tree branch cane: How I became blind and then what. In D. Frye (Ed.), *Bridging the gap: Living with blindness and diabetes* (pp. 3–6). The National Federation of the Blind.

Castellano, C. (2005). *Making it work: Educating the blind/visually impaired consumer in the regular school.* Information Age Publishing.

Castellano, C. (2010). *Getting ready for college begins in third grade.* Charlotte, NC: Information Age Publishing.

Castellano, C. (2017). A new mobility system for toddlers? *Future reflections.* https://www.nfb.org/sites/www.nfb.org/files/images/nfb/publications/fr/fr36/3/fr360302.htm

Center for Disease Control and Prevention. (CDC). (2017). *Blindness and vision impairment.* https://www.cdc.gov/healthcommunication/toolstemplates/entertainmented/tips/Blindness.html

Chamberlain, M. N. (2005). Saturday school: A holistic approach to educating children with visual impairments. *Future Reflections, 24*(4). https://nfb.org/Images/nfb/ Publications /fr/fr20/fr05ci16.htm

Chamberlain, M. N. (2013). Orientation and Mobility: One instructor's perspective. *Future Reflections, 32*(3), 28–32. https://nfb.org/images/nfb/publications/fr/fr32/3 /fr320309.htm

Chamberlain, M. N. (2015). Sighted/human guide: One instructor's perspective. *Future Reflections, 34*(1). https://nfb.org/images/nfb/publications/fr/fr34/1/fr340110.htm

Chamberlain, M. N. (2017). Orientation and Mobility for babies and toddlers: A parent's guide *Future reflections.* https://www.nfb.org/sites/www.nfb.org/files/images/nfb/publications/fr/fr36/3/fr360301.htm

Chamberlain, M. N. (2017b). The Orientation and Mobility goal bank. *Future Reflections: Special issue: The individualized education plan (IEP).* https://nfb.org/images/nfb/ publications/fr/fr36/2/fr360206.htm

Chamberlain, M. N. (2018). Helpful hints for paraprofessionals working with students who are blind or visually impaired. *Future Reflections, 37*(3). https://www.nfb.org/sites/www.nfb.org/files/images/nfb/publications/fr/fr37/3/fr370302.htm

Chamberlain, M. N. (2019). *Self-confidence levels in sequential learning versus structured discovery cane travel, post Orientation and Mobility instruction: A comparison study.* https://digitalcommons.csp.edu/cgi/viewcontent.cgi?article=1298&context=cup_commons_grad_edd

Chamberlain, M. N., & Mackenstadt, D. (2018). Teaching orientation & mobility to students with visual impairments and additional disabilities. *Future Reflections, 37*(1). https://nfb.org/images/nfb/publications/fr/fr37/1/fr370103.htm

Cmar, J. L. (2015). Orientation and Mobility skills and outcomes expectations as predictors of employment for young adults with visual impairments. *Journal of Visual Impairment and Blindness, 109*(2), 95–106. https://files.eric.ed.gov/fulltext/EJ1114561.pdf

COMS Handbook. (2018). *Certified Orientation and Mobility specialist (coms) handbook. Section 2—Scope of practice for Orientation and Mobility certification.* https://www.acvrep.org/certifications/coms-scope

Coulter, A., Entwistle, V., & Gilbert, D. (1999). Sharing decisions with patients: Is the information good enough? *BMJ.* https://www.ncbi.nlm.nih.gov/pmc/articles/PMC1114785/pdf/318.pdf

Crow, N., & Herlich, S. (2012). *Getting to know you: A social skills/ability awareness curriculum.* American Printing House for the Blind.

Crudden, A. (2015). Transportation issues: Perspectives of Orientation and Mobility. *Journal of Visual Impairment and Blindness, 109*(6), 457–468.

Cutter, J. (2001). The need for pre-cane: Fact or Fancy? *Future reflections.* https://www.nfb.org/images/nfb/publications/fr/fr5/frfa0109.htm

Cutter, J. (2001b). *Rights, roles, and responsibilities in the Orientation and Mobility process.* https://nfb.org/images/nfb/publications/bm/bm01/bm0107/bm010708.htm

Cutter, J. (2007). *Independent movement and travel in blind children: A promotion curriculum.* Information Age Publishing.

Deverell, L. (2011). O&M environmental complexity scale. *International Journal of Orientation & Mobility, 4*(1), 64–77. DOI: 10.21307/ijom-2011-008. https://www.exeley.com/International_Journal_of_Orientation_and_Mobility/doi/10.21307/ijom-2011-008

Dictionary.com. (2018). *Consumer.* https://www.dictionary.com/browse/consumer

Dodds, A. (1984). *A report to N.R.I.B. on a visit to Nebraska Services for the Visually Impaired: Blind mobility research unit* (Report No. 138 to the Royal National institute for the Blind). Nottingham, England: University of Nottingham.

Dodds, A. (1988). *Mobility training for visually handicapped people: A person-centered approach.* Croom Helm.

Dodds, A. (1993). *Rehabilitating blind and visually impaired people: A psychological approach.* Springer.

Dodge, D. T., Dombro, A. L., & Colker, L. J. (1998). *A parent's guide to infant/toddler programs.* Teaching Strategies, Inc.

Dodge, D. T., & Heroman, C. (1999). *Building your baby's brain, a parent's guide to the first five years.* Teaching Strategies, Inc.

DuFour, R., DuFour, R., Eaker, R., & Many, T. (2006). *Learning by doing: A handbook for professional learning communities at work.* Solution Tree.

Dweck, C. S. (2008). *Mindset: The new psychology of success: How we can learn to fulfill our potential.* Ballantine Books.

Education Reform. (2015). *Curriculum.* https://www.edglossary.org/curriculum/

Ensing, G. (2016). Orientation and Mobility for children: A conversation for parents. *Cincinnati Association for the Blind and Visually Impaired.* https://yt.ax/watch/orientation-and-mobility-for-children-a-conversation-for-parents-37807179/

Fabio, M. (2019). *How the Socratic method works and why is it used in law school.* https://www.thoughtco.com/what-is-the-socratic-method-2154875

Family Lives. (n.d.). *Why play matters.* https://www.familylives.org.uk/advice/early-years-development/learning-and-play/why-play-matters/

Fay, J., & Funk, D. (1995). *Teaching with love & logic: Taking control of the classroom.* The Love and Logic Press.

Fazzi, D. L., & Barlow, J. M. (2017). *Orientation and Mobility techniques: A guide for the practitioner: Second edition.* American Foundation for the Blind Press.

Fazzi, D. L., & Petersmeyer, B. A. (2001). *Imagining the possibilities: Creative approaches to Orientation and Mobility instruction for persons who are visually impaired.* American Foundation for the Blind.

Ferguson, R. J. (2001). *We know who we are: A history of the blind in challenging educational and socially constructed policies, a study in policy archeology.* Caddo Gap Press.

Ferguson, R. J. (2007). *The blind need not apply: A history of overcoming prejudice in the Orientation and Mobility profession.* Information Age Publishing.

First Steps. (n.d.). *Museum of the American Printing House for the Blind.* .

Flaherty, E., Hawkins, A., & Heaton, S. (1997). *The family of Owen M.: Off we go to learn everyday things about Orientation and Mobility.* Hill Publications.

Foundation Fighting Blindness. (n.d.). *Mobility & Orientation packet.* http://www.blindness.org/sites/default/files/pages/pdfs/Mobility-and-Orientation-Packet.pdf

Geruschat, D. R., & De L'Aune, W. (1989). Reliability and validity of O&M instructor observation. *Journal of Visual Impairment & Blindness, 83,* 457–460.

Geruschat, D. R., & Turano, K. A. (2002). Connecting research on retinitis pigmentosa to the practice of Orientation and Mobility. *Journal of Visual Impairment & Blindness, 96*(2), 69–85. https: //www.afb.org/jvib/newjvibabstract.asp?articleid=JVIB960202

Ginsburg, K. R. (2007). The importance of play in promoting healthy child development and maintaining strong parent-child bonds. *Pediatrics, 119*(1), 182–191. DOI: https://doi.org/10.1542/peds.2006-2697

Glasser, W. (1990). *The quality school: Managing students without coercion.* HarperCollins.

Glasser, W. (1998). *Choice theory: A new psychology of personal freedom.* HarperCollins.

Glossary of Education Reform. (2013). *Locus of control.* https://www.edglossary.org/locus-of-control/#:~:text=Locus%20of%20control%20is%20a,experiences%20that%20affect%20their%20lives

Golon, A. S. (2017). *Visual-spatial learners: Understanding the learning style preference of bright but disengaged students.* Sourcebooks, Inc.

Gould, P., & Sullivan, J. (1999). *The inclusive early childhood classroom: easy ways to adapt learning centers for all children.* Gryphon House, Inc.

Gravel, E. (2006). Learning to walk. In B. Karg, & R. Sutherland (Eds.), *Letters to my teacher: Tributes to the people who have made a difference* (pp. 23–25). Adams Media.

Guerreiro, J., Ahmetovic, D., Kitani, K. M., & Asakawa, C. (2017). *Virtual navigation for blind people: Building sequential representations of the real-world.* http://web.ist.utl.pt/joao.p.guerreiro/publications/assets17_virtualNav.pdf

Hallowell, E. (2011). *Shine: Using brain science to get the best from your people.* Harvard Business School Publishing.

Halpern-Gold, J., Adler, R. W., & Faust-Jones, S. (1988). *Travel tales: A mobility storybook.* Mostly Mobility.

Hansen, E. (1998). Creating teachable moments . . . and making them last. *Innovative Higher Education, 23*(1), 7–26. https://doi.org/10.1023/A:1022916412432

Heinen, N. (2014). White cane is symbol of independence. *News 3 Editorial.* https://www.youtube.com/watch?v=I7C3PwYa9jE

Herbert, J. T. (2000). Simulation as a learning method to facilitate disability awareness. *Journal of Experiential Education, 23*(5), 5–11. DOI: 10.1177/105382590002300102

Hill, E. W., & Ponder, P. (1976). *Orientation and Mobility techniques: A guide for the practitioner.* American Foundation for the Blind.

Hilliker, A. (2013). Email correspondence.

Ho'opano. (n.d.). *Helpful hints when you're with a blind person.* Rehabilitation Center for the Blind and Visually Impaired. State of Hawaii/Department of Human Services.

http://citeseerx.ist.psu.edu/viewdoc/download?doi=10.1.1.463.1039&rep=rep1&type=pdf.

Hudson, L. J. (1997). *Classroom collaborations.* Perkins School for the Blind.

Iskow, C. I. (2010). From war injured to the elderly, brain injuries are on the rise for vision rehabilitation practitioners. *Journal of Visual Impairment & Blindness, 104*(10), 597–602.

Jacobson, W. H. (1993). *The art and science of teaching Orientation and Mobility to persons with visual impairments.* American Foundation for the Blind.

Jensen, H., Pyle, A., Zosh, J. M., Ebrahim, H. B., Zaragoza Scherman, A, Reunamo, J. , Hamre, B. K. (2019). *Play facilitation: the science behind the art of engaging young children.* The LEGO Foundation, DK.

Johnson, T. (2012). *Beginner's guide to echolocation for the blind and visually impaired.* CreateSpace Independent Publishing Platform.

Kaiser, J. T., Cmar, J. L., Rosen, S., & Anderson, D. (2018). *Scope of practice in Orientation and Mobility.* Association for Education and Rehabilitation of the Blind and Visually Impaired O&M Division IX. Association for Education and Rehabilitation of the Blind and Visually Impaired.

Kalinowski, T. (2013). *Blind man dragged by TTC bus after door closes on his cane.* https://www.thestar.com/news/city_hall/2013/01/09/blind_man_dragged_by_ttc_bus_after_door_closes_on_his_cane.html

Kappan, D. (1994). On simulating blindness. *Viewpoints.* https://files.eric.ed.gov/fulltext/ED378743.pdf

Kelley, M. (2004). How empowerment changed my life: "I don't have to live in my car anymore . . . " *American Rehabilitation, 28*(1). U.S. Department of Education. Office of Special Education and Rehabilitative Services. https://www2.ed.gov/news/newsletters/amrehab/2004/autumn/kelley.doc

Kim, D. S., & Wall Emerson, R. (2012). Effect of cane length on drop-off detection performance. *Journal of Visual Impairment & Blindness, 106*(1), 31–35.

Koestler, F. (1976). *The unseen minority: A social history of blindness in the united states.* American Foundation for the Blind.

Koestler, F. (2004). *The unseen minority: A social history of blindness in the united states.* American Foundation for the Blind.

Kosciulek, J. F. (2004). Empowering people with disabilities through vocational rehabilitation counseling. *American Rehabilitation, 28*(1). U.S. Department of Education. Office of Special Education and Rehabilitative Services. https://www.thefreelibrary.com/Empowering+people+with+disabilities+through+vocational+rehabilitation...-a0126791480

Kratz, L. E., Tutt, L. M., & Black, D. A. (1987). *Movement and fundamental motor skills for sensory deprived children.* Charles C. Thomas.

LaGrow, S. J., & Weessies, M. J. (1994). *Orientation & Mobility: Techniques for independence.* The Dunmore Press Limited.

Lazear, D. (1999). *Eight ways of knowing: Teaching for multiple intelligences* (3rd ed.). SkyLight Training and Publishing, Inc.

Leonard, J. A. (1968). Towards a unified approach to the mobility of blind people. *American Research Bulletin, 18,* 1–21.

Long, R., & Giudice, N. (2010). *Establishing and maintaining orientation for mobility.* https://umaine.edu/vemi/wp-content/uploads/sites/220/2016/08/Long-Giudice2010-Orientation-and-mobility-RedBook.pdf

Long, R. G. (1990). Orientation and Mobility research: What is known and what needs to be known. *Peabody Journal of Education, 67*(2), 89–109.

Lost and disorientated. (2016). Retrieved 2020, July 25, from https://thesaurus.plus/related/disorientated/lost

Lumadi, M. W., Maguvhe, M. O., & Dzapasi, A. (2012). Transformational efficacy of a curriculum for people with visual impairment. *Anthropologist, 14*(4), 291–303.

Macmillan, F. (2018). Kinesthetic learner characteristics: what are they? https://engage-education.com/aus/blog/kinesthetic-learner-characteristics-what-are-they/#!

Malik, S., Abd Manaf, U. K., Ahmad, N. A., & Ismail, M. (2018). Orientation and Mobility training in special education curriculum for social adjustment problems of visually impaired children in Pakistan. *International Journal of Instruction, 11*(2), 185–202.

Martinez, L. (2007). A lesson from life: Take your cane! *Future Reflections, 26*(2). https://www.nfb.org/sites/www.nfb.org/files/images/nfb/publications/fr/fr26/issue2/fr07sum03.htm

Maurer, M. M. (2011). Examining highly skilled cane travelers: A preliminary study. *Journal of Blindness Innovation and Research, 1*(2).

Maurer, M. M., Bell, E. C., Woods, E., & Allen, R. (2007). *Structured discovery in cane travel constructivism in action.* https://nfb.org/images/nfb/publications/ bm/bm07/bm0704/bm070405.htm

Mettler, R. (1995). *Cognitive learning theory and cane travel instruction: A new paradigm.* State of Nebraska, Department of Public Institutions. Division of Rehabilitation Services for the Visually Impaired. Department of Education.

Mezirow, J. (1991). *Transformative dimensions of adult learning.* Jossey-Bass.

Mezirow, J. (2000). Learning to think like an adult. Core concepts of transformation theory. In J. Mezirow & Associates (Eds.), *Learning as transformation. Critical Perspectives on a theory in progress* (pp. 3–33). Jossey-Bass.

Mino, N. M. (2011). Problem-solving in structured discovery cane travel. *Journal of Blindness Innovation and Research, 1*(3). https://www.nfb.org/images/nfb/ publications/jbir/jbir11/jbir010302abs.html

Miyagawa, S. (1999). *Journey to excellence: Development of the military and VA blind rehabilitation programs in the 20th century.* Galde Press.

Morais, M., Lorensen, P., Allen, R., Bell, E. C., Hill, A., & Woods, E. (1997). *Techniques used by blind cane travel instructors: A practical approach: Learning, teaching, believing.* National Federation of the Blind.

Moskowitz, M. (2007). *The Oregon project for preschool children who are blind or visually impaired: Overview and new developments.* Southern Oregon Regional Program for the Visually Impaired Medford, Oregon, USA. http://imc16.com/wp-content/uploads/2017/07/M.-Moskowitz.pdf

Moss, C. M., & Brookhart, S. M. (2012). *Learning targets: Helping students aim for understanding in today's lesson.* Association for Supervision and Curriculum Development (ASCD).

Museum of the American Printing House for the Blind. (n.d.). *Orientation and Mobility: Part one.* https://www.aph. org/museum/programs/main-gallery/callahan-gallery/28-o-and-m-part-1/

National Blindness Professional Certification Board (NBPCB). (2018). https://www.nbpcb.org/pages/lookup.php

National Orientation and Mobility Certification (NOMC). (2017). https://www.nbpcb.org/nomc/

NMSBVI Orientation & Mobility Inventory (New Mexico School for the Blind and Visually Impaired Orientation & Mobility Inventory). (2012). http://www.nmsbvi.k12.nm.us/WEB/O&M_INVENTORY/O&M_Inventory. htm#:~:text=The%20NMSBVI%20Orientation%20%26%20Mobility%20(O%26M,of%20need%20for%20 individual%20students

O'Donnell, B. A. (1988). Stress and the mobility training process: A literature review. *Journal of Visual Impairment & Blindness, 82,* 143–47.

Omvig, J. (2005). *Freedom for the blind: The secret is empowerment.* National Federation of the Blind.

Omvig, J. H. (2002). *Freedom for the blind: The secret is empowerment.* Region VI Rehabilitation Continuing Education Program. University of Arkansas.

Orr, A., & Rogers, P. (2001). Development of vision rehabilitation services for older people who are visually impaired: A historical perspective. *Journal of Visual Impairment & Blindness, 95*(11).

Parent Institute. (1998). *Parents are teachers, too.* http://www.parent-institute.com/product/1104

Payne, R. K. (2002). *Understanding learning: The how, the why, the what.* Aha! Process, Inc.

Perla, F., & O'Donnell, B. (2004). Encouraging problem-solving in Orientation and Mobility. *Journal of Visual Impairment & Blindness, 98*(1), 47–52.

Pogrund, R., Healy, G., Jones, K., Levack, N., Martin-Curry, S., Martinez, C., ... , & Vrba, A. (1995). *Teaching age appropriate purposeful skills: An orientation & mobility curriculum for consumers with visual impairments.* Austin, TX: Texas School for the Blind and Visually Impaired.

Pogrund, R. L., & Griffin-Shirley, N. (2018). *Partners in O&M: Supporting Orientation and Mobility for students who are visually impaired.* American Foundation for the Blind Press.

Pogrund, R. L., & Rosen, S. J. (1989). The preschool blind child can be a cane user. *Journal of Visual Impairment & Blindness, 83*(9), 431–439.

Roberts, J. (2009). *A sense of the world: How a blind man became history's greatest traveler*. Harper Perennial.

Rodgers, M. D., & Wall Emerson, R. W. (2005). Human factor analysis of long cane design: Weight and length. *Journal of Visual Impairment & Blindness, 99*(10), 622–632.

Rowland, M. P., & Bell, E. C. (2012). Measuring the attitudes of sighted college students towards blindness. *Journal of Blindness Innovation and Research, 2*(2) .

Salisbury, J. M. (2018). Cultivating feelings of first-class status. *Journal of Blindness Innovation and Research, 8*(1), 8–25.

Saltzman, J. (1978). *The seven minute lesson-acting as a sighted guide*. Video. American Foundation for the Blind. https://www.youtube.com/ watch?v=3q0jmpdE454

Salus University. (n.d.). *Careers in blindness and low vision*. http://www.salus.edu/Colleges/Education-Rehabilitation/Low-Vision-Rehabilitation-Programs/Careers-in-Blindness-Low-Vision.aspx

Sarid, A. (2012). Between thick and thin: Responding to the crisis of moral education. *Journal of Moral Education, 41*(2), 245–260.

Sauerburger, D. (2007). *"Traditional" O&M in the modern environment: Hallmarks of a quality O&M program*. http://www.sauerburger.org/dona/ncsab.htm

Sauerburger, D., & Bourquin, E. (2010). Teaching the use of a long cane step by step: Suggestions for progressive methodical instruction. *Journal of Visual Impairment and Blindness, 104*(4), 203–214.

Scholl, G. T. (1986). *Foundations of education for blind and visually handicapped children and youth: Theory and practice*. American Foundation for the Blind.

Schreiber, J. B., & Moss, C. M. (2002). A Peircean view of teacher beliefs and genuine doubt. Teaching and Learning. *The Journal of Natural Inquiry and Reflective Practice, 17*(1), 25–42.

Schroeder, F. K. (1997). Implications of final regulations on O&M instruction. *American Rehabilitation, 23*(3).

Schwartz, N. (1987). *My friend Jodi is blind*. The Lighthouse.

Silverman, A. (2014). On long lines and tax breaks: A mindful approach to special blindness benefits. *Future Reflections, 33*(3). https://www.nfb.org/sites/www.nfb.org/files/images/nfb/publications/fr/fr33/3/fr330312.htm

SKI-HI Institute. (2010). *Deafblindness and the role of the intervener in educational settings*. http://intervener.org/wp-content/uploads/2011/05/Deafblindness-and-the-Role-of-the-Intervener.pdf

Smith, C., & Rigby, P. (2015). *The bee book: A tale of leadership and chance*. CreateSpace Independent Publishing Platform.

Social Security Administration. (2018). *Disability evaluation under social security 2.00 special senses and speech-adult*. https://www.ssa.gov/disability/professionals /bluebook/2.00-SpecialSensesandSpeech-Adult.htm#2_02

Soong, G. P., Lovie-Kitchin, J. E., & Brown, B. (2000). Preferred walking speed for assessment of mobility performance: Sighted guide versus non-sighted guide techniques. *Clinical and Experimental Optometry, 83*(5), 279–282. DOI: 10.1111/j.1444-0938.2000.tb05017.x

Soong, G. P., Lovie-Kitchin, J. E., & Brown, B. (2001). Does mobility performance of visually impaired adults improve immediately after Orientation and Mobility training? *Optometry and Vision Science, 78*(9), 657–666.

Stein, H. A., Slatt, B., & Stein, R. (2000). *The ophthalmic assistant: A guide for ophthalmic medical personnel.* Mosby.

Strickling, C. A., & Pogrund, R. L. (2002). Motor focus: promoting movement experiences and motor development. In R. L. Pogrund & D. L. Fazzi (Eds.), *Early focus: Working with young children who are blind or visually impaired and their families* (2nd ed., pp. 287–325). American Foundation for the Blind.

Sullo, B. (2007). *Activating the desire to learn.* Association for Supervision and Curriculum Development.

Tennyson, R. D., & Rasch, M. (1988). Linking cognitive learning theory to instructional prescriptions, *Instructional Science, 17,* 369–385, Kluwer Academic Publishers.

Thorpe, M. J. (2007). The teaching cane. *Future Reflections.* Retrieved from: https://www.nfb.org/images/nfb/publications/fr/fr25/fr07spr10.htm

Tigges, S. (2004). Slaying dragons: Building self-confidence and raising expectation through orientation center training. *American Rehabilitation, 28*(1), U.S. Department of Education. Office of Special Education and Rehabilitative Services. https://www.thefreelibrary.com/Slaying+dragons%3A+building+self-confidence+and+raising+expectations...-a0126791479

Tovey, H. (n.d.). *Outdoor play and exploration.* Proebel Trust. Retrieved from: https://app.pelorous.com/media_manager/public/209/Froebel/FT%20Play%20Pamphlet.pdf

Trudelle, M., & Jones, K. (2020). *Mobile app wayfinding webinar!* Notes.

Tuttle, D., & Tuttle, N. R. (1996). *Self-esteem and adjusting with blindness: The process of responding to life's demands.* Charles C. Thomas Publisher.

Tuttle, D. W. (1984). *Self-esteem and adjusting with blindness: The process of responding to life's demands.* Charles C. Thomas Publisher.

Vaughan, E. (1993). *The struggle of blind people for self-determination: The dependency-rehabilitation conflict: Employment in the blindness community.* Charles C. Thomas.

Vaughan, E., & Omvig, J. H. (Eds.) (2005). *Education and rehabilitation for empowerment: A volume in critical concerns in blindness.* Information Age Publishing.

VisionAware. (2018). *Travel/O&M training: AFB directory of services listing.* http://www.visionaware.org/directory.aspx?action=results&CategoryID=105

Wainapel, S. F. (1989). Attitudes of visually impaired persons toward cane use. *Journal of Visual Impairments & Blindness, 83*(9), 446–448.

Wall Emerson, R. S., & Corn, A. L. (2006). Orientation and Mobility content for children and youth: A delphi approach pilot study. *Journal of Visual Impairment and Blindness, 100*(6), 331–342.

Wells, K. (2008). The missing link: A collaborative approach to early childhood orientation and mobility. *International Journal of Orientation & Mobility, 1,* 57–61. 10.21307/ijom-2008-007

Wang, K. (2014). Every scout can earn a disability awareness badge. https://www.friendshipcircle.org/blog/2014/12/23/how-scouts-can-earn-a-disability-awareness-badge/

Wehmeyer, M. (2004). Self-determination and the empowerment of people with disabilities. *American Rehabilitation, 28*(1). U.S. Department of Education. Office of Special Education and Rehabilitative Services.

Welsh, R. L. (2005). Inventing Orientation and Mobility techniques and teaching methods: A conversation with Russell Williams (part 2). *RE:view, 37*(2), 61–76.

White, K. (1991). *Training program for individuals working with older American Indians who are blind or visually impaired: Training manual.* Rehabilitation Services Administration.

Wiles, J. (2009). *Leading curriculum development.* Corin Press.

Williams, M. A., Hurst, A., & Kane, S. K. (2013). *Pray before you step out: Describing personal and situational blind navigation behaviors.* University of Maryland. DOI: 10.1145/2513383.2513449

Williams, R. (1967). Development of mobility programs which used canes as aids. *Conference for mobility trainers and technologists; Proceedings.* Massachusetts Institute of Technology Faculty Club. Social and Rehabilitation Services.

Willoghby, D. M., & Duffy, S. L. (1992). Cane travel and young students: Handbook for Itinerant and Resource Teachers of Blind and Visually Impaired Students. *Future Reflections, 11*(4). https://www.nfb.org/sites/www.nfb.org/files/images/nfb/publications/fr/fr11/issue4/f110405.htm

Winter, B. (2015). *10 fascinating facts about the white cane.* Perkins School for the Blind. https://www.perkins.org/stories/10-fascinating-facts-about-the-white-cane

APPENDIX

Blind	**Legally Blind**	**Partially Sighted**
In order to be verified as a child with a visual impairment as listed above, the evaluations need to include the analysis and documentation of:		In addition, the child needs to meet the requirements of either criterion listed below:

• No more than light perception as stated in a signed report by a licensed ophthalmologist or optometrist • The need for adapted curriculum, method, materials, and equipment for learning; and what is listed below.	• A visual acuity of 20/200 or less in the better eye with correction or a contiguous field restricted to 20 degrees or less as stated in a signed report by a licensed ophthalmologist or optometrist. • The need for adapted curriculum, methods, materials, and equipment, or any combination thereof for learning; and what is listed below.	• A signed report by a licensed ophthalmologist or optometrist to certify a structural defect, condition, or disease of the eye, which may affect the ability to learn visually; and what is listed below plus what is listed to the right →	• A Functional Vision assessment. All assessed behaviors need to be elicited by both light and pattern. Significant delays in three or more of the visual behaviors could be detrimental to functional vision. The observable visual behaviors need to include but are not limited to: peripheral orientation, fixation, ability to shift gaze, ability to track, and ability to converge. **OR** • A visual assessment as stated in a signed report by a licensed ophthalmologist or optometrist to certify at least one of the following: a) a distant visual acuity of 20/70 or less, in the better eye with correction; b) a near visual acuity equivalent to or less than 8-point type at 40 centimeters, in the better eye with correction; c) a central visual field loss of any degree in both eyes; or d) a peripheral visual field of 60 degrees or less in the better eye.

The educational significance of the visual impairment including:
- Documentation of behaviors which appear to impede the overall function as observed in appropriate settings by someone other than the classroom teacher; and
- Deficiencies in one or more of the following areas: activities of daily living, social interaction, academic achievement, performance in the educational setting, or orientation & mobility.　　(NDE, n.d.)

Nebraska Verification Guide for Blind, Legally Blind and Partially Sighted

RESOURCES FOR PARENTS

American Printing House for the Blind. P.O. Box 6085, Louisville, KY 40206-0085 (502) 895-2405 http://www. aph.org/products http://www.aph.org/cvi/index.html

Cane Travel and Young Students. Willoughby, Doris and Duffy, Sharon. Featuring excerpts from the *Handbook for itinerant and resource teachers of blind and visually impaired students. Future reflections*. Fall 1992, Vol. 11 No. 4. https://www.nfb.org/sites/www.nfb.org/files/images/nfb/publications/fr/fr11/issue4/f110405.htm

Cane Travel at Home: Lesson Ideas for Parents and Instructors. Wisecarver, Liz. Future Reflections, Spring 2020 Instruction at Home. https://www.nfb.org/images/nfb/publications/fr/fr39/3/fr390303.htm?fbclid=I-wAR3bPFByHFotWIdvM36OwkZA7EYTkxM3xXJLoVGpraYFd7sZNcEHbm2JrI4

Future Reflections Magazine. A quarterly magazine for parents and teachers of student who are blind or visually impaired; offers resources and information based on the National Federation of the Blind's positive philosophy of blindness. https://www.nfb.org/resources/publications-and-media/future-reflections

Getting ready for College Begins in Third Grade: Working Toward an Independent Future for Your Blind/ VI Child—Pre-K to Middle School. Castellano, Carol (2010). Series: Critical Concerns in Blindness. Information Age Publishing

Growing Up with Independence: The Blind Child's Use of the White Cane. Schroeder, Fredrick. K. Braille Monitor. 1986. https://www.nfb.org/sites/www.nfb.org/files/images/nfb/publications/bm/bm86/bm8612/bm861209.htm

Independent Movement and Travel in Blind Children: A Promotion Model. Cutter, Joe (2007). Series: Critical Concerns in Blindness. Information Age Publishing

Making It Work: Educating the Blind/Visually Impaired Student in the Regular School. Castellano, Carol (2005). Series: Critical Concerns in Blindness. Information Age Publishing

My Journey. Chamberlain, Merry-Noel. (1999). https://www.nfb.org/images/nfb/publications/slate/slfw9907.htm

National Organization of Parents of Blind Children. http://www.nopbc.org or Connect via Facebook: https://www.facebook.com/nopbc

Orientation and Mobility: One Instructor's Perspective. Chamberlain, Merry-Noel. (2013). Future Reflections, 32(3), 28–32. https://nfb.org/images/nfb/publications/fr/fr32/3 /fr320309.htm.

Saturday School: A Holistic Approach to Educating Children with Visual Impairments. Chamberlain, Merry-Noel. (2005). *Future Reflections, 24*(4). https://nfb.org/Images/nfb/ Publications /fr/fr20/fr05ci16.htm.

Self-Confidence Levels in Sequential Learning Versus Structured Discovery Cane Travel, Post Orientation and Mobility Instruction: A Comparison Study. Chamberlain, Merry-Noel, (2019). Ed.D. Dissertations. Concordia University, https://commons.cu-portland.edu/edudissertations/266

Sighted/Human Guide: One Instructor's Perspective. Chamberlain, Merry-Noel, Future Reflections, Winter 2015, Travel. https://www.nfb.org/sites/www.nfb.org/files/images/nfb/publications/fr/fr34/1/fr340110.htm

The Orientation and Mobility Goal Bank. Chamberlain, Merry-Noel. (2017). *Future Reflections,* 36:2. https://nfb.org/ images/nfb/publications/fr/fr36/2/fr360206.htm

The Preschool Blind Child Can Be a Cane User: An Article Review. Chamberlain, Merry-Noel (2019). *Future Reflections, 38*(3). Orientation and Mobility. https://www.nfb.org/images/nfb/publications/fr/fr38/3/fr380305.htm

The "Teaching Cane." Thorp, Mary Jo. (2007). *Future Reflections,* Winter/Spring, 26:1. https://nfb.org/images/nfb/ Publications/fr/fr25/fr07spr10.htm

Website: Orientation and Mobility for Children. http://www.pdrib.com/pages/omkids.php

NOTES

_____

_____

_____

_____

_____

_____

_____

_____

_____

_____

_____

_____

FREE WHITE CANE APPLICATION
https://www.nfb.org/programs-services/free-white-cane-program

Fill out this form or go to the link above. Thank you very much for your interest in the Free White Cane Program. Please be sure to complete all fields on this application form because incomplete forms cannot be processed.

First name:
Last name:
Address:
City: State:
Zip Code: Phone Number:
Birth Date: _____   (month)   (day)   (year)
E-mail: (optional)
Member of NFB? _____ Yes _____ No
Braille Reader? _____ Yes _____ No
Circle cane size: 25,   27,   29,   31,   33,   35,   37,   39,   41,   43,   45,   47,   49, 51,   53,   55,   57,   59,   61,   63,   65,   67,   69
By requesting this white cane, I acknowledge that: *   I am blind or visually impaired. *   This cane is for my personal use. *   It has been more than six months since a previous request for a white cane.   Signature: _____
Please mail completed application to: **Free White Cane Program** **National Federation of the Blind** **200 East Wells Street at Jernigan Place** **Baltimore, MD 21230**

Consent for Orientation and Mobility Instruction

Student's Name:	*Date:
School Name:	School Phone #

My name is _____ and I give consent for my child, _____
          (Print name)   (Print name)

to participate in Orientation and Mobility (O&M) instruction. I understand:

a) Orientation and Mobility is specialized instruction which addresses my child's need to learn the specific skills and techniques necessary to individuals who are blind or visually impaired to travel safe and effective within the community.

b) My child's O&M instruction will be provided by a trained and certified O&M instructor.

c) Instruction will take place in my child's school, and/or in the neighborhood or businesses near my child's school, when appropriate.

d) Transportation for my child will be provided by_____.

e) O&M instruction may include working with the long, white cane, and/or low vision optical aids.

f) The O&M instructor will accompany my child at all times during mobility lessons.

g) In the event of any incidents that affect my child's safety during the course of the mobility lesson, I specifically give consent for the O&M instructor listed below to obtain appropriate assistance for my child. Accordingly, I agree to provide the information requested below along with my signature.

If you have any questions or concerns, please feel free to contact:

O&M's business card	O&M's supervisor's business card

Parents, please provide the information requested below, sign, and date this form to be included in your child's Individual Education Plan (IEP).

Parent Signature	* Only valid for one year.
Parent phone #	
Emergency contact (Please Print)	
Emergency phone #	
Child's doctor's name	
Child's doctor's phone #	

NOTES

ABOUT THE AUTHOR

Merry-Noel Chamberlain grew up with bilateral amblyopia. After being a homemaker for several years, she attended the University of Nebraska and earned a BA in Elementary Education. Although she enjoyed being an elementary teacher, she later accepted an Orientation Counselor position at the Nebraska Commission for the Blind. That position required her to spend three months wearing sleep-shades to learn the alternative skills of blindness, including Orientation and Mobility (O&M) under the direction of Richard Mettler (1995). Later, she went to Louisiana Tech to earn a Master's Degree in Educational Psychology with a concentration in O&M, which was a new program at that time and required an additional year in sleep-shade training. While there, Merry-Noel learned she was legally blind with an added visual diagnosis of glaucoma. She was among the second graduating class, pioneering as their first legally blind female to graduate from this new Structured Discovery Cane Travel program.

From Louisiana, the family moved to Iowa where she became an Independent Living Service Coordinator at the Iowa Department for the Blind. After spending another six months in sleep-shade training, she worked with visually impaired adults over the age of 55. However, she missed working with children, so she transitioned to the public-school system and became a Teacher of the Visually Impaired (TVI). This position required her to obtain a Master's Degree in Special Education—Visual Impairment, which she earned from Western Michigan University. However, at that time, Iowa did not accept National Orientation and Mobility Certification. So, after seven years as a TVI, she packed up the family and followed her dreams to accept an O&M position at the Virginia School for the Deaf and the Blind, in Staunton, Virginia.

Currently, the family lives in Nebraska where Merry-Noel loves being a TVI and an O&M instructor for an Educational Service Unit serving children birth to age 21 in several school districts. However, ever since graduating from Louisiana Tech, she deeply wanted to investigate the difference between Sequential Learning (SL) and Structured Discovery Cane Travel (SDCT). This desire led her to Concordia University where she earned a Doctorate Degree in Education: Transformational Leadership. Completing her dis-

The ABCs of Structured Discovery Cane Travel for Children, pages 247–248.

sertation study *Self-Confidence Levels in Sequential Learning Versus Structured Discovery Cane Travel, Post Orientation and Mobility Instruction: A Comparison Study* proved SDCT consumers have higher self-confidence than SL consumers by 32%. The results of that study and teaching O&M to children led her to the creation of *The ABCs of Structured Discovery Cane Travel for Children.*

Not only is Dr. Chamberlain a TVI and an O&M, she is also a parent of a blind young adult. Therefore, she has a holistic approach to education. She understands both sides of the educational environment—the professional and the parent.

During her free time, Dr. Chamberlain enjoys spending time with her family, writing, crocheting, and creating educational games for her students. She believes the cane needs to be used at every walking opportunity outside the home and with SDCT transformational skills—there are no mobility limits!

To learn more about Dr. Chamberlain, she describes the many different stages she traveled through comprehending her vision loss in the following article, **My Journey:** https://www.nfb.org/images/nfb/publications/slate/slfw9907.htm

CPSIA information can be obtained
at www.ICGtesting.com
Printed in the USA
LVHW051600101222
734842LV00008BA/679

9 781648 025556